Dr Charlotte Wolff was born near Danzig, eastern Germany (now Gdansk, Poland). She went to the local grammar school and studied medicine at a number of German universities, starting at the University of Freiburg where she also attended lectures on phenomenology by Professor Husserl and Dr Heidegger, one of the founders of existentialism. She received her M.D. at Berlin University in 1928. At the same time she was developing as an artist, her chief interests being poetry and philosophy.

While working in Berlin she attended a course in hand-reading arranged for the medical profession by Julius Spier. She recognized the immense value of hand analysis and began her own research in Paris where she settled in 1933 after fleeing from the Nazis. She started there to develop her own method of hand interpretation. Her work attracted great interest inside and outside medical circles, it was much appreciated by the protagonists of Surrealism, especially André Breton, Paul Eluard and Antoine Saint-Exupéry who became Dr Wolff's close friends.

In 1936 she settled in London with the help of Aldous and Maria Huxley through whom she met many literary figures, Virginia Woolf, T. S. Eliot, Osbert Sitwell and Thomas Mann among them. She is well known as a psychiatrist, as a pioneer authority on the psychology of the human hand and gesture and as a pioneer of sexological research. Her books are *The Human Hand* (1942), *A Psychology of Gesture* (1945), *The Hand in Psychological Diagnosis* (1952), *On the Way to Myself* (an autobiography, 1969), *An Older Love* (a novel, 1976) and the much praised *Love Between Women* (1971) out of which developed many of the themes more fully explored in *Bisexuality*.

BISEXUALITY
A Study

CHARLOTTE WOLFF M.D.
Fellow of the British Psychological Society

QUARTET BOOKS   LONDON MELBOURNE NEW YORK

Published by Quartet Books Limited 1979
A member of the Namara Group
27 Goodge Street, London W1P 1FD

First published by Quartet Books Limited, London, 1977

Copyright © 1977, 1979 by Charlotte Wolff

ISBN 0 7043 3253 1

Typeset by Bedford Typesetters Limited
Printed in Great Britain by
Billing & Sons Limited, Guildford, London and Worcester

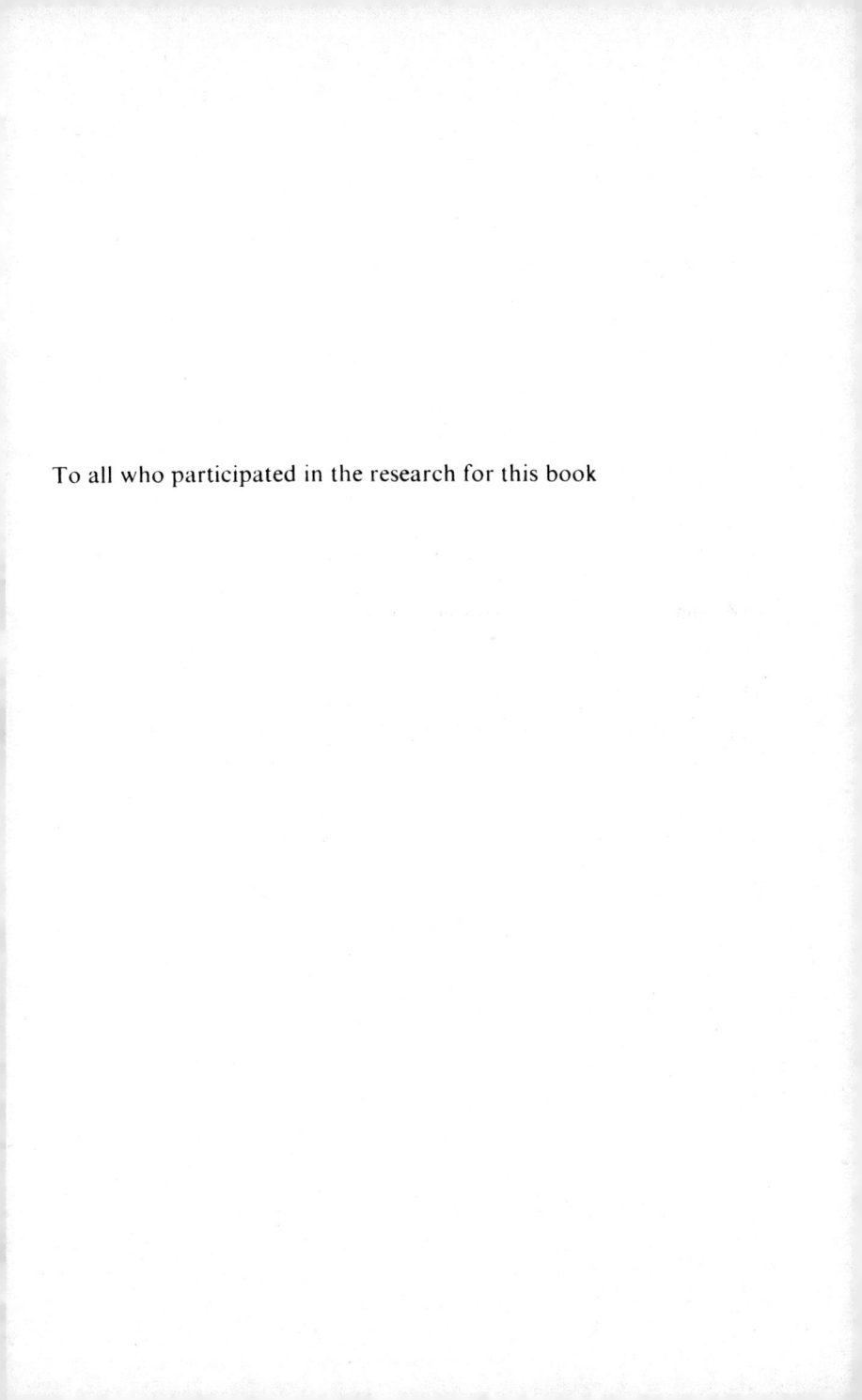

To all who participated in the research for this book

CONTENTS

Introduction to the paperback edition viii
Preface and acknowledgements ix
    I Bisexuality: as others saw it 1
   II Biological inferences 40
  III Gender identity and sexual orientation 52
  IV Procedure of study 66
   V Early influences 72
  VI Later relationships 88
 VII Interviews 110
VIII Autobiographical documents: as they saw themselves 123
Appendices: 1 Bisexuality and Androgyny 199
             2 Statistical Tables 208
Glossary 245
Bibliography 251
Index 256

INTRODUCTION TO THE PAPERBACK EDITION

I have added an Appendix and another autobiography to the paperback edition for the following reasons.

The concept of bisexuality had been used as an umbrella for many different sexual variations for over 100 years, and one of the aims of this book was to reach a *clear* understanding of its meaning. It did not occur to me while writing it that another semantic problem could exist which might once more affect the understanding of bisexuality: namely, its confusion with androgyny. In the first chapter I mention some American psychologists who used the term androgyny in a purely psychological sense, and their approach did not impinge on the concept of bisexuality as set out in my book.

But after publication, I became aware that many people identified androgyny with bisexuality. This was evident at discussions following talks I gave on the subject of bisexuality, as well as in conversations, letters and reviews about my book. This lack of understanding of the differences between the two concepts led to wrong comparisons and conclusions about both.

I think that authors who substituted androgyny for bisexuality were motivated to do so because of the manifold subjective interpretations of bisexuality. But they failed to define the term, nor did they explain how it differed from bisexuality. Only the American analytical psychologist, June Singer, made an attempt to do so. Her book *Androgyny* appeared after I had written my book. Her definition of both terms is, however, so limited and idiosyncratic that it is more confusing than explanatory. She understands bisexuality as a primitive form of androgyny, and her definition of the latter strays into such esoteric regions as to become abstruse.

As no detailed explanation of either term has been given up to now, I have tried to do so in this Appendix. And the additional autobiography is included to illustrate the points I have made.

Charlotte Wolff

PREFACE AND ACKNOWLEDGEMENTS

This book is a sequel to my study on lesbianism. Homosexuality has its roots in bisexuality, which has been recognized for more than a hundred years by psychiatrists and psychologists. Yet a clear-cut definition of bisexuality has not been given by any of those who used the concept for the purpose of explaining other sexual variations. No large-scale study on the subject itself has ever been attempted, and I decided to fill the gap.

While I did research on lesbianism my understanding of bisexuality grew considerably, and the seed for this book was sown at that time. It covers a wider field than *Love Between Women*, but is also designed for both the professional and lay reader. It could not have been written without the generous help of many people, organizations for sexual minorities and the Press. I owe a great debt of gratitude to them all.

In the first place, I want to thank those who participated in the research, and made the whole enterprise possible. I was a trustee of the Albany Trust when I started the investigation, and my thanks go to the then Director, Mr Antony Grey, who published the first appeal for my study in a Newsletter. I am equally grateful for the help I received from Sappho, Kenric, the Beaumont Society and the Friends Homosexual Fellowship. Many subjects contacted me through their good offices.

Statistics were essential for this study in order to summarize and illustrate the results of the questionnaires. I was fortunate to have the help of Dr A. R. Jonckheere, senior lecturer in the Department of Statistical Psychology at University College, London. He entrusted

Dr David Caudrey with the statistical work. Both gave me the greatest help in discussing the methods used, and the preparation of the Tables. They further assisted me by making many important suggestions for the planning of my book. They were generous enough to give me much of their time at my frequent visits to the Department. Dr Caudrey not only carried out the laborious task of computing the data and analysing the results, but he never failed to answer my questions about certain complexities of the statistics and the composition of appropriate Tables. I am most grateful to them both for their personal interest and kindness.

I am also very grateful for the generous co-operation of two American friends, Mrs Kyle Johnson and Mr Hal Trafford, who took every trouble to be of help in my research.

Last, but not least, I want to thank my friend Miss Audrey Wood, O.B.E., who devoted herself not only to typing the manuscript, but also to taking care of much of the burden of daily life while I prepared this book.

1 BISEXUALITY: AS OTHERS SAW IT

Man has been preoccupied with bisexuality from the dawn of history. The earliest legends of an androgynous origin of human beings came from the Middle East and probably China. But Greek mythology gave permanence to this idea through the legend of Hermaphroditus. He was the son of Hermes and Aphrodite, a beautiful youth, half male, half female. The nymph of the fountain Salmacis had been responsible for his bisexual nature. She fell so deeply in love with him, that she begged the Gods never to be parted from him. They fulfilled her wish by uniting her sex with his. The Greeks immortalized the hermaphroditic image in numerous sculptures and in literature. In Plato's *Symposium*, Aristophanes spoke of hermaphrodites as the third sex. He said: 'In the first place there were three sexes, not, as with us, two, male and female; the third partook of the nature of both the others and has vanished, though its name survives.' (From the translation by W. Hamilton.)

The hermaphrodite was the original model of man in primitive thought. The concept of hermaphroditism survived its legendary past. It was taken up by science where it became indispensable for the understanding of certain biological and medical phenomena. It also found a niche in the language of psychology under the name of psychical hermaphroditism, later called bisexuality. But neither term was ever clearly defined.

In my own definition, *bisexuality is the root of human sexuality, and the matrix of all bio-psychical reactions, be they passive or active.* Bisexuality is expressed first and foremost in bi-gender identity, which may or may not lead to bisexual orientation.

*

C. G. Jung scored a bull's eye when he incorporated the hermaphroditic legend into his archetypal images, of which the anima and the animus are the principal protagonists. They stand for the hidden other-sexed self, and symbolize undying wishes and ideals common to all of us. The animus is the male aspect in a woman, and the anima the female one in a man. They represent the most powerful forces in the life of both sexes. It is the man's anima which drives him to search for his love partner, who corresponds to the female part of himself. And a woman's animus longs to find her own male-self in the person she loves.

In *The Syzygy* (*Collected Works IX*, Vol. 2, chp. 3, 1963) Jung gives a more detailed description of the bisexual nature of human beings. The anima is an all-embracing and devouring element in a man's character, and is linked to the eternal mother. But it is also connected with the real mother's possessive love, which makes a man want to escape from the world and its problems. The anima leads to a secret conspiracy between the actual mother and her son, while the archaic maternal image is embedded in the dark regions of his unconscious mind.

Jung identified the anima with Eros, which he considered to be the essence of 'femininity'. Its equivalent, the animus, represents the male in a woman, and is mirrored in an archaic or idealized father image. But it is also related to the actual father. The animus stands for Logos, creative intellect, which, according to Jung, is the essence of 'masculinity'.

Jung's ideas of 'masculinity' and 'femininity' are of historical interest only as they have no relevance to women and men of our time. The following quotation from his *Memories, Dreams, Reflections* (1963) illustrates his naivety and ignorance about the nature of women: 'In its primary "unconscious" form, the animus is a compound of spontaneous, unpremeditated opinions which exercise a powerful influence on the woman's emotional life ... Consequently the animus likes to project itself upon intellectuals and all kinds of heroes.'

Legendary symbolism is supreme in analytical psychology, but has also a place in Freudian psychoanalysis. The latter would not have made such an impact without references to Oedipus, Electra, Narcissus and Eros, whose figures symbolize fundamental human situations and conflicts. The idea of psychical hermaphroditism was already familiar to nineteenth-century psychiatrists before Freud. It became the corner-stone of psychoanalysis when he adopted Fliess's idea of bisexuality.

Freud used Greek legends as imaginative examples of his intellectual theory, while Jung was steeped in mythology itself, both in his way of thinking and style of writing. He was in direct line with the legendary past of Greece and the Far East. Freud, on the other hand, was a highlight in late nineteenth- early twentieth-century psychiatry, which had an eye on rational interpretation and biological conditioning.

It may appear incongruous to put Melanie Klein side by side with Jung, but she too was in line with a legendary concept of love. It closely resembled the one Aristophanes proposed in the second part of his discourse in Plato's *Symposium*. In this version, man was not only created a sexual hermaphrodite, but was a double-being altogether. He had four hands, four feet and two faces. The muscular and perceptive powers of this creature were immense. He moved with immense speed, turning round like a barrel, and he perceived everything around and behind him, as he could see forwards and backwards. Such powers displeased the Gods and they cut the creature in half with the help of Apollo, who applied the artist's skill to this surgical operation.

How does this freakish saga relate to Melanie Klein's ideas of bisexuality?

Melanie Klein charted a new territory of psychoanalysis through her discovery that children, already in early infancy, experience intense libidinal sensations. These are projected onto both parents, and exhibit the ambivalence and ambiguities of such attachments: love turning into hate, and desire into destructive impulses. In being able to put the age for these happenings into the first year of life she considerably extended the boundaries of psychoanalytic knowledge. Her observations, drawn from her analysis of infants, provided her with the yardstick to do so. Her discoveries of the infant's earliest experiences of love and hate gave her a place of her own, and were instrumental in creating the Kleinian psychoanalytic school.

The most striking of her observations were those of the fantastic images the infant has of his parents, the objects of his violent and ambivalent desires. He sees them as a monstrous hermaphroditic unit. Babies, in the first year of life, already have impressions of their parents redolent of the hermaphroditic monsters which Aristophanes described. The mother is furnished with a penis and the father with breasts, and both are entwined in an 'everlasting' sexual intercourse. The infant's desires are directed to one or the other parent in turn, and sometimes to both simultaneously. But the first love-object is always the mother's breast which, apart from its natural purpose, is the source of oral pleasures, and other sensual reactions. The latter interpretation is, of course, stereotyped psychoanalysis.

Klein's innovation consisted in pre-dating the infant's sexual development. According to her, the baby had passed the pre-Oedipal phase, when parents were pictured as hermaphroditic beings, in the second year of life. By then, little girls already experienced unconscious vaginal reactions. This claim put Klein right outside Freudian psychoanalysis.

In this early period of life bisexuality is certainly ambisexual. Love, jealousy and hatred are the intrinsic ingredients of the infant's attachments. They are directed either towards the mother or the father, depending on the situation of the moment. The change-over of these emotions from one parent to the other illustrates the naturalness of bisexuality as well as its early ambivalence, and evidences at the same time that homosexuality is part and parcel of bisexuality.

According to Klein, the effect of early infantile fantasies cannot be overrated. The baby sees his parents, not only as a combined hermaphroditic creature, but each of them furnished with single organs of the other. These monstrous pictures become imprinted in the imagination. Inevitably the child, confronted with such a mental burden, feels overpowered and confused. But his sense of self-preservation and his healing powers are remarkable. He finds comfort and clings with gratitude to his first love, the 'good breast' (the mother), which helps him to manage his guilt feelings, envy and hatred.

The observations by Melanie Klein give a macabre slant to early bisexual manifestations, which may become the underlying cause of serious psychological disturbance in childhood and later life. But a compensating factor is the identification with the mother, particularly where the girl is concerned. The Kleinian analyst, P. Heimann, expressed this in *Developments in Psychoanalysis* (1952) as follows: 'Identification with the first love-object, the mother, resulting from introjection, intensifies the girl's heterosexual and the boy's homosexual components of inborn bisexuality.' (p. 166)

It seems clear that even the revolutionary Kleinian school takes sexual 'normality' as a yardstick for the 'good life'. It is therefore out of touch with present-day sexological knowledge. But Klein, like Jung, had much to teach us about the nature of love, of which her original interpretation of the Narcissus myth is an example (Heimann, op. cit. pp. 167, 168). Klein considered the equation of narcissism with self-love to be wrong. The story goes that Narcissus fell in love with his own image in a fountain, and narcissistic love, as generally understood, stopped at this point without going into the depth of the legend. In fact, the myth relates that a nymph called Echo fell in love with Narcissus, but he rejected her. Echo begged Aphrodite to avenge her, and so it happened that Narcissus fell in love with his own reflection in the water, mistaking it for that of a beautiful water-nymph. He tried to catch and embrace her, but the frustration he experienced through his vain attempts made him believe that she could not respond because she was in distress. He wanted to save her. And so he tried and tried to get hold of her, but there was nothing to get hold of. He got more and more desperate, until he died from sorrow and depression. His way of loving seems to show that the Greeks did not believe in so-called 'self-love': Narcissus did not love himself but an object. Melanie Klein's interpretation corresponds to the real content of the Greek myth. Narcissus, who looked into the water, appeared to look at the outside world, but in fact gazed into himself where he perceived unconsciously the image of the beloved with whom he was identified. The new meaning which Klein gave to the old legend is closely related to Jung's concept of the anima and animus. Both authors imply that bisexuality is at the very root of love.

But Klein's view of bisexuality in women was flawed. She, the revolutionary who went ahead of Freud in her own discoveries of psychosexual life in earliest infancy, did not cut herself loose from orthodox theory in other respects. She remained stuck with the outmoded idea of the girl's penis envy and the woman's sexual inferiority. She went along with Freud's assumption that girls want to be boys, and that their self-confidence shrivels at the sight of the male organ. For her, the girl was still a 'mutilated' boy, and had no sexual identity per se. She was set on the way to sexual 'normality' through identification with her mother.

These ideas have been contested and corrected by psychoanalysts like Deutsch, Horney and others, as well as by my own research on female homosexuality. But Klein's unique merits in psychoanalytical research give her enough credit to be set against her failure to liberate herself and her work from conventional ideas about women's sexuality. Among her many outstanding achievements is the discovery that the infant's forlorn position with his parents is due to the fact that 'greed, hate and persecutory anxieties in relation to the primary object, the mother's breast, have an *innate* basis'. She wrote: 'In this book, I have also shown that envy, as a powerful expression of oral- and anal-sadistic impulses, is also constitutional.' (*Envy and Gratitude*, 1953, p. 81)

One could argue about the term constitutional, unless its meaning is qualified. The negative emotions Klein described are, in my view, conditioned reflexes. But this is a verbal disagreement only, because the reactions of the infant to his parents (and siblings) are fundamental, and help to form his temperament and mentality. I am convinced that emotionally cannibalistic desires have broadened our minds and propelled us into awareness of our primary anxiety and destructiveness.

Klein's discovery that earliest feelings of envy might become the unconscious source of neurotic symptoms later on, has been illustrated in her psychoanalysis of adults. She demonstrated, in the analysis of a male patient, that unrecognized, destructive impulses originated in inborn bisexuality. Envy and hatred of the mother, which were the other side of love for her, reinforced homosexual tendencies directed towards the father. Klein recounted two dreams of one of her patients, which illuminate the situation. Here is a résumé.

In the first dream he caught a fish, but he could not kill it. He put it into a woman's laundry basket to let it die a natural death. The fish turned into a beautiful baby, but the baby had swallowed the hook. According to Klein, both fish and baby were the analyst herself, and showed the patient's envy of her. The symbol of the basket revealed his early desire to be a female, possessing the maternal functions of his mother he so much envied. The analyst had swallowed the hook, which meant that she had been taken in by the patient. His ambiguity about the killing of the fish indicated that he left open the question as to whether the analysis with all its pain was, after all, useful to him. When the patient recognized the cause of his destructive impulses, he went into a deep depression because he hated himself for what he had done.

The fish dream continued in a different form the following night. This time, a pike, whales, sharks and a sucker fish dominated the scene. The pike was old and worn out, but the sucker fish, sitting upon it, could not do it any harm. It sucked itself instead. According to Klein, the pike was herself, worn out and old, badly treated by the patient who was represented by the sucker fish. The pike, as well as the whales and sharks, boded danger, warning the patient of the analyst's persecutory powers.

This dream became the turning point in the patient's treatment. Although it led to an even deeper depression than he had experienced before, he had gained insight into the causes of his predicament.

The ambivalent feelings about the analyst mirrored problems of the underlying bisexuality of this patient (and many others). Melanie Klein expressed this most vividly when she interpreted another dream of the same patient in which she often stood for his father, changing quickly into his mother, and at times representing both parents simultaneously. He felt guilty about his homosexuality for which he made his father responsible, because he believed that envy and hatred of his mother had engendered this 'wrong' love. The truth was that the patient was unable to come to terms with his bisexuality, which included, *eo ipso*, the love for another male (his father). His hermaphroditic image of the analyst bore striking witness to the lasting power of infantile imagery, and certain vicissitudes connected with bisexuality, according to Klein. I disagree with many of Klein's views. And I have investigated the subject of bisexuality through the research of ordinary people not patients. My point of departure was essentially different from Klein's. In any event, one cannot fail to suspect conclusions drawn from patients as being rather unrealistic, or at least one-sided, in excluding 'ordinary' subjects.

Although bisexuality as such has not been investigated through systematic research up until now, most authors mentioned in this chapter have given evidence, in one way or another, of its manifestations. The development of ideas does not proceed in a straight line. Time is a tricky human invention. It not only moves forwards but can also move backwards. Individual people and whole communities can be closer to the distant than to the immediate past. The passage of time follows the ups and downs of waves, and we see, after an interval which may be long or short, the return of fashions or the reinstatement of authors and artists who had been rejected or forgotten. Klein and Jung came so close to ancient times in their imaginative understanding of the human condition, that their work forged a link with the mythology of a distant past. The 'puritan' doctrine of behaviourism pushed them into the background, but they are coming to the fore again. This is already the case with Jung, and perhaps to a lesser degree with Klein. Freud, who suffered much insult and denigration from behaviourists, is on the way to being reinstated to his proper stature. I shall speak of his outstanding contribution when I review ideas on bisexuality in the nineteenth and twentieth centuries. But before doing so, I must mention the Greek philosopher Parmenides (515–460 B.C.), probably the first theoretician of homosexuality which he considered to be an inherited and natural disposition; and so did Aristotle, as Dr R.

Klimmer reported in his book *Die Homosexualität* (1963, pp. 63, 64). I mention these Greek savants, in spite of the fact that they wrote only about male homosexuality, because they are the earliest sources of theoretical information about sexual non-conformity. They might or might not have known that homosexuality cannot be isolated from bisexuality, a fact which was only clearly comprehended in the second half of the nineteenth century.

Heterosexuality and homosexuality had always been polarized. Homosexuality was openly practised in the hellenic period as an ideal way of life. The same was (and is) true of other cultures outside Judaic and Christian influences. But bisexuality was either taken for granted or not recognized.

It is a long jump from the philosophers of ancient Greece to the enlightened physicians of the nineteenth century who treated sexuality in a new way. They studied 'sexual pathology' through observation of patients, and based their conclusions on experience. In the dark ages, homosexuality was a sin punishable by death, and it is understandable that this taboo subject could come under medical scrutiny only when the time was ripe. The German physician, Dr Casper, was the first medical author who wrote about homosexuality which he called paederasty. He understood that it was part of a wider condition, a kind of psychical hermaphroditism. The term bisexuality was then unknown. In 1852, Casper published an article, *Uber Notzucht und Pederastie* (On Rape and Paederasty), where he equated paederasty with male homosexuality which he thought to be congenital. Dr Casper was an authority on forensic medicine and a leading physician in public service (Havelock Ellis, *Studies in the Psychology of Sex*, Vol. I, Part IV, 1942, p. 66).

The Austrian, Ulrichs, himself a homosexual, wrote in a similar vein twenty-five years later. He was not a medical man, but had studied law and worked as an assessor. He wrote articles and novels on homosexual themes under the pseudonym, Numa Numantius. He must have been aware of the bisexual root of homosexuality because he made the point that 'mental sex is not connected with bodily sex'. He considered himself to be a man with feminine sensibilities, a condition which he regarded as normal. He demanded that people like him should have the same social status as heterosexuals, and be allowed to marry persons of their own kind. He equated 'mental' hermaphroditism with male homosexuality. Ulrichs deserves a special mention because of his progressive views, anticipating the trends of today more than a hundred years ago. His ideas are as radical as those one finds in the Gay Liberation Front. Ulrichs stands out as one of the very few nineteenth-century authors who dissociated themselves in their work from Christian morality (Ellis, ibid. p. 66).

Charles Darwin was the first to use the word bisexuality. He wrote in *The Variation of Animals and Plants under Domestication* (1868), that bisexuality alone could explain certain hereditary traits. Latent characteristics of the opposite sex can be transmitted to future generations in both fauna and flora.

It is regrettable that the term mental (psychical) hermaphroditism has practically gone out of use, because it is not only more imaginative, but also less equivocal than bisexuality.

The Hungarian physician, Dr Benkert, coined the word homosexuality in the year 1869. He had the courage to ask the Prussian Minister of Justice to repeal the law against homosexuality, because he said it was a congenital condition, almost impossible to control (R. Klimmer, op. cit. p. 66).

Vague terms reflect uncertainty about conditions they are meant to describe. Even far-seeing authors of the nineteenth century dealing with homo- and bisexuality, did not escape confusion about either. Alternative designations for homosexuality were at this time: paederasty, sodomy, contrary sexual feelings, inversion, antipathetic sexual reactions, and uranism. The alternative expression for bisexuality was mental (psychical) hermaphroditism, which was not properly understood as a separate entity before Krafft-Ebing.

The German psychiatrist, Dr Westphal, who edited the *Archiv für Psychiatrie*, published in 1869 an article *Konträre Sexualempfindung* which made history. He was the first physician to investigate female homosexuality, which he considered to be congenital. His article did not deal with female bisexuality per se, but implied it. His contribution is of importance not only because he was a pioneer in research on female homosexuality, but also because he sympathized with the emotional and sexual leanings of lesbians, for whom he expressed the greatest admiration (Ellis, op. cit. p. 65).

There can be no doubt that the French psychologist, A. Binet, had insight into bisexuality, which came to light in an article he published in the *Revue Philosophique* (1887). He showed himself to be an iconoclast in the proposition that the choice of a love object was determined by accident, and depended on outer circumstances. One falls in love for the first time with what 'the eye beholds' when in a state of sexual hyperaesthesia, which prepares the right condition for the *choc fortuit* (accidental shock). At such a moment, the eye might behold a person of the same or the opposite sex, and either could fix one's love-life for good. Binet's ingenious theory anticipated much of behaviourism. Although he was mentioned by other authors, Freud among them, his theory was either sharply criticized or dismissed altogether.

Some years earlier, E. Gley also published a paper in the *Revue Philosophique* under the title *Les Aberrations de l'Instinct Sexuel* (1884). He suggested that bisexuality was the root cause of homosexuality. Freud mentioned him as a pioneer for having done so in *Three Essays on the Theory of Sexuality* (1905). This made Gley appear more important as an innovator than he really was.

R. von Krafft-Ebing was, in fact, the great pioneer in sexology who gave a fresh vista to the whole range of sexual variations and bisexuality in particular. A new era of knowledge began with the publication of *Psychopathia Sexualis* in 1886. This book became a sexological bible, which went into numerous editions and was translated into many languages. Although Freud's eminence dimmed Krafft-Ebing's fame, it is unquestionable that he laid the foundation of modern sexology. Like many pioneers, he stood with one foot in the future and the other in the past. He shared with most nineteenth-century authors on sexual 'deviations' the Christian hangover of sexual morality. But this did not affect the sympathy he felt for both his male and female patients, which was vividly demonstrated in many case histories in *Psychopathia Sexualis*.

Judaism and Christianity had condemned homosexuality as a deadly sin, and the severity of the law had persecuted these 'sinners' for longer than a millennium. But in the latter part of the nineteenth century homosexuality became a nervous and moral illness: the sinner had advanced to the status of a patient. It is important not to overlook the probability that many homosexual people of the dark ages were, in fact, married bisexuals. (Krafft-Ebing was one of the first authors to use the term bisexuality side by side with psychical hermaphroditism.) The discovery that bisexuality is part and parcel of human nature was made through a slow process of trial and error. Krafft-Ebing differentiated clearly between psychical hermaphroditism and homosexuality. In the numerous case histories of *Psychopathia Sexualis* he let 'life' speak, and the reader not only learns about bisexuality as such, but also about its specific manifestations in homosexuality and transsexualism. Krafft-Ebing did not name the latter condition, but anticipated much present-day knowledge about it. His clinical observations taught him that: 'Hermaphroditism and sexual inversion stand in no relation to each other. This is clear from the fact that the hermaphrodite does not offer inverted sexuality, while, on the other hand, hermaphroditism has never been anatomically observed in cases of antipathetic sexual instinct.' (*Psychopathia Sexualis*, pp. 228, 229)

A strange case of sexual change in a woman may have stimulated his avant-garde ideas of transsexualism. A Professor Kaltenbach had consulted him about her. She was married, thirty years of age, and Kaltenbach thought her to be a case of precocious onset of the change of life. Hair grew all over her body, and she developed acne on a skin formerly white and smooth. Her voice broke, and both her expressive and psycho-motor behaviour changed into the 'masculine'. At the same time her character had altered. Formerly mild and obedient, she was now energetic, aggressive and hard to control. Both Krafft-Ebing and Kaltenbach were amazed about this metamorphosis. Krafft-Ebing's explanation was: '. . . loss of former feminine sexuality. Physical and psychical development of male sexuality, hitherto latent. Interesting illustration of the bisexual predisposition, and of the possibility of the continued existence of a second sexuality in a latent state, under conditions hitherto unknown.' (ibid. p. 230)

Krafft-Ebing had occasion to observe two similar cases, but with them the change of sex was only on a psychical level. Krafft-Ebing was, in my opinion, the most important investigator of psychosexual problems in the nineteenth century, and prepared the ground for the Freudian revolution. It is regrettable that neither Freud nor his followers gave him the recognition he deserved. And modern authors on transsexualism altogether fail to recognize their debt to him. R. Stoller dismissed him out of hand, and R. Green mentioned him as of historical significance only. In his biography of Freud, E. Jones wrote about his ambivalent feelings towards Krafft-Ebing, who was Professor of Neurology and Psychiatry at the University of Vienna when Freud started his career in psychoanalysis. He did not agree with Freud's novel ideas on hysteria, and openly disapproved of them. The younger man was hurt by the rejection, and resented the narrow-minded attitude of his senior colleague. But when Krafft-Ebing tried, though unsuccessfully, to get him a Professorship at Vienna University, he seemed to be reconciled. He mentioned his work on a number of occasions, but not with the appreciation it deserved. Perhaps the carousel of time will reinstate Krafft-Ebing to his true significance.

I am relating a case history from *Psychopathia Sexualis*, and some general passages from this book in order to show his clinical acumen and his progressive ideas. To start with, here are some examples of his thoughts:

> Sexual feeling is really the root of all ethics, and no doubt of aesthetics and religion . . . Observation teaches us that the pure type of man and woman is often enough missed by nature, that is to say that certain secondary male characteristics are found in women and vice versa. This shows, for instance, in vice versa occupations. In both instances particular cleverness in the inverted – and pronounced awkwardness in the originally proper occupations, will be noticed. (p. 27)

In a section dealing with gynecomastia (development of breasts in men), he wrote: 'Such men are feminine, also in secondary characteristics – soft skin, high voice, wide pelvis and pubic hair of the feminine type develops.'

On the grounds of these physical signs he asked the pertinent question: 'What determines the development of an individual of that definite type – man or woman?' And: 'That the sexual glands are important so far as the sex itself is concerned, is hardly open to controversy, but they are not necessarily *the determining factor*.' [italics mine] (p. 28)

Krafft-Ebing thus expressed modern ideas on gender identity and assignment.

These quotations show that Krafft-Ebing was ahead of his time. But he was also rooted in the past, being held back by the mores of his time, which became apparent in his quotation from Chevalier's *L'Inversion Sexuelle* (1893): 'This destruction of antipathetic sexuality [homosexuality] is at present not yet completed. In the same manner in which the appendix points to former stages of organization, so may also be found in the sexual apparatus – in the male as well as the female – residua, which point to the original bisexuality.' (p. 227)

Many present-day psychiatrists and psychologists would not argue with this citation. The view that bi- and homosexuality are immature states of psychosexual development is still held by many. They are convinced that heterosexuality represents sexual maturity, an attitude to which Freud also subscribed. In the context of Krafft-Ebing's far-reaching insights, his leaning towards normality and conventional morality is particularly disappointing. But it does not diminish his outstanding merits, of which the most striking are: the anticipation of modern ideas about gender identity and gender assignment, and the clearly designed profile of transsexualism which he classified as a form of psychical hermaphroditism. This is illustrated in the autobiography of a physician, Case 129, published in *Psychopathia Sexualis*, which is one of the outstanding case histories in Krafft-Ebing's *chef d'œuvre*. It is also by far the longest, and I am re-telling it here in a shortened version.

Born in 1844 of a great Hungarian family, he was for many years an only child. His family had a bad record of nervous and psychological illnesses, and sisters as well as brothers had died from a constitutional weakness. Only one brother, born a long time after him, survived.

His eccentric mother, whom he adored, dressed him as a girl. His blond, curled hair and clear skin completed the feminine attributes of his appearance. He was a precocious child who could read and write at the age of four. Gifted and cursed with a vivid imagination, he was disturbed by nightmares. This strange little boy was compliant, very obedient and docile. People liked him, particularly the older generation, because he never upset anyone with tantrums or any other display of 'temperament'. He had male playmates whom he liked, but he felt just as content with their sisters. They treated him as one of themselves, and he recounts that he was well on the way to becoming 'altogether a girl'. Although he liked the company of other children he preferred, above all else, staying at home with his mother.

This childhood paradise was not to last. Boys teased him about his girlish appearance and pursuits. He reacted by trying to be one better than them, imitating 'masculine' behaviour. He climbed trees, played at soldiers, fought with his mates and avoided girls. From then on, he kept his predilection for a 'feminine' appearance to himself. But he could not avoid looking like a girl in spite of his new-found boyish manners.

When his family had to move to Germany because of his father's profession, his old problem became acute again. His schoolmates teased him mercilessly about his girlish looks and his involuntary 'feminine' gestures. They even gave him the name of a girl. Strangely enough, his mother did not react to 'social' opinion, and continued to dress him in a coquettish manner. He reacted again by taking the opposite direction, assuming attitudes alien to his nature. Yet he felt awkward in long trousers and, of course, in the whole masquerade. He felt uncomfortable in the genital region, particularly at gymnastics. He was unable to execute all the exercises, and had to restrict himself to those which girls could do without pain. He disliked undressing in the company of other boys, and already at the age of thirteen realized full well that he wanted to be a woman. Yet he never wanted a male lover. His feelings for other men remained entirely in the realm of friendship. He thought of himself as a 'double' creature, a real man with feminine sensibilities. He experienced paradoxical feelings in all his contacts. He wanted to be with girls but his approach to them was not that of a male. On the other hand, he had grown tall, and had started to grow a beard, which made him physically inconspicuous. It also helped him to 'act' in a virile fashion. He joined a dissolute group of students, drank and fought with them, and went to bed with women as they did. But he always knew that his behaviour was nothing but a mask to disguise his real nature. He had no coital difficulties, but desired to lie underneath the woman, a preference which lasted throughout his life. Uncertainty about his sexual identity drove him to onanism, which aggravated rather than helped his inner tensions.

And so he lived a double life. Family obligations forced another problem on him: marriage. The uncertainty about such an important step made him hesitate for quite a time.

As it happened, he fell deeply in love with a 'masculine' woman, and married her. He was by then a dedicated physician and the satisfaction he found in his job may have given him a better sense of balance in his personal life. He enjoyed the physical side of marriage, but with the proviso that he had to take the conventional female role, lying on his back, making love as a woman in the shape of a man. His wife had a complete understanding of him, and their marriage which produced five sons was a happy one. But this happiness was broken by illness. After an attack of gout, he became more and more neurasthenic and hypochondriacal. He was tormented by migraine and angina pectoralis. He felt pain all over his body, and frequently visited spas in order to find relief. Failure to get help turned him to drugs and he became dependent on hashish. The drug altered his life. His perception of his body (his body image), changed radically: he thought that his genitals had undergone a transformation. His male parts had shrivelled, and he was now also physically a woman. His small breasts swelled at sexual excitement and every month he experienced period pains. His pelvis had broadened and taken on a definitely feminine shape. In fact, he had gone through a metamorphosis in every respect. While he had formerly been a man with feminine tastes and sensibilities, he was now a woman from top to bottom, in every fibre of his being. His former sexual identity complex had been solved, though in the 'opposite' direction. His moods now stabilized, he became a contented person who endured his illnesses, actual or imagined, with patience and equanimity. He still functioned as a male in the sexual situation, but in the conventional female position and with female sensations.

The doctor as patient, remained an observer of his hallucinatory state. His sense of reality must have been unconsciously preserved, which prevented him from ending his life as a psychotic. He came through the amazing episode of a sexual transformation without being irreparably damaged. In a letter to Krafft-Ebing which accompanied his life-story, he wrote: 'I also thought it might interest you from the pen of a physician, how such a worthless human or masculine being thinks and feels under the imperative idea of being a woman.'

Krafft-Ebing commented that this patient was able to control his abnormal feelings, and thus escaped the danger of becoming a paranoiac.

The physician's story contains all the characteristics of male transsexualism as mentioned in recent research studies by Stoller and others:

1 obsessional preoccupation with the physical and mental phenomena of 'contrary' sex
2 compulsive desire to be of the opposite sex
3 indifference towards homosexuality
4 dichotomy between male sexual function and female sexual sensations during coitus
5 complete introversion
6 abnormally close mother/son relationship during childhood
7 predominance of auto-eroticism.

Female bisexuality is also described in *Psychopathia Sexualis*, where, as in the story of Mrs M., love for women is overwhelmingly emotional, and that for men mainly physical. Krafft-Ebing himself held the view that homosexual inclinations predominated in bisexual men and women.

It is of considerable interest that he not only extended sexological knowledge, but, later in life, shed the moralistic prejudices of his generation. He abandoned his former opinion that bi- and homosexuality were morbid and immoral, and saw them as sexual variations, consistent with psychic health (Ellis, op. cit. p. 70). He was also in agreement with progressive legal thinking, in that, except under certain circumstances, neither homosexuality nor gross indecency should be punishable offences. Otherwise, consenting adults should be free to live according to their sexual inclinations when they reached the age of maturity, which he proposed should be sixteen. (Ellis, op. cit. p. 354) Psychiatry owes a great debt to the father of sexology, and remembrance of his merits would go some way towards paying it.

Past achievements are the foundation of present-day knowledge. Without their proper evaluation, science and psychology would stand on clay feet. It is also a matter of integrity to pay respect to those who prepared the paths which we now tread. Unfortunately, it has happened all too often that authors have claimed priority of discoveries which were made by others before them. In his delightful book *Nonscience* (1971), Brian Ford satirized many famous authors who claimed priority which belonged to authors of the past.

The immediate heirs of Richard von Krafft-Ebing were Sigmund Freud, Havelock Ellis and Magnus Hirschfeld, a triumvirate who determined the next stage of sexological knowledge. They were contemporaries, Freud and Havelock Ellis being practically the same age, and Hirschfeld a few years younger. None of them denied their debt to their eminent predecessor, but each acknowledged it with a personal slant, which made all the difference. Freud's acknowledgement was tainted by the resentment of his earlier years. He mentioned Krafft-Ebing on several occasions in *Three Essays on the Theory of Sexuality*, more often than not in footnotes. He gave him, though, full praise in his *Collected Papers* (1949) for his original description of the sado-masochistic syndrome. He acknowledged his merit in having coined the terms sadism and masochism, but he failed to give him the respect he deserved in the field of sexual variations, where he made so much progress himself. Havelock Ellis allotted to Krafft-Ebing ample space in the book already cited. His name appeared there almost as often as that of Magnus Hirschfeld, on whose work he much relied. He acknowledged Krafft-Ebing's importance for the theory of 'inversion', and gave him due credit for his concept of psychical hermaphroditism. He praised *Psychopathia Sexualis* as a storehouse of psychological facts, and the only book of lasting value that had been published for a long time. He paid tribute to Krafft-Ebing's clinical enthusiasm, and applauded him for having claimed sexual pathology as a branch of medicine (Ellis, op. cit. pp. 69–70). Magnus Hirschfeld dedicated his *Sexual Pathology* (1947) to the spirit of Krafft-Ebing's *chef d'œuvre*, which he commended as a magnificent work.

*

Freud gave a new meaning to the concept of bisexuality. He greatly enlarged its significance by recognizing that it played a vital part in the unconscious mind. He made bisexuality one of the corner-stones of psychoanalytical theory and practice. It is strange that the importance of psychical hermaphroditism had escaped him at the beginning of his career. He only got hold of it when Fliess handed it to him on a plate. Freud had ample opportunity to be acquainted with it through the writings of his eminent predecessor, Krafft-Ebing. Was it an inhibition, or were other preoccupations preventing him from grasping the fact that bisexuality was the essence of his work? In his introduction to Freud's *The Origins of Psychoanalysis*, E. Kris attributed the advance of his theory to the incorporation of the idea of bisexuality which he had taken over from Fliess, and accepted because of its magnificent simplicity. But he rejected Fliess's claim that cross-sexed qualities always remained unconscious, and were identical with the unconscious mind itself. Freud argued that this was too narrow and physical a view, as it excluded the wider psychological significance of bisexuality.

Freud had the ability to mix elements of thought which, by usual standards, could not be mixed. He succeeded in introducing myth into psychoanalytic thinking which was essentially rational. Although Melanie Klein surpassed him in her imaginative insights into the mystery of ancient legends, he recognized that mythological thought could be integrated into the logical system of his own theory. Logos took the lead in everything Freud wrote. For this reason, his use of mythological ideas was veiled and implied rather than directly stated. The intellectual sharpness of his formulations diminished their imaginative impact. One can look at this as either a loss or a gain. What Freud's approach lost in imaginative power, it gained in rational persuasiveness. He realized that the language of myth was the code language of man's archaic inheritance, which expressed unconscious desires common to all mankind. The French anthropologist, Lévi-Strauss, made a special study of mythology on similar lines, and accepted the Freudian method of looking at it.

Freud's interpretation of dreams and free associations is a subjective key of de-coding the unconscious. It is open to question whether or not it is the right one. Similar doubt can be cast on his priority in the discovery of the unconscious.

'And there is no new thing under the sun,' said Ecclesiastes (the Preacher, chp. I, v. 9) over 2,700 years ago. His saying has only too often been proved true, which puts the whole concept of priority into disarray anyway. Freud's attitude to Fliess is a case in point.

He had rejected his friend's suggestion that qualities of the opposite sex were repressed into the unconscious, but he used this very idea in his explanation of neurotic states and particularly hysteria. And worse, he claimed the concept of bisexuality to be his own. It is however to Freud's credit that he admitted having had a *lapsus memoriae* about Fliess's priority. It is likely that his own conflicts, particularly his resentment of hostile criticism of psychoanalysis, were responsible for this misplaced self-assertion. He was indeed ingenious in moulding the ideas of others anew. His unusual mental powers enabled him to lighten the underground territories of the mind. He revolutionized psychology in freeing it from the shackles of Christian morality, and in realizing the intricate connection between bisexuality and unconscious processes of the mind. He recognized that bisexuality was the driving force of the psyche, ruling mind and emotion in health and disease. Yet he failed to define it clearly. In the end, he admitted that he was unable to understand it fully. As a psychiatrist, Freud's attention was drawn primarily to emotional and mental disturbances, and he considered bisexuality to be a decisive factor in neurosis and psychosis. He saw its particular significance in the emotional and erotic development of the child. This is no small achievement. Whether or not one agrees with his theory, the way in which he made the concept of bisexuality fit into the psychoanalytic system is admirable. Freud claimed that bisexuality was the root cause of incestuous impulses in children. He based this assumption on the psychoanalysis of adult neurotics, which exposed him to severe criticism from the start. He tried to counter such allegations in the case history of 'A Phobia in a Five Year Old Boy' (1909), where he wrote: 'That no sharp line can be drawn between neurotic and normal people – whether children or adults . . . and that a number of individuals are constantly passing from the class of healthy people into that of neurotic patients, while a far smaller number also make the journey in the opposite direction.'

He must have been aware of the weakness of his explanation because he repeatedly urged his pupils to psychoanalyse children, a task which Melanie Klein had made her own. His method of psychoanalysis gave him the tools for a delicate mental surgery with which to diagnose and treat his patients. Krafft-Ebing lacked this advantage, but his simple case histories perhaps carry more conviction because they were not forced into the corset of a theory. Be that as it may, Freud's contribution was outstanding because of the new vista he gave to unconscious processes of the mind in general, and to bisexuality in particular. His paper *Hysterical Fantasies and Bisexuality* (1908) is a masterpiece. His talmudic method of arguing, tortuous as it may be, led in the end to a lucid explanation of a condition which has puzzled the medical profession up to the present time. Freud assumed the existence of unconscious fantasies which once had been conscious, and were intimately related to hysterical symptoms. He enumerated nine 'points' to show how this worked, and concluded that the condition was related to infantile and repressed sexuality. The ninth point contained the essence of them all, and runs like this: 'An hysterical symptom is the expression of both a masculine and a feminine unconscious sexual fantasy.'

He concluded from this that a bisexual disposition can be seen most clearly in emotional disturbances. This was true for his generation, but loses its significance in our time. It does not, however, diminish his merit because no psychological insight is timeless. Social conditions inevitably affect the psyche of both investigators and investigated. Freud was still bound to the Victorian era with its pronounced sense of male superiority. In later life he realized he had suffered from the fact that the psychological research of his time was entirely male orientated, and that he had failed to understand the female psyche. His exploration of bisexuality in the male is original and penetrating, whereas it is faulty and confused where the female is concerned. His paper 'A Child Is Being Beaten' (1919) is a good example of this imbalance. He deals here with sado-masochistic fantasies manifested in sexual reactions to images of children being beaten. He acquired his knowledge about this phenomenon through the analysis of four women and two men. He had found, in his tortuous, roundabout way, that all of them showed repressed incestuous wishes. He equated the sadistic fantasies of girls with their male component, and the masochistic ones of boys with their female component. He believed that the male's condition was related to suppressed libidinous wishes for his father. Yet the person who did the beating was generally represented by the mother. The boy unconsciously changed her image into that of the father. This twist would appear to be ludicrous, if Freud had not added that the mother was the boy's 'normal' love object. In doing so, he somewhat balanced his interpretation. One may or may not believe in his analysis. I personally think it suspect because I doubt that the repressed incestuous libido could be responsible for sado-masochistic fantasies. Sadistic and masochistic impulses are, in my view, common reactions in every human being, and have a constitutional root.

Although Freud equated the sadistic fantasies of girls with their male component, yet he related their libidinous wishes always to the father. This makes no sense at all, as, according to his ideas of the female Oedipus complex, they should be yielding (masochistically) to the object of their love. Freud apparently did not realize that girls might desire their mothers in the same way as boys did. But it is to his credit that he ended his paper in a spirit of uncertainty, and practically admitted that he did not know the answer to the girl's bisexuality. He never got away from seeing her as a mutilated boy who always felt deprived, and suffered from a congenital castration complex. He never stated clearly that boys also wished to be of the opposite sex, in spite of the fact that he was made aware of this through a psychoanalytic session reported in 'A Phobia in a Five Year Old Boy', whose bisexuality could not have been better expressed than through the following dialogue, which took place between him and his mother:

I [the mother]: What were you playing at with your doll?
Hans: I said 'Grete' to her.
I: Why?
Hans: Because I said 'Grete' to her.
I: How did you play?
Hans: I just looked after her like a real baby.
I: Would you like to have a little girl?
Hans: Oh yes. Why not? I should like to have one, but mammy must not have one. I don't like that.
I: But only women have children.
Hans: I'm going to have a little girl.

This extract shows not only the boy's confusion about sexual differences, but also his envy of the reproductive function of the mother.

In the end, Freud learned by trial and error to have some understanding of women, and of female bisexuality. Late in life he wrote *Female Sexuality* (1931) which is essentially an apologia for his misunderstanding, if not ignorance, of the girl's early attachment to her mother, without which her bisexuality could not be explained. He realized that the cause of his inadequacy was his maleness, which always induced his women patients to have a father-transference on him. He admitted that women analysts had a better chance of dealing with women's problems, because they had the advantage of being mother figures.

His failure to see clearly where he went wrong had, however, a deeper reason than he thought. It was the result of his upbringing in a heavily male-dominated society. His Jewish origin might have accentuated his male arrogance. Although in the end he progressed somewhat in his understanding of women, he was never able to come to terms with the whole complexity of female psychosexuality. But he deserves credit for his 'apologia', and for the correction of his view that male and female bisexuality were analogous. In the paper mentioned he underlined the difference between the two. Although his conclusions were flawed by old prejudices, he appreciated that a girl's 'pre-Oedipal' attachment to her mother exceeded in intensity and passion that of the boy. In comparing female and male development, he wrote: 'First of all there can be no doubt that the bisexual disposition which we maintain to be characteristic of human beings, manifests itself much more plainly in the female than in the male.'

So far so good, but he went wrong in the explanation of this statement. He thought that the clitoris and vagina represented two sexual zones, a 'masculine' and a 'feminine' one, while the male had to be content with only the penile region. Firstly, the division into clitoral and vaginal zones is artificial, because both are interdependent in their response to sexual stimuli. Secondly, the anal zone tends to be more sensitized in males than females, and can serve as a sexual zone in itself. Freud saw bisexuality and homosexuality in black and white terms. For him, the 'masculine' or active component of the girl made her desire her mother, while she turned to her father armed with 'feminine' charms and the wish for submission. Freud was in error about the girl's situation with both. In an earlier study (*Love Between Women*, 1971) I have shown that, in lesbians, sexual responses are both male and female. The emphasis can be either on one or the other, at the same time or at intervals, which gives considerable variation and flexibility to lesbian love. My present research has shown that the same holds good for female bisexuality.

Freud could be as enlightened as he could be uncertain. He expressed long ago the modern idea that the words 'masculine' and 'feminine' had no real meaning. For a time, he preferred instead to differentiate between active and passive qualities but also felt uncertain about this classification. One cannot but agree with him that it is questionable whether any division between specifically male and female qualities is justifiable at all. Unfortunately, he never got to the truth about female psychosexuality, but he went some way towards it. He progressed because he was not afraid to admit that his former views were mistaken. He was an eternal student, which made him, finally, a master, in spite of obvious flaws in his teaching. The way he developed the theme of bisexuality is crystallized in a number of papers, and in *Three Essays on the Theory of Sexuality*,

Freud produced some excellent formulations of bisexuality. For example, he wrote in one of his 'Letters to Fliess': 'In every sexual act four persons are involved' (p. 289). This is, indeed, the very essence of bisexuality.

The same lucidity is evident in the following from *Three Essays on the Theory of Sexuality*: 'The sexual object [in homosexuality] is not someone of the same sex, but someone who combines the characteristics of both sexes.' No better explanation of the intrinsic connection between bi- and homosexuality could be given.

But perhaps the most impressive of his verbal 'pearls' is this:

> It is well known that at all times there have been, as there are, human beings who can take as their sexual objects persons of either sex without the one trend interfering with the other. We call these people bisexual ... But we have come to know that all human beings are bisexual in this sense, and that their libido is distributed between objects of both sexes, either in manifest or latent form. But the following point strikes us. While in the individuals I first mentioned the libidinous impulses can take both directions without producing a clash, in the other, more frequent, cases, the result is an irreconcilable conflict. (*Collected Papers*, Vol. V, p. 347)

I consider this statement to be perfect, though the conflict is, in our time, less irreconcilable.

Freud's ideas and research about bisexuality might never have come to fruition without his long-standing friendship with Wilhelm Fliess. On the other hand, Fliess's name would not be known outside Germany if he had not been instrumental in stimulating Freud's thoughts on bisexuality. But Fliess was his own man and pioneered the idea of periodicity, which is a special form of numerology. He assumed that two vital days in the life of every woman and man directed their destiny and that of their descendants. The lucky or fatal days depended on the numbers twenty-eight and twenty-three, the former signifying the female, the latter the male period. Both periods were active in either sex because of the innate bisexuality of human beings. In Germany, his theory aroused enormous interest beyond medical circles. Fliess had the misfortune to be plagiarized by two contemporaries, Weininger and Swoboda, and to be dismissed as an 'unsound' investigator by foreign colleagues up to this day. But I maintain that he should be taken seriously for the following reasons: firstly, the rhythmical course of events goes far beyond the biological side of life. Time's eternal return makes incisions in the inner and outer life of man and beast, and does so at regular intervals. And secondly, bisexuality creates tensions in human beings (and animals) without which progress and vivacity would vanish. Nothing exists without polarity. There must be a time for action and a time for rest, which is the conditio sine qua non of our inner and outer existence. Male and female periods introduce the time factor into bisexuality.

I do not know whether Fliess's calculations of such definite days as he suggests were justifiable. But the fundamental idea behind them is a signpost which points to a valuable area of research into biopsychological functions. There is another aspect of his thought to which attention should be paid, namely that of the significance of right and left. Fliess was convinced that the asymmetry of left and right of the human body represented the 'masculine' and 'feminine' qualities of the person. Their denomination is wrong, but nobody can doubt that we sway between more active and expansive and more imaginative and reflective moods. Whatever name we may give to them, these reactions express our bisexuality. I have a personal reason for giving prominence to Fliess's fascinating theory. My studies of the human hand produced evidence that the right represented the rational and active, and the left the imaginative and intuitive side of the personality. The American psychologist, Werner Wolff, came to similar conclusions about the human face. His experiments proved that we were indeed 'double-faced'. The right half of the face presented the mask we show to the world, while the left mirrored what we really are – our Self. In his book, *Vom Leben und Vom Tod* (1914), Fliess claimed that the left part of the face was related to the 'feminine' side in men and to the 'masculine' in women. He gave a number of examples of left-accentuated faces in famous artists. Among them were Michelangelo, Leonardo da Vinci, Schumann and Goethe. The two great Italians were left-handed, too. He rightly stated that bisexuality was most obvious in artists, and that the names mentioned belonged to those who were known to have loved men and women. Fliess's assumption that left-handedness followed the same pattern was not borne out by my own studies, though confirmed by Magnus Hirschfeld.

One cannot write about Fliess without mentioning Weininger, the philosopher whom he accused of having plagiarized his ideas. Weininger's book *Geschlecht und Charakter* (1903) was a bestseller in Germany, was translated into many foreign languages, and has always been recognized as an important contribution to sexology. He made use of Fliess's 'law' of periodicity, but mentioned his name only in a reference in small print. But he developed this theory in connection with bisexuality in his own way, and presented it with considerable élan, notwithstanding sensationalism. The book is as full of insights as of irrational assumptions. Weininger was a desperado and a Jew, who hated Jews and women. His 'male superiority' and his anti-semitism were expressed in emotive language. They clouded his judgement and faulted his book. His utterances about women were so idiosyncratic and ridiculous that one can only take them as a bad joke. He claimed that the features of every 'great' woman were of a decidedly 'masculine' type. It was the male in the female who craved emancipation. He also proposed that the highest form of love a woman could attain was lesbian love. All 'feminine' qualities were despicable in his eyes. Weininger was a creature of extremes, and one comes across remarkable insights side by side with naiveties. He maintained that every human being oscillated between the male and female. These oscillations were great or small in different individuals, but also varied considerably in the same person. Sometimes they were enormous, sometimes minimal, but they were always there. And when they were considerable, they affected the appearance of the person (for example, expression, gesture). Apart from day-to-day changes in their strength, the accent on 'masculinity' or 'femininity' was subject to a general periodicity. It was Weininger's original idea to recognize the flexible character of bisexuality, which manifested itself in sequences (*im nacheinander*) and not simultaneously.

Although Fliess's contribution to bisexuality has nothing to do with psychoanalysis, his influence on Freud justifies my inclusion of his ideas in connection with him. And I think it right to mention at the same time Weininger's work, which was greatly influenced by Fliess.

Helene Deutsch, one of the most distinguished analysts of her generation, was both a great theoretician and a great practitioner. The theme of bisexuality played a considerable part in her book, *The Psychology of Women* (1946), which revealed her as an innovator who let 'fresh air' into psychoanalytic thinking. She was one of the women analysts who filled the gap in Freud's truncated knowledge of female sexuality. Her emphasis on the influence of female bisexuality in pre-puberty and adolescence is of particular interest. At that time, according to Deutsch, the girl is not quite sure of her gender identity, and uncertain whether she loves men or women. She vacillates between the two. Her bisexuality produces conflicts, and, in some cases, emotional instability. Love and hatred of the person she favours follow in rapid succession, as she experiences difficulties in integrating her 'masculine' and 'feminine' components. Deutsch's merit lies in her meticulous observation of bisexual tendencies throughout a woman's life, which she illustrated with many case histories.

A most vivid example is her detailed account of George Sand's bisexuality. As a child, she used to play in front of a mirror: now she was her father, now her mother. She changed from boy to girl, and saw herself dressed either as a fashionable man or an elegant woman. She continued to play the two parts all her life. Deutsch understood that emotional difficulties of bisexual women were not always reflected in personal relationships, but sometimes in general aggressiveness and over-ambitious pursuits. She observed that environmental influences determined the direction which bisexuality took in individual women. She stressed the mother-daughter relationship as the prime mover of a girl's need for female love. She underlined the desirability of their mutual bond, and acknowledged the naturalness of lesbianism. Deutsch modified the notion of the girl's penis envy, which was a considerable advance; she did not deny its existence, but did not think that the comparison of the clitoris with the penis was its cause. She believed in a 'secondary' penis envy. But in some respects, Deutsch remained old-fashioned. She retained the notions of 'masculinity' and 'femininity', and considered feminine qualities to be tainted by passivity and masochism. Her re-formulation of penis envy lacked a clear definition. Although she wanted the term to be changed to envy of men, she believed it to be due to 'inner' causes. Deutsch referred to this subject in the chapter 'Environmental Influences' of the book mentioned; she overlooked the overwhelming social evidence for female 'sexual inferiority'. My research on female homosexuality has shown that 'outer' causes, namely a woman's social disadvantages, are at the back of her envy of the male.

Karen Horney proved in her book *Feminine Psychology* (1967) that she had the same independence from psychoanalytic orthodoxy as Helene Deutsch. One could claim that she went further, because she rebelled more strongly against its dogmatic views on infantile sexuality. Her wide practical experience as a therapist, combined with her brilliant intellectual acumen, quashed certain long-held convictions of the psychoanalytical school. She countered some of them in the following:

> Freud's statement that 'it is well known that a clearly defined differentiation between the male and the female character is first established at puberty'... On the contrary, I have always been struck by the marked way in which little girls between their second and fifth year exhibit specifically feminine traits... From the beginning I have found it difficult to reconcile these impressions with Freud's view of the initial masculine trend of the little girl's sexuality. (ibid. p. 150)

She refuted Freud's concept of penis envy. It was not true that only girls were envious of the opposite sex. She wrote: 'Boys expressed, at the same age, a parallel tendency in the form of wishes to possess breasts or to have a child.' And: 'In neither sex have these manifestations any influence on the child's behaviour as a whole' (ibid. pp. 151–2).

She thus dismissed the idea of the girl's assumed sexual inferiority. All her statements have the hallmark of simplicity and indisputable authority. Freud referred to her in his paper *Female Sexuality* as the analyst with whom he did not see eye to eye. She belonged to the small group of psychoanalysts who denied Freud's assertion that a girl's sexual sensations were only clitoral. Horney and one of her colleagues, Josche Hiller, had observed vaginal masturbation during the first five years of life. Their observations were confirmed by Professor Liepmann, a well-known German gynaecologist and my own teacher.

Horney gave the concept of castration-fear in the male a new slant, when she said: 'Once we realize that masculine castration is very largely the ego's response to the wish to be a woman, we cannot altogether share Freud's conviction that bisexuality manifests itself more clearly in the female than in the male'. (ibid. p. 144)

In the chapter 'The Neurotic Need for Love', Karen Horney gave a warning not to confuse sexual orientation with the need of the neurotic to lean and to be loved. She drew attention to the difference between authentic homosexuality and the dependency of neurotic people on members of their own sex. Her wise admonition holds good also for bisexual people, who might turn to either sex for reasons other than natural choice.

Karen Horney was probably the most 'liberated' psychoanalyst of her generation, but Georg Groddek was the *enfant terrible* among them. His reputation rested on his personality rather than on theory. He was a 'natural', an intuitive man, with magnetic power over those who sought his help. He went his own way without fear or favour, and everything he wrote had the marks of authenticity and originality. He went further than other psychoanalysts in rejecting the idea that heterosexuality certified a person's sexual maturity. He maintained that bisexuality was the natural way of loving, and did not agree with his colleagues that it was (or should be) limited to childhood and puberty. He wrote in *The Book of the Id* (1950, first German edition 1923):

> Man is bisexual all his life long, and keeps his bisexuality. At the most he consents at one or another period of his life, as a concession to the moral code in fashion, to repress a portion – and it is a very small portion – of his homosexuality and in doing so, he does not destroy it, but merely narrows its range. And just as no-one is purely heterosexual, so no-one is purely homosexual... For my part, I hazard the question that the woman's eroticism is much freer than the man's in relation to the two sexes: it seems to me as if she had a fairly equal capacity of love for either sex.' (pp. 234, 236)

I have been able to test his challenging statement in interviews with, and autobiographies of, women participants, with the proviso that their love for women was distinctly different from that for men.

Bisexuality is a foregone conclusion in psychoanalytic theory, but its meaning and importance was seen in different ways by different analysts. Ronald Fairbairn deserves a special mention in this context. He rejected Freud's version of the Oedipus complex. In his book *Psychoanalytic Studies of the Personality* (1952), he accepted its existence, but denied a primary bisexual attachment to the parents. The first need of the baby was safety, and all his/her impulses were directed towards it. The infant's bisexual libidinous expressions came second. They were the means to an end, designed to ensure the goodwill of both parents. Fairbairn's view is close to my own, of which I gave a detailed exposition in *Love Between Women*.

Havelock Ellis was without doubt the most colourful person ever to engage in psychosexual studies, for the simple reason that his mind extended far beyond the work for which he became most famous, *Studies in the Psychology of Sex*.

In his later photographs he looked like an English Rabindranath Tagore. This might give a clue to his foremost vocation. He was essentially a poet for whom the aesthetic principle was paramount. The integrity in everything he stood and worked for gave his writings the stamp of authenticity and authority. His autobiography reveals him as a man of many facets. He had an enormous curiosity for all things of the mind, and experienced considerable difficulty in being definite about anything. An idealist and romantic, he made considerable allowances for other people's behaviour, but very few for himself. Havelock Ellis's personality was so strongly connected with his work, that one cannot give a just estimate of the latter without taking the former into account. He tried a number of professions before he studied medicine; he was a 'literateur' before he became engaged in psychology. He was a man of progressive politics who fought for women's rights and associated with anarchists. At the same time he read and wrote voluminously, to the point of overstretching himself and his writings. His *Studies in the Psychology of Sex* is an encyclopaedia of sexological knowledge, and there can be no doubt about his scholarship. But his ideas relied much on those of others, which created a disproportion between the voluminous size of his books and their originality. I spoke of his difficulty in taking a definite stance. This aspect of his character was reflected in his work. He tended to contradict himself, particularly on the subject of bisexuality. He was sure that bisexuality was a biological condition, but seemed uncertain whether it existed in a psychological sense also. Here are two examples of his ambivalent attitude: 'If indeed we really accept the very reasonable view that the basis of the sexual life is bisexuality . . . it becomes difficult to see how one can speak of a spurious class of homosexuals.' (Ellis, op. cit. Vol. II, 'Sexual Inversion in Men', p. 86) Two pages further on, he stated: 'The bisexual group introduces uncertainty and doubt, because homosexuals may be made bisexual through social pressure.' In the same chapter, he compared bisexuality with ambidexterity, which affirmed his biological view of it. Havelock Ellis could not really come to terms with psychical hermaphroditism, yet he believed in Freud's discovery of the link between bisexuality and neurotic and mental disturbances. He agreed with Freud's observation that the clitoris was larger in childhood than in later life, and assumed that lesbians retained this trait. He equated lesbianism with physical masculinization, which was consistent with his biological view of homosexuality. On the other hand, he almost went along with Moll, the famous German psychiatrist and researcher in sexual 'pathology', who claimed that homosexuality could be cured because homosexual men could be made to love boyish women on account of their bisexuality. Ellis conceded: 'In the case of bisexual individuals or of youthful subjects whose homosexuality is not fully developed, it is possible that this method is beneficial' (ibid. p. 330). He went into every aspect of sexual behaviour, and also made a study of the dreams of 'inverts'. He found that most homosexuals dreamed of people of their own sex. Those who did not were bisexuals. His observations were not confirmed by my own research. The situation is far more complex. A study of 108 lesbians revealed in many cases dreams of intercourse with men.

Ellis produced interesting information about the periodicity of sexual desire. It roughly corresponded with the theory of Fliess, who, as Ellis reported, had not been the first to pioneer the idea. Already in 1846, an English author, Laycock, wrote that the nervous system in women underwent periodical changes in the seasons, particularly during the equinoxes, and that these changes were largely sexual. He also mentioned a Dr Koster, a German physician who wrote a book *Uber die Gesetze des periodischen Irreseins und verwandter Nervenzustände* ('On the laws of periodic insanity and related nervous states', 1882). Ellis claimed that the periodical rhythm of sexual activity was more marked in women than men. He failed, however, to recognize the cyclic recurrence of a male/female erotism in women, which pointed to a bisexual periodicity.

Havelock Ellis had an unusual depth of understanding for women of every sexual orientation, which bore witness to his intuitive power and his own femaleness. His notion that lesbians were always 'masculine' women was typical of his generation. His wife, an overt homosexual of the 'masculine' type, a woman of brilliant intelligence, was probably the model for his attitude to lesbians. His love for her might have been responsible for his belief in their mental superiority, a belief which he shared with Magnus Hirschfeld. In the chapter 'Sexual Inversion in Women' of the book cited, Ellis praised them as being far more adventurous, intelligent, and sexually more susceptible than 'normal' women. He believed that aesthetic sensibilities were an outstanding ingredient of lesbian love. He agreed with Moll that married lesbians had not the same horror of intercourse with the opposite sex as homosexual men, because of their greater passivity. In *Love Between Women*, I have shown that the real reason is the underlying bisexuality in lesbianism, which is of a different brand to that of male homosexuality.

Havelock Ellis was also a man of action who worked for sex reform and sex education. And he was a novelist, a translator of literary works as well as a political thinker. He approached his studies on sexual psychology in quite a different spirit from that of Freud. Although psychoanalysis was fundamentally alien to him, he had a great admiration for Freud's achievements, and quoted him abundantly in his books. For a time, his own reputation was on a par with Freud's, but in the end he was overshadowed by him. Ellis's life was marked by extremes. At one time he was prosecuted for obscenity, at another praised as one of the greatest writers ever on sexual matters. His fate mirrored the extremes of his personality. It is impossible to pigeon-hole him, but the impression I gained from his books, especially his autobiography, is that he was both a great savant and a great amateur.

Magnus Hirschfeld had much in common with Havelock Ellis. They shared many ideas on homosexuality and were dedicated to the pursuit of an enlightened sex education. They founded, together with August Forel, the World League for Sexual Reform for the purpose of propagating a more knowledgeable and understanding attitude towards sexual 'abnormalities'. Magnus Hirschfeld was on a par with Ellis in both his wide sexological knowledge and his humanitarian ideals.

Less of a romantic, but as much of an idealist as Ellis, he was one of the most eminent and successful practitioners of psychological medicine before the Second World War. He founded the *Institut für Sexualwissenschaften* (Institute of Sexological Science) in Berlin and claimed to have met several thousand homosexual people whom he advised and helped. His reputation in Germany and all over Europe equalled that which Krafft-Ebing once enjoyed. His main contribution to sexological literature was his book *Die Homosexualität des Mannes und des Weibes* (1914), which Ellis cherished as a masterpiece. Magnus Hirschfeld diverged from him in his view of psychoanalysis. He was in full agreement with Freud about the concept of bisexuality as a bio-psychological condition. Practically all other authors of the time believed in its biological basis, and explained sexual 'abnormality' as an innate condition. Only Ulrichs and Binet were exceptions to the rule.

Hirschfeld was much impressed by the endocrine experiments of Steinach and Ischlondsky. He believed that hormones had a vital bearing on homosexuality and other 'perversions', but appreciated the importance of psychological influences on these conditions. Even progressive sexologists of the period classified sexual orientations which were not heterosexual as 'abnormal'. Hirschfeld observed that sexual hyperaesthesia was frequent in bi- and homosexuality. He anticipated Kinsey when he wrote: 'In the case of bisexual people, the degree to which they are attracted to the one sex or the other, is usually widely different. The patient himself expresses this numerically, such as that he is attracted ninety per cent to the feminine and ten per cent to the masculine, or vice versa.' (*Sexual Pathology*, p. 148) In *Sexual Anomalies and Perversions*, which contains extracts from Hirschfeld's books, he is quoted as having written: 'Psychical hermaphroditism is a factor that has been considerably underrated by nearly all the experts.' And: 'Thus psychoanalysis has proved that all homosexuals of both sexes have had heterosexual inclinations in their youth . . . There is no exception to this rule . . .' (p. 212)

He dismissed Adler's theory that both sexes valued maleness and despised femaleness, and he disagreed with Adler's view that male homosexuality results from sexual failure with women. Hirschfeld had special praise for Ivan Bloch, who proclaimed that anthropological knowledge had changed the pathological view of 'perversions'. Bloch pointed out that bi- and homosexuality were sexual orientations common to all peoples of the world at any time of their existence. Hirschfeld accepted bi- and homosexuality as sexual variations, but classified them still as anomalies. Unfortunately, the old terms such as inversion, deviation and perversion, die hard. And their use continues even today, in spite of the 'permissive' society and a great number of progressive books on sexology. Hirschfeld differentiated between real and pseudo-homosexuality, and explained the latter through bisexuality. Like Kinsey, he graded homosexuals, but, unlike him, he classified a person as bisexual when the emphasis on the homo- and heterosexual components was about equal. It is noteworthy that Magnus Hirschfeld set up the first German marriage bureau in connection with his Institute. It became the model for similar enterprises in other countries. In doing so, he was the first advocate for an organization which catered for the greatest possible variety of partners. Present-day marriage bureaux and computer dating agencies could take a leaf out of his book, because his system included all sorts of human beings, from the more or less typical to the atypical – to use these wrong but easily understood terms. But he spoke out against the marriage of 'gays', as he had rarely seen it to be successful.

Hirschfeld's view that bi- and homosexual people tend to excel in the arts and literature was well known. A community of these 'outsiders' flocked around him; they regarded him not only as an understanding doctor and a humanitarian, but also as a real friend.

Alfred Kinsey and his collaborators undertook the largest statistical study ever made on sexual behaviour in men and women. The results were published in *Sexual Behaviour in the Human Male* (1945) and *Sexual Behaviour in the Human Female* (1948). It is paradoxical that I can only make the most meagre contribution on Kinsey and his team, who produced the most complete work of its kind. But the fact is that bisexuality did not come into Kinsey's rating scheme, and was only mentioned on one page in each of the two books. All that Kinsey wrote about the subject was: 'There remains, however, among both females and males, a considerable number of persons who include both homosexual and heterosexual responses and/or activities in their histories ... This group of persons is identified in the literature as bisexual' (second book cited, p. 468).

Kinsey explained that he omitted to introduce bisexuality into his rating scheme of sexuality because the 'common' reader would not know the meaning of the word. And he thought that many academics might also be ignorant about it. People tried to dichotomize the classification of phenomena, he argued, and, for this reason he confined himself to measuring homosexuality only, graded in accordance with its hetero- and homosexual components. His former collaborators and other research workers followed in his footsteps in applying the same model.

Hirschfeld and Moll rightly believed that the pathological view of sexual variations had been modified through anthropological evidence. There is no doubt that anthropology can teach psychology a great deal as, for example, Margaret Mead has shown.

Margaret Mead studied primitive societies of the South Sea Islands in the twenties. In *Coming of Age in Samoa* (1928) she made an important contribution to our knowledge of their sex-life. It is wholesome to learn that the physical appearance of certain men and women suggested characteristics of the opposite sex. But this was deceptive. In Bali, for example, both sexes looked very much alike. Some of the men were small, slender, with no specific muscular development. But they were proud of their maleness, and, as a rule, heterosexual, as was expected of them. In her book *Male and Female* (1949), Mead emphasized that the Balinese male would look feminine to us, but our criteria of 'masculinity' and 'femininity' were inoperative among the Balinese and other 'primitive' groups. The same holds good for the female. Some women were as tall as men or taller, of athletic build, and with as powerful a musculature as males. The development of their breasts and hips was scanty. Neither did they show 'feminine' qualities of temperament. They behaved in a fiery and aggressive manner, and enjoyed adventure. Yet they were by no means devoid of strong maternal impulses and sexual desire for the male.

Mead warned the reader not to confuse different 'racial' types with sexual orientation. In small and primitive communities, life was streamlined and sexual roles defined. But there were considerable differences between tribes in their assignment and appreciation of sex roles. In most of them, the place of the woman was very high, if not equal or even superior to that of the man. But there can be no doubt about the manifestations of bisexuality in a number of the tribes in their customs, beliefs, and educational system. In one of the tribes of New Guinea, boys and girls were treated alike. Boys developed the same tenderness towards babies as girls and their manners were wholly 'feminine'. Although the boys had to leave their 'bisexual' world at the onset of puberty in their early teens, nostalgia for 'womanhood' remained with them for good. But the men who performed their initiation ceremony watched over them and forbade any indulgence in their former habits. Homosexuality was strictly forbidden. Yet with many of the youngsters, it became an irresistible need which they pursued secretly (ibid. pp. 104–5).

In other 'primitive' societies Margaret Mead met individuals who did not follow the sexual stereotype. They experienced sensations, interests and attitudes which should be those of the opposite sex. And if their sense of identity was strong enough, they expressed them in spite of the rules of the community. Their sexual identity clashed with their gender identity which made them self-conscious. They felt out of touch with the great majority of their tribe. Although the latter conformed in day-to-day living with their sexual roles, their underlying bisexuality found spectacular expression in initiation ceremonies. Mead ascribed this phenomenon to men's envy of the female sex. The male of these tribes suffered from a basic insecurity:

> The underlying structure of the initiatory cult . . . provides such cogent counterpoint to our Western ideas of the relationship between the sexes. In our occidental view of life, woman, fashioned from Adam's rib, can, at most, strive unsuccessfully to imitate man's superior powers and higher vocations. The basic theme of the initiatory cult is, however, that women, by virtue of their ability to make children, hold the secrets of life . . . Men's role is uncertain, undefined, and perhaps unnecessary . . . Men can get the male children away from the women, brand them as incomplete, and themselves turn boys into men. Sometimes more overtly, sometimes less, these imitations of birth go on, as the initiates are swallowed by the crocodile that represents the men's group, and come out newborn at the other

end, as they are housed in *wombs* [my italics] or fed on blood, fattened, hand-fed and tended by male 'mothers'. Behind the cult lies the myth that in some way all this is stolen from the woman ... Men owe their manhood to a theft. (ibid. pp. 110–11)

In *Coming of Age in Samoa* Margaret Mead mentioned bi- and homosexuality in girls, but only as an aside. She dealt mainly with the diversity of sexual behaviour in men. Her observations confirmed the discovery of progressive psychoanalysts (mainly women) that the male-envied the female sexually. Manifestations of bisexuality in primitive societies bear witness to its universality, independent of race, colour and cultural evolution.

In her studies of primitive tribes in the South Sea Islands, Margaret Mead has shown that their ideas of 'masculinity' and 'femininity' are quite different from those of the Western world.

Earlier, Freud had felt uneasy about dividing human qualities according to sex. He tried to replace the words 'masculine' and 'feminine' with a more meaningful terminology, but was dissatisfied with his attempt. Since my study on lesbianism, I dismissed the supposition of sex-bound characteristics as a mental straight-jacket, and left it at that. Different schools of psychology still accept the existence of 'masculine' and 'feminine' qualities, and base their theories of bi- and homosexuality on this assumption.

It is odd that the concept of bisexuality which is basic to the understanding of sexual variations, has never been fully understood. The different interpretations given to it reflect uncertainty about its nature. I believe that the erroneous acceptance of 'masculine' and 'feminine' attributes is responsible for the failure to grasp its meaning. It is inconceivable that bisexuality could be the sum total of characteristics which are either amorphous or non-existent. Unfortunately, the old terms are ingrained in the vocabulary of professionals and laymen alike. I have therefore found it necessary to use them, but do so with inverted commas.

The struggle to come to terms with the meaning of bisexuality still goes on. Considerable strides towards a clearer notion were made during the last twenty-five years through the study of *transsexualism*. Harry Benjamin, an American psychiatrist, coined the word, and initiated the study of this phenomenon. Krafft-Ebing gave an example of it seventy years earlier in publishing the autobiography of a physician (Case 129). Transsexualism puts bisexuality into relief perhaps more concretely than other sexual variations. In his book *The Transsexual Phenomenon* (1966), Benjamin reported on his treatment of a great number of transsexuals. He always suggested conservative therapy first, and only gave way to their desire for surgery in suicidal cases.

Transsexuals are people who believe that their mind is trapped in the wrong-sex body, and they want to get rid of it by any means possible. Male transsexuals desire to live as women, and female transsexuals want to live as men. Some are satisfied with hormonal treatment, but many insist on a surgical transformation. Men who feel and react like women, women who feel and react like men, experience a violent clash between sexual and gender identity. It is not the dubious 'masculinity' and 'femininity' which bothers them, but a sense of belonging to the opposite sex.

Benjamin admitted that the etiology of transsexualism was still unclear. He believed in a mixture of causes, some biological and some psychological. He noted that the condition occurred far more often in men than women. He described it as the culmination of transvestism (the desire to dress in the clothes of the opposite sex).

The impetus which Benjamin gave to the study of an extreme manifestation of a contra-sexual urge, was taken up by a number of research workers in America.

John Money and Anka Erhardt of Johns Hopkins University worked on the whole range of human sexuality, but gave special consideration to bisexuality and transsexualism. They were biologically orientated and interpreted psychological reactions in these conditions in the light of genetic and hormonal influences.

Robert Stoller, psychiatrist and psychoanalyst, probably made the greatest advance in a theory of bisexuality in general and transsexualism in particular. In his books *Sex and Gender* (1968) and *The Transsexual Experiment* (1976), he showed that bisexuality played the major part in this conflict of gender identity. In the first book he wrote that bisexual mothers were the root cause of transsexualism in boys. Stoller, being a psychoanalyst, considered the mother-child relationship as basic in the making of cross-sexual identity. At the same time, he assumed that prenatal conditioning of the nervous system could predispose a child to this particular form of psychosexual hermaphroditism. Stoller greatly admired Freud's theory of bisexuality, which he accepted as the basis for his own ideas on the subject. Unfortunately, he still used the terms 'masculinity' and 'femininity' in describing its characteristics: but he did not agree with Freud's view that 'masculinity' was the ideal of every boy, and superior to 'femininity'. Stoller completely failed to understand early female bisexuality, but he had a perfect grasp of bisexuality in a grown-up woman, to which his book *Splitting* (1974) bears witness.

He described there the case of a Mrs G., a woman he had psychoanalysed for seven years. She alternated between experiencing herself as female and as male. She believed she had a penis when she loved a woman, but was a normal female when she loved a man. She was married and had a number of children, yet her homosexual side seemed to be the stronger.

In *Splitting*, Stoller still described Mrs G's bisexuality as a mixture of 'masculinity' and 'femininity'. Yet in *Sex and Gender* he had already coined the terms 'a sense of maleness' and 'a sense of femaleness', which he considered to be the essential features of a core gender identity. With the introduction of this concept, Stoller had made a real leap forward in the understanding of bisexuality.

Apart from individual research workers, a collective of transvestites and transsexuals, represented in the Beaumont Society, contributed significantly to the knowledge of bisexuality. One of its representatives, himself a transvestite, gave these definitions: 'The transvestite finds that he is both a "he" and a "she" together at one and the same time, or alternating from one to the other when opportunity or desire permits.' And: 'While the transsexual is either neutral or feminine in sexual behaviour (real or imaginary), the transvestite usually remains *entirely heterosexual*.' (from an article in the *Guardian*'s Miscellany page, September 1973)

It is the belief of the Beaumont Society that with transvestites, bisexuality is *within* the personality rather than expressed in sexual orientation. Their view that they are generally heterosexual is, however, not confirmed by Dr Randall (Director of the Sexual Identity Clinic at Charing Cross Hospital) nor by this study. In any case, the Beaumont Society, which caters for men only, discourages homosexual behaviour in its members. It was founded in America as an 'International Foundation of Full Personality Expression', encompassing both male and female reactions in every individual.

Over the last fifteen years, the school of Developmental Psychology researched 'masculinity', 'femininity' and psychical androgyny. Developmental Psychology teaches that the maturation processes of the brain determine the selection of stimuli the child can make use of at different phases of his development. H. Wallon and J. Piaget were the founding fathers of this school, and both wrote extensively on the correlation between brain maturation, psycho-motor function and the environment. Their followers differed in their emphasis on the biological or social factor, but most of them agreed that the environment had the 'last word'.

John Nash tried to throw some light on 'masculine' and 'feminine' behaviour in a paper 'Sex Differences and their Origins' (in *Developmental Psychology*, 1975). He discussed firstly the biological aspect, referring to a 'masculine' and 'feminine' brain, which, in my view, confused the issue from the start. Nash emphasized that environmental and cultural conditions were decisive factors in the understanding of 'masculinity' and 'femininity'. It is to be regretted that he and other authors of the same school continued to use these outdated terms. But he has to be credited for his remark that measurements of both had so far not ceded any definite results. And he wisely posed the question whether or not there was any sexual difference in mental and emotional reactions. He attached great weight to the mother's different attitudes to her male and female children, which could account for the difference in their behaviour patterns. The boy generally received the more favourable treatment because of the mother's preference for the male. He started life with an advantage which could explain his greater aggressiveness and sense of enterprise. The girl's docility, receptivity and lack of self-esteem, attributes which are supposed to be 'feminine', might in fact be the outcome of her less favourable position with the mother. He mentioned that expectancy of what is desirable for either sex is the outcome of parental preferences.

A. Heilbrun and D. Fromme, both American psychologists, dealt, in a paper 'Parental Identification of Late Adolescents' etc, with the young person's imitation of the life style of one or both parents. 'Masculinity' is highly esteemed in American culture, and boys who identified with a 'masculine' father would be well rewarded. The proposition of same-sex identification went astray where females were concerned. The authors quoted several investigators who had reported that women who identified with their mothers were badly adjusted. Heilbrun and Fromme measured 'masculinity' and 'femininity' in 400 students in relation to these qualities in their parents. They omitted to indicate the number of male and female students. They justified their choice of adult subjects because the 'masculine/feminine' behaviour pattern did not change over twenty years, so they said. Their most interesting finding was that identification with the same-sex parent was related to the ordinal position with siblings. Eldest and only children identified, as a rule, as they were supposed to do, but not so the younger ones. Girls who resisted modelling themselves on their mothers were better adjusted than those who did. The opposite was true of boys. The 'masculine' girls showed less anxiety and other negative emotions than the 'feminine' ones, but the 'feminine' boys suffered from emotional disturbances of various kinds.

Although I disagree with the premise – the existence of sex-bound character attributes – the paper has significance for my subject. It gave evidence that *androgynous* girls had a greater chance to develop their personality to the full than those who conformed with the 'feminine' stereotype (*Journal of Genetic Psychology*, 1965).

Sandra Bem, of Stanford University, studied psychological androgyny (psychological hermaphroditism), and her two papers on the subject take the 'masculinity/femininity' ratings onto another plane. In spite of her reiteration of these misleading terms, her ideas on psychological bisexuality are based on meticulous research and point in the right direction. In 'The Measurement of Psychological Androgyny' (1974), she measured androgyny as a function of a person's 'masculinity' and 'femininity' in their own eyes. It is to Sandra Bem's credit that she criticized the polarization of 'masculine' and 'feminine', which obscured the meaning of androgyny. The androgyny score reflected the amount of 'masculinity' and 'femininity' which the person included in his/her self description. According to her: 'Androgynous sex role represents the equal endorsement of both masculine and feminine attributes.'

She expressed the hope that her research would encourage investigators on sex differences to question the assumption that sex stereotypes were correlated with mental health. In her view, the androgynous personality will, perhaps, come to define a more human standard of psychological health.

In 'Sex Role Adaptability: One Consequence of Psychological Androgyny' (1975), Bem continued the theme of her previous paper. She had been impressed by the argument of the Women's Liberation Movement that stereotyped sex roles did not encourage psychological health in the individual and society. The *real* androgynous person, who is flexible in the expression of both his/her 'feminine' and 'masculine' sides, will adjust to life situations as they come. She mentioned a paper by Cosentino and Heilbrun (1964), which confirmed that androgynous women scored in self-reliance, self-confidence and intelligence, in comparison with stereotyped females. High 'masculinity' in men went with high anxiety and neuroticism.

The two main results of a number of tests which Bem applied to androgynous and stereotyped males and females were the following: firstly, that 'feminine' and androgynous males showed more involvement in a playful pursuit than 'normal' men, who didn't know how to react. And secondly that 'feminine' women were no more playful than androgynous and 'masculine' women. This result was contrary to expectation. 'Feminine' women showed less involvement in playful pursuits because they lacked spontaneity. They funked unexpected tasks with obvious inhibition and anxiety.

Androgyny had the best of both worlds. The paper ends: 'it may well be, as the Women's Liberation Movement has urged, that the androgynous individual will some day come to define a new and more human standard of psychological health.'

Bem and some other developmental psychologists have underlined the social importance of androgyny and emphasized its significance for the mental health of society.

II BIOLOGICAL INFERENCES

The long-held view that bisexuality was an inborn condition waned under the influence of psychoanalysis. But psychologists never doubted the existence of a biological factor. They could not, however, identify it before the recent advances in genetics, brain research and endocrinology, which contributed to a greater knowledge of the interaction between constitutional tendencies and environment. The discovery of chromosomes was a turning point in biology. It led to a great leap forward in genetics and sexology.

Two sex chromosomes decide whether an embryo develops into a female or male human being. There are forty-six chromosomes in all, two of which are sex chromosomes, the result of impregnation with either male or female germ cells. They are signified by an X or Y. A female develops when both are X, a male develops when one is X and the other Y. The differentiation into sex glands is caused by sex-determining genes and a hormonal factor. The X chromosome is larger than the Y. Another striking difference between them is that two of the former are necessary for the formation of ovaries, but only one of the latter for the development of testes. For about two months of foetal life the embryo can potentially develop into either sex. During the seventh week the undifferentiated sex gland gets structurized through forming the Wolffian and Müllerian ducts. In the male the Wolffian duct develops and the Müllerian atrophies, while the opposite process takes place in the female. But the atrophy of one or the other duct is not absolute, a situation which is responsible for some residues of the opposite sex: for example, the clitoris in women, the prostate gland and breasts in men. The decisive development into either sex only occurs in the third month. Secretions from the foetal testes are necessary to produce male genital structures, while the development of female genitals is not dependent on secretions from its foetal ovary. *The female is therefore biologically the more primitive sex.* The greater vulnerability and lower life expectancy of the male might be the result of this genetic difference between the sexes.

Normally, the sex chromosomes are XX or XY, but other combinations can occur, as if our genetic make-up were able to play many tunes on two notes. Combinations which diverge from the normal are called chromosome errors. They lead to genital abnormalities of different degrees, which present considerable psychological and social difficulties for both parents and children. I am very briefly describing such pathological conditions because they go with a *congenital* disposition to bisexuality, in contrast to the *normal* bisexuality which is the heritage of every human being. Pathological conditions highlight those which are not abnormal. Here is a very brief summary of the most important pathological syndromes.

The Klinefelter Syndrome, in which the number of sex chromosomes is three instead of two, XXY, is characterized by a dwarfed male body with under-developed genitals, emotional infantilism and mental retardation.

In Turner's Syndrome one X chromosome is missing. In rare cases two X are present, but one has a faulty structure. Turner's syndrome produces a dwarf-like female body with certain congenital defects, such as a webbed neck, obesity and infantile sex organs.

Two other abnormal chromosome combinations are XXX and XYY. They are not as uncommon as the previous ones. One could have expected that the first condition would produce a hyper-female, but women so affected are often sterile and mentally retarded. The second chromosome error also has dramatic consequences. Men with this condition are very tall and look particularly virile. They suffer from behaviour disorders, with a tendency to delinquency.

The most striking chromosome abnormality occurs in *physical* bisexuality or hermaphroditism. The sex glands of hermaphrodites contain testicular and ovarian tissue. It is therefore not surprising that hermaphrodites have double the normal number of sex chromosomes or more. They are either XX,XY or XX,XXY. Other combinations are also possible. Hermaphrodites possess both male and female sex glands. They vary considerably in physical appearance and shape of external genitalia. Some show more female, some more male, physical traits, but there is always a uterus present.

The endocrine system also plays a crucial role in embryonic and postnatal life. Hormonal influences can make or mar the normal course of foetal development. The whole repertoire of endocrine functions is not yet fully understood, but it is known that an intrinsic link exists between the endocrine glands and the autonomic and central nervous systems. Hormonal secretions of the sex glands, the adrenals and the pituitary gland, play a signal part in determining the psychosexual constitution of a person. It is of particular interest that testes, ovaries and adrenals, secrete androgens and oestrogens (male and female hormones). Androgenic hormones are responsible for the development of musculature, hair growth and sex drive in both men and women. The output of male and female hormones independent of sex, is a clear declaration in the language of biology that bisexuality is part of human nature.

The adrenals have a special place in sexual development in pre- and postnatal life. Hormones of the pituitary gland ensure their enlargement in foetal existence and puberty, which accounts for their powerful activity during these critical periods. The pituitary has therefore a key role in psychosexual functions.

In his *Textbook of Endocrinology* (5th edition, 1974), Williams indicated that psychosexual characteristics were directly related to the potential bisexuality of the embryo. Investigations in America, Western Europe and Russia have shown that the sexual development of the foetus is represented in 'nuclei', called sex-centres, in the hypothalamus, which is a part of the mid-brain. They are formed during the period of sexual differentiation into male or female. The most remarkable research work in this field was, in my view, undertaken by Professor G. Dörner (Humboldt University, Berlin). The main motivation for his research was the quest for the origin of homosexuality, with an eye to preventive therapy (1969). He was the first to show, in his investigation on about 1,000 rats (1976), that sexual behaviour in the male became feminized through different methods of changing hormonal balances. This could be done by means of castration, the implant of female sex glands into the hypothalamus region of the mid-brain, or injections of either oestrogen or androgen. The effect was a reversal of the specific sex-centres. Instead of a male, the animals developed a female sex-centre, and, soon after birth, showed either homo- or bisexual behaviour. Dörner believed that the behaviour of rats was also applicable to human beings. But can one really speak of rats and men in the same breath? I am not a biologist, and cannot refrain from keeping a question-mark in my mind.

As a matter of fact, clinical research by Mascia, Money and

Erhardt and others verified Dörner's claim. In human beings, certain endocrine disturbances in prenatal life do affect the relevant sex-centres in the hypothalamus region for good. They lead to pseudo-hermaphroditic conditions, for example the androgen-insensitivity syndrome. This is an hereditary disorder in which androgen (male hormone) produced by the foetal testes has no effect on the corresponding sex-centre in the hypothalamus region. The internal genitalia are immature but male, while the external genitals have a female appearance. This is probably due to testosterone (male hormone) deficiency in foetal life.

A number of other endocrine anomalies also alter the normal course of prenatal development in the direction of pseudo-hermaphroditism in both sexes, due to different degrees of androgen deficiency in males, and androgen or oestrogen overdoses in females. Dörner mentioned that, in these cases, one and the same sex-centre in the hypothalamus region was formed for males and females (1973). Many different shades of pseudo-hermaphroditism can occur, depending on the extent of hormonal disturbance in prenatal life. The milder forms may never be diagnosed, yet may play a part in the perception of a person's gender identity. Pseudo-hermaphroditism can also be due to maternal hormones circulating in the placenta. The pregnant woman's contribution to a possible hormonal disturbance in the embryo can be due either to her own endocrine make-up, or to an alteration of her hormonal balance through medical treatment. Mascia, Money and Erhardt mentioned several cases of masculinization of female children through progestine (a female hormone) which was given to the mother in order to prevent an abortion. The prenatally androgenized girls showed signs of having developed the male sex-centre in the hypothalamus region instead of the female one. Their external sex organs were masculinized, the clitoris being more or less hypertrophic. In some cases, the masculinization went so far as to produce a penis and empty scrotum. Yet the ovaries functioned normally, and the body was feminized at puberty. Menstruation was normal, though generally delayed in onset. Treatment of the mother with injections of male hormones, before her pregnancy was known, produced similar results. Recently, Ingeborg Ward found that stress during pregnancy can decrease the mother's androgen output, leading to the feminization of a male child. Ward's finding opens a new vista on hormonal influences on the embryo, namely the importance of the pregnant woman's emotional state.

Money and Erhardt investigated girls whose masculinization

was due either to injections of progestine (female hormone preventing abortion), or to an hereditary condition. In both cases the adrenal glands are over-stimulated, and produce too much androgen (male hormone). Both conditions go under the name of *adrenogenital syndrome*. The result is masculinization of the external sex organs in a major or minor degree, but the internal genitalia are always female. Children with the hereditary condition have a higher degree of masculinization, and their pseudo-hermaphroditism is more pronounced than in the non-hereditary cases. Their sex assignment is therefore of particular importance. If they are given regular cortisone treatment as well as feminizing surgery of the external genitals, they can develop a feminine physique and even menstruate, though usually much later than normal. Money and Erhardt found that the behaviour of the girls of either category did not differ significantly. They studied altogether twenty-five girls, ten of one, and fifteen of the other variety. They were matched with suitable controls. Unlike these, they all thought of themselves as tomboys. Some would have preferred to be male, but were not really unhappy with their female status. They were energetic, liked outdoor activities, and disdained playing with dolls.

The particular interest of this investigation lies in the authors' claim that only 'masculinized' females are tomboys. This has not been found to be so either in my earlier investigation of lesbians or in the bisexual women of my present study. Thirty-eight out of seventy-five bisexual women showed tomboyish behaviour as children, and wanted to be of the opposite sex. But the situation changed when they were grown up. Only five would have preferred to be male in adulthood and this only for reasons of a better professional and social status (see Tables 12, 13). The women concerned were no different in appearance from other women, but they were distinguished by a remarkable dynamism, freedom of expression and unprejudiced social and personal attitudes. Equally erroneous is Money and Erhardt's claim that masculinized girls have a particularly high intelligence. In a sample of ten girls, six had an I.Q. of over 110. The authors attributed this result to the effect of androgen on the cortex of the brain, but 'one swallow does not make a summer', and a high I.Q. in sixty per cent of a sample of ten has no claim to significance. I fail to understand how a surplus of foetal androgen could be responsible for a high I.Q. in men or women. I cannot help wondering where all those over-sexed male simpletons come from who obviously have an overload of pre- and postnatal androgens. Furthermore, how can it be explained that eminent women of different races, who had no chance to be hyper-androgenized, show exceptional intelligence and abilities? One need only think of Dame Kathleen Lonsdale, Indira Ghandi, Margaret Thatcher or Shirley Williams, to mention only a small, selected group, in order to question whether it was an excess of androgen which gave them their brilliant intelligence. They bear no marks of difference in appearance or expressive behaviour from other women. The claim that an increased amount of androgen increases a woman's mental capacity is untenable. It recalls Weininger's crazy idea that all intelligent and remarkable women such as Sappho, George Eliot, Helene Blawatsky and the painter Rosa Bonheur, looked like – and equalled – men. It is a matter of fact that prenatal genetic and hormonal disturbances lead more often to mental deficiency than to superior intelligence.

Another hormonal disturbance in prenatal life concerns women only. It is the Stein-Leventhal Syndrome, which is characterized by an excess of androgens, resulting in hirsutism and obesity. The condition is probably due to a dysfunction of the ovaries which form multiple cysts. A hypertrophic clitoris and a deepened vocal range add to the virility of these women.

Cushing's Syndrome is caused by adrenal dysfunction. It afflicts both men and women in their appearance, and their circulatory and other functions. The most conspicuous feature is obesity. A surplus of androgen produces female hirsutism, and often a hypertrophic clitoris. The fat faces and obese trunks of male and female patients are at odds with their thin arms and legs. They have a fine kinaesthetic sense and are often good dancers.

Frölich's Syndrome also concerns both sexes, and shows some resemblance to Cushing's Syndrome. The main characteristics are infantile genitalia, combined with a fat face and trunk. Everybody knows the fat girl and boy, often mercilessly teased by their mates. Yet they are the 'darlings' of their milieu. Their placid temperament and congeniality endear them to everyone. They are late developers, but their endocrine dysfunction does not single them out from other people. They live and love, as a rule, like the majority.

The last condition to be mentioned is Kallman's Syndrome which only occurs in the male and is hereditary. Degenerative processes in the hypothalamus region, which lead to dysfunction of the pituitary, are responsible for an undeveloped, small penis, and the absence of the sense of smell. The latter is probably due to the close proximity of the area of smell to the sex-centres in the hypothalamus region.

*

One would expect that in all the abnormal conditions I have described, sexual behaviour would be in line with biological make-up, where a physical disposition to bi- and homosexuality is acquired on pathological grounds. But this is not at all the case. Children born with genital abnormalities undergo the most severe brainwashing from their parents with the assistance of the medical profession. Everything is done to make them into 'normal' stereotypes in appearance and psychosexual behaviour. They are forced to become what they are not by nature.

In both its normal and abnormal developments, embryology has given us clues about the all-embracing sexual unity at the start of life. It has also taught us that 'destiny' can be overruled by the suggestive brainwashing of family and society. The gross abnormalities I have described highlight hidden potentials in everybody. And the 'normal' endocrine make-up shows many different shades in different individuals. The endocrine constitution can predispose to personal magnetism, energy and joie de vivre. The lucky ones who possess such advantageous equipment have a good chance to withstand the onslaught of environmental brainwashing. Otherwise, where would all those rebels come from, who differ from the majority not only in their sexuality, but also in ideology and social attitudes, through obeying their natural bent.

Although the influence of the endocrine glands can be decisive, I do not agree with Magnus Hirschfeld, and research workers like John Lorraine, Griffiths and others of our time, who believe that hormones alone hold the key to psychosexual behaviour. The endocrine make-up can overrule conventional codes and become imperative for behaviour, but an unconventional way of life will only be chosen under the psycho-endocrine dictate of a strong personality. Others will suppress their needs, and bow to the rules of normality; people who live first-hand lives are the exception rather than the rule. Although society has in many ways become more tolerant, prejudice against sexual variations still persists, except for a broad-minded minority of professional and lay people. They fight for the rights of sexual minorities to live in accordance with their individual needs and to be their *real selves*.

Corinne Hutt claimed in her book, *Males and Females* (1972), that essential differences existed between men and women in perceptive, intellectual, sensory and other functions. Her detailed study appeared to prove the superiority of the male in many fields. According to her, men are superior in intelligence, energy, creativity and visuo-spatial capacity. Women, however, have more articulate verbal and manual skills, a higher auditory acumen, a better sense of smell, and other minor advantages. But the summa sumaris of her claims left the female where she always was – the second sex. Hutt's book misses the essential point: the influence of parental expectations, which represent stereotyped attitudes transmitted from one generation to the next. The superior qualities of the male claimed by Hutt could be the outcome of parental preferences and/or the mother's way of holding the boy child and expressing a particular closeness to him, while she shows more distant attitudes to a female infant.

In the English language both sexes are referred to as 'he'. The girl has to hide under the male umbrella from the start. This is the symbolic expression of negation, if not annihilation, of the female child, and represents an indelible trauma to her identity and self-esteem. Hutt prefaces her analysis of different abilities in men and women by describing differences in cerebral lateralization. The right hemisphere controls non-verbal and spatial capacities, while verbal and language functions are represented in the left. According to her, girls showed an earlier maturation of the brain than boys, and were superior to them in reacting to auditory stimuli. This finding explained the female's greater verbal and language skills. Males scored better in visuo-spatial abilities. Money and Kinsey had observed that men reacted more strongly than women to visual erotic material. Their finding was in line with Hutt's observation that visuo-spatial abilities were more highly developed in the male than in the female. The question arises whether these differences, if they exist, are innate qualities or conditioned responses. The brain of the newborn baby is malleable enough to be indelibly inscribed by peri- and post-natal experiences. The parents' preference for the boy, the mother's more magnetic and emotional closeness to 'him' than to 'her' (there are exceptions of course), could stimulate a better auditory perception in the girl child, simply by causing her to listen harder. When a situation is not fundamentally secure, tension and attention are increased. Sensitivity to sound (noise in particular) is related to anxiety and the sense of balance. The latter affects spatial ability. Sight is the instrument of looking *at*, of regarding the world *outside*. Inner peace and a feeling of security encourage the mind to look outwards. I argue, therefore, that the higher development of the auditory sense in the female and the visuo-spatial ability in the male is conditioned by environmental influences, primarily the mother-child relationship. Hutt found that women scored higher than men in verbal intelligence tests, as was to be expected, and that their short-term memory was better. But men had a better long-term memory, and scored higher in solving arithmetical problems. Although the brain of a female matured earlier and showed up better in the beginning, that of a male surpassed it at a later stage. According to Hutt, women's intelligence remained within average limits, while that of men had a very wide range. Their I.Qs were among the lowest and highest, comprising idiots and geniuses. Their capacity for quick repartee and easy chatter did not equal that of the female, but they excelled in logical and abstract thought and creativity. This picture of women as second-class citizens displays every conventional and prejudiced notion one can think of. It makes a comical showing in the years of the female revolution, which should have taught Hutt and other investigators of so-called innate male and female abilities how to ask *relevant* questions. In the first place, Hutt should have queried the validity of measurements of intelligence. The significance of the I.Q. is doubtful because emotions, anxiety in particular, can interfere with intellectual performance and falsify results. The same holds good for the Wechsler and non-verbal tests.

Hutt's findings implied that women were better listeners and communicators than men. Their gift for both can be explained by the fact that second-class citizens share with social minorities a fine power of observation, verbal fluency, and considerable talent for communication. They are conditioned from the start to be 'on the look-out', and to pre-empt negative attitudes. Hutt's book was published in 1972, and she must have been aware that women's performance, intellectual and otherwise, had by then taken a great leap forward and that this was the general trend, not confined to the exceptional few. She mentioned the claim made by Money, Erhardt and others that intelligence was positively correlated with androgen levels. This claim contributed to the idea of women's lower brain capacity. But she rightly had her own reservations about it.

Creativity has been denied to the female sex by authors past and present, and Hutt is no exception. In her view, creative women were rare anyway, and the few who did produce works of art or literature had not achieved real greatness. Hutt claimed that creativity depended on two aspects of thinking: fluency and originality of response. In a test designed by her and Bhavnani, boys scored higher than girls in both. The authors thought that, apart from intellectual gifts, drive and ambition played a part in creativity. They failed to see that its mystery lies in the power of the emotions and the imagination. Fluency and originality of responses to questions have, in my view, no direct relevance to creativity. The answers of the subjects tested might have been the product of 'lateral thinking' which, according to de Bono, can be taught. Hutt's explanation of why so few women are creative does not correspond with facts. The long line of great female novelists in this country from George Eliot to Virginia Woolf, disproves her point in the literary field; there were geniuses among women painters – Gonsharowa, Soutine, Modersohn-Becker, to name only a few; and, since Ethel Smythe, more than a few female composers have left their mark on the musical world. It is undeniable that up until now there have been fewer creative women than men. This is not due to lack of creative gifts, but to women's position in society, and the inferior status accorded to them over 2,000 years.

Drive and ambition heighten creative urges. Aggressive impulses, activated by adrenal androgens, are supposed to be at the root of both. As androgen levels are higher in men than women, it seemed logical to conclude that men were superior in drive and ambition. But the idea that the sexes differ in aggressiveness is both simplistic and open to doubt. Hutt realized that the concept of aggression cannot be clearly defined as it depends on extraneous variables. She therefore investigated the fighting behaviour in male and female rats, hoping to get some clarification about aggressive behaviour in humans. She found that male rats were more aggressive than female rats. Castration of adult females made no difference to their fighting performance, while males castrated at birth or in infancy had little fighting spirit left. But females who were treated with androgens at birth or in infancy showed a raised level of aggression. Although Hutt warned against applying findings like these to humans, her classification of male and female abilities suggests that she nevertheless accepted their relevance for human behaviour. She did not realize that a warning must be given in regard to any experimental situation: that there is an element of subjectivity in the investigator. It is well known that an unconscious bias cannot be eliminated, and might influence the study. Hutt's experiments might or might not have been so affected. In any case, her experimental findings on the behaviour of rats are inconsequential for human beings for the following reasons: firstly, according to investigations by Money and Erhardt, girls with a progestine-induced masculinization were not particularly aggressive, though they were full of energy and drive. Secondly, aggression fired by ambition is necessary for any kind of conquest. It is just as evident in women as men. It may be more subtle in the former, yet it is no less strong and effective. And finally, drive and ambition are not necessarily related. Ambition is a form of exhibitionism. People with little energy indulge in ambitious schemes and actions as much as vigorous individuals if not more.

In order to understand that human beings are bisexual, it is necessary not to take stereotyped qualities of men and women for granted. We cannot know about differences between them, apart from morphogenic data. Men and women must be looked at as individuals who draw their bio-psychical characteristics from the same source. Bisexuality would be an illusion if there were a fundamental difference in the emotional and mental make-up of male and female. Most research workers have studied sexual differences in the light of conventional stereotypes. Although developmental psychologists distinguished between stereotyped and non-conformist behaviour, they did not go to the root of the problem. They accepted the concept of 'masculinity' and 'femininity' which is misleading because it is the result of conditioning. In discussing Hutt's investigation in detail, I have tried to show that those qualities which, in her view, indicated fundamental differences between the sexes, might in fact be conditioned responses.

Bisexual people reject stereotyped sex-roles and attributes. They feel that they have a common ground with both the male and female, and that bisexuality assures the full development of a human being. Kate Millett expressed the same idea when she wrote in her book *Flying* (1975): 'Homosexuality was invented by a straight world dealing with its own bisexuality.'

There are only two of Hutt's findings with which I agree: the differences in the sense of touch and the sense of smell in men and women.

Sensitivity to touch depends on the qualities of the skin, which are obviously different in the sexes. This sense is more highly developed in women. Even extreme climatic conditions and female hirsutism cannot alter this. Touch and pain are twinned and so are touch and pleasure. The tolerance level for both is lower in women than men, which accounts for the female's more intense experience of pain and pleasure. Through the ages, these sensibilities have been played upon in the art of love when women take the guiding role, be it active or passive.

The greater sensitivity to smell in women is caused by their higher level of oestrogen. Smell can be an aphrodisiac. Its magnetic power is in line with that of the animal world, and women's particular sensitivity to smell is another indication that the female is the more primitive sex. Perhaps it also conveys the truth that women's sexual needs are stronger than men's because they reach into the very depths of being in their closeness to animal nature.

The bisexual nature of human beings, women in particular, has been emphasized by certain militant members of the Women's Liberation Movement. It is understandable that they want the pendulum to swing towards matriarchy. This could present a danger to women and men alike. Women's emotional matriarchate has existed since the great days of the Egyptian Queen Nefertiti and probably before. I support the Women's Liberation Movement, but am as much opposed to female as to male chauvinism. Women and men together – not women superior to men – is the conditio sine qua non for a balanced society. Women have always been the guardians of wisdom and humanity which makes them natural, but usually secret, rulers. The time has come for them to rule openly, but together with and not against men.

III GENDER IDENTITY AND SEXUAL ORIENTATION

A subtle difference between sexual and gender identity has led to semantic confusion. Some authors, Green and Money among them, identify the two, but they must be differentiated because the first has a far more limited meaning than the second. Sexual identity is the awareness of belonging to either the male or female sex. It is the first stepping-stone in the formation of gender identity which, in its turn, develops with the growth of personality.

Gender identity reflects a person's erotic and sexual self-image, and is therefore part and parcel of the imagination. It is, of course, basic to the sense of personal identity which it can either strengthen or weaken. This explains its importance for mental and physical health. An uncertain gender identity can lead to states of gross anxiety and even self-alienation. The part played by gender identity in the imagination and in relationships, has made it a vital concern for psychological investigation and therapy.

Although gender identity has, as a rule, a direct influence on sexual orientation, it must not be confused with it. In their book *Man and Woman, Boy and Girl* (1972), Money and Erhardt mistakenly do just that when they speak of a homosexual gender identity.

Gender identity is either consciously male or female or a mixture of both. The latter situation represents the *natural* human condition. But through the agencies of family and society, either the male or female component is suppressed, and may only show its face in dreams or day dreams.

The difference between sexual and gender identity is dramatically illustrated by transsexualism, which has received growing attention through the investigations of Benjamin, Stoller, Money, Green and others. The independence of gender identity from biological sex could not be more strikingly shown than by transsexuals who insist that they live in a wrong body. They wish to become what nature did not mean them to be.

In a minor degree, we are all in the same boat, because nobody's gender identity can be really natural. Family and society impose their conditioned and conditioning ideas on the child, and influence or distort the way he/she perceives his/her self-image. It is a sad fact that the majority of human beings never live according to their own nature. Only a minority by-passes stereotyping by parents and society, and lives more authentically than the rest. Even sexual identity has its roots in parental suggestion, that of the mother in particular. The constantly repeated statements: 'You are a little boy', and 'You are a little girl', make the child only too aware of his or her own sex. When parents would have preferred a child of the opposite sex, gender identity might be influenced by their wishes. This goes to show how much first environmental influences are decisive. Nature only gets a word in edgeways, but does not fail to teach us the basic lesson that human beings are essentially *artefacts*, made by their culture. One of the most telling examples of how both sexual and gender identity can be changed through environmental influences was described by Money and Erhardt, in a tale which has become famous in sexological history (ibid. p. 118). It concerned a male child who suffered ablation (removal) of the penis through an accidental burn during circumcision, and was surgically 'made' a girl. The parents followed expert advice to treat the child accordingly. His name was changed, and he grew up as a girl in every way. His reactions, attitudes and tastes became completely 'feminine', and so did his looks. Reversal of gender identity can happen to people who are neither mentally nor physically abnormal. I knew two lesbians who suffered from gender confusion under great emotional stress in late adolescence, when they thought of themselves as hermaphrodites. Their cases are not isolated ones. Imagination can play tricks with people driven by wishful thinking to take for reality what is only in their minds.

Stoller used the irrelevant notions of 'masculinity' and 'femininity' as terms of reference in his definition of gender identity, which was repeated by many other authors. In every human being, female or male, there are the seeds of activity and passivity, extroversion and introversion, spontaneity and reserve, impulsiveness and patience, brutality and tenderness, and so on. These human properties have no sex markings. They are interchangeable in the same person, which gives elasticity to the concept of gender identity. One of my subjects, a married man of twenty-five, was fully conscious of the incongruity between his own gender identity and the stereotyped 'masculine' and 'feminine' sex roles imposed by society. I quote from his unedited autobiography (published in full at the end of this book):

It was our aim . . . to create a situation where both men and women cooked and cleaned, or fixed a shelf and did the decorating. A place where our child could see that she would not have to be good at cooking in order to get a man. A place where she could see the importance of women having freedom to do their own work, and not just look after the kids and house. A place where she could experience the strength of women and the tenderness of men. A place where reality could exist, where people could be themselves regardless of their sex. A place where people whose sexuality was of their own choosing could be together. A place where she could be cared for by people other than her biological parents . . . Now that a more equal responsibility for child care has developed in the household, I enjoy living with Bronnie. I find that having a child has brought me out . . . I am learning about how we are conditioned into having prejudices and guilts. How we are stereotyped and are unable to be ourselves. Bronnie is constantly harassed by people, the media, to be a sweet, pretty, innocent little maid who sucks up to men. It is sickening to see the power society wields over our children . . . I joined a group of men who aim to break down the barriers of sexist stereotyping.

Inner and outer events can modify the gender identity of adults for a time. Persons who see themselves as predominantly male or female might, under certain circumstances, change their erotic self-image. Mental shocks and physical illness for example, can bring into the open the other-sexed part of themselves. This is a therapeutic process. A man who always thought of himself as aggressive and virile (a 'proper' man) might become passive and receptive under the impact of a severe illness or any other traumatic experience, in order to release inner tension and resolve conflicts. It is well known that adverse circumstances can transform an independent person into a clinging one, and reverse emotional reactions. This process is generally called retrograde, but in my view it is the very opposite: the attempt to realize oneself as a whole person.

As a rule, gender identity directs sexual orientation. Persons aware of their bi-gender identity usually love people of either sex, but this is not necessarily so. Male transvestites are a case in point. They are aware of their natural bisexuality, but most of them live a heterosexual life. However, some of those who participated in this study, admitted homosexual inclinations.

An example of a modified sexual orientation without a change in gender identity, was that of a male respondent in his late fifties. For a long time he had lost his bisexual urges, and had become exclusively homosexual. But one day his old desire for women was re-kindled. He wrote to me about a year after I had interviewed him: 'An interesting sidelight on my condition which may be of value to your research: I have recently come to know a woman member of my group much better. The surprise and delight of our mutual attraction has led to another surprise – the weakening of my heterosexual inhibitions.' The experience obviously meant much to him. His letter expressed surprise and delight about the event, which he considered a gift from heaven. He would not have believed a few months ago that he would be capable of feeling as he felt now. His homosexual pursuits had made him feel guilty and depressed. He was going through the male climacterium, which had re-awakened long lost emotions. This is a time when endocrine changes tease both the senses and the imagination, and encourage new flings of adventure.

Stoller believed in a core gender identity, the main characteristics of which were a sense of maleness and a sense of femaleness. He differentiated between core gender identity and gender identity itself, a distinction which, in my view, is unnecessary if not unjustifiable. A sense of maleness and a sense of femaleness adequately describe basic features of gender identity proper. They should replace the ill-conceived notions of 'masculinity' and 'femininity'. Maleness and femaleness make themselves felt in the first place under the impact of endocrine influences. Let us take the example of a woman. On many occasions she is bound to be aware of her femaleness, pleasantly or unpleasantly, both in her imagination and life experience. She is likely to experience her femaleness at menstrual periods either with relief or displeasure, and she is bound to be entirely absorbed by it in childbirth. This is not to say that a sense of femaleness could not pierce her being at any time, provoked by sexual attraction, erotic images, impressions and emotions. Again, a man's sense of maleness does not only make itself felt through libidinous desire and erections, but is also aroused through perceptive, emotional and imaginative processes, which in turn stimulate endocrine functioning. A sense of femaleness or maleness is not the exclusive property of one sex or the other, but belongs to either. Why? Because bio-psychological bisexuality is the keynote for the experience of a sense of maleness in a woman, and a sense of femaleness in a man. The awareness of both is subjective and differs individually in both sexes. Such experiences cannot be communicated verbally, but their impact may be grasped through imaginative empathy. A woman's experience of a sense of maleness may differ from that of a man, and a man's experience of a sense of femaleness may differ from that of a woman. In neither case can these sensations be verified as factual because of their subjective quality, but exist they do. One might, of course, ask whether they are fictitious. But this would not necessarily devalue their significance. It can rightly be argued that fiction may be more informative than fact. It can even predict scientific discovery. As we know, the science fiction of today can become the reality of tomorrow. Perhaps the concept of the unconscious itself is fiction. But where would we be without Freud's and Jung's theories which have contributed so much to our understanding of human beings and history? One might also wonder whether certain schools of psychology which claim to be scientific, are but fiction dressed up as science. The truth is: we simply don't know. We should not underrate the creative power of the imagination, which permeates every aspect of life. It is reasonable to regard human beings as a symbiosis of biology and fiction. The greatest part of our life is spent in fiction through the agency of the imagination. The advanced technology of the age has made us, to a great extent, independent of the wear and tear of existence, leaving us free for the pursuits of the mind fired by the imagination.

The new understanding of gender identity in its sometimes fantastic forms, has not only been gained through research but also through imaginative empathy. A striking example of this is to be found in Stoller's *The Transsexual Experiment*, where he described how he understood in a flash of inspiration the gender identity of transsexual boys. He realized that a little boy had far more difficulty in accepting his maleness than a little girl in accepting her femaleness. He did not want to be anatomically different from his mother, with whom he was linked in symbiotic existence. Not so the little girl who had, according to Stoller, no conflict of this sort. Stoller's idea that the male did not want to be male in the first place, might be a stepping-stone towards a global understanding of human psychosexuality. His findings were confirmed by Margaret Mead who observed that in some primitive communities, grown-up men wanted to be female. They envied woman's capacity to produce children which, to them, was a sign of superiority. While Stoller may have seen one truth, he failed to recognize another. His 'fiction' led him into a cul-de-sac where the girl's bisexuality was concerned. I have shown a very different picture of the situation in *Love Between Women*. The girl has the same longing for union with the mother as the boy. She does not identify with her as a female because it would make her less desirable to her mother who feels closer to a male. The girl's bisexuality is aroused through the wish for complete union with the mother, which I called 'emotional incest'. Stoller's lack of understanding of the girl's bisexuality is the result of a blind spot, evident in most male psychiatrists. In *Women and Madness* (1974), Phyllis Chessler rightly claimed that they are unable to understand the female psyche. But Stoller's insight into the gender identity of transsexual boys made it clear enough that bisexuality is the point of departure for all psychosexual life.

Fully established gender identity is a late product. It is particularly uncertain in adolescence, when hormonal influences are overwhelming. They can lead young people to make psychosexual relationships not in tune with their real gender identity. Contrary to other authors, Gagnon and Simon wrote in *Sexual Conduct, the Social Sources of Human Sexuality* (1974), that *sexual* identity was only established in adolescence, and might influence a person's life for good. But they muddled the issue because they did not take into account the comparative transitoriness of puberty. If Gagnon and Simon were right, a great number of people would never be true to their gender identity in their emotional and sexual relationships.

Significant findings by I. Ward have shown that emotional stress reduces the output of androgens. The opposite is the case during periods of heightened well-being. Increased androgen output increases vitality, eroticism and sexual drive, and stimulates the imagination. It is important to realize that gender identity needs both environmental and imaginative feeding in order to maintain its stability. The imagination can be enriched through the environment and personal relationships, through literature and the arts. One must remember that the imaginative power of the child plays an important part in the development of gender identity. Nursery rhymes, fairy stories, picture books, and now television, excite children's imaginations, lead to hero worship and produce idols on whom they model themselves and their erotic self-image.

Gender identity gains in strength at any age through reciprocal love, achievement of any kind, and the pursuit of desired goals, even when the journey might have been more rewarding than the arrival. But for some people, adversities have a more invigorating effect than the benevolent deals of fate. The gender identity of bisexual people, for example, can be strengthened through the rather isolated position in which they find themselves with both hetero- and homosexuals.

Society, motivated by the need for self-preservation and the extension of territory, required a clear-cut dichotomy between men and women which made bi- and homosexuality undesirable. The distribution of labour between the sexes became a necessity. Times have changed, but old ideas have not been replaced by suitable modern ones. Family and society continue to mould gender identity according to outmoded stereotypes. Without their interference, bi-gender identity would be the norm, and bisexuality a foregone conclusion. This is still the case in the 'paradise' of childhood, before the taboos imposed on gender identity become conscious. Without the repression of the other-sexed side of oneself, gender identity would always be male/female. Some vague notion of their other-sexed part does remain even in those who proclaim that they are strictly heterosexual. Such a dim memory cannot be equated however with 'unconscious awareness', a psychoanalytic concept which is a contradiction in terms. We are not aware of our unconscious, except on those occasions when it hits us either through *lapsus* of tongue and gesture, or premonitions and unexpected situations. It is true that more and more people realize that human beings cannot be defined by their anatomical sex alone, but the majority continues to hold narrow-minded views.

One could reasonably expect that those who *are conscious* of their bi-gender identity would be bisexual, but this is not always the case. Gender identity and sexual orientation can diverge for the following reasons:

1 Mores of convention, the guarantors of approval by society, exert heavy pressure to conform. Those who step out of line could put at risk their financial security and social acceptability.

2 Rebellion against parental expectations could cause feelings of guilt and alienation from the family.

3 A powerful cause of psychosexual self-negation is the need to be in tune with one's immediate surroundings. The fear of isolation which might otherwise ensue is unbearable to many. Organizations of sexual minorities have been formed as an antidote. But they cater first and foremost for homosexuals. This point was frequently made during interviews with subjects of this study. At several conferences of sexual minority groups, bisexual members discussed this difficulty among themselves, and at the C.H.E. gathering at Sheffield (1975) the formation of a separate organization was seriously considered, but it did not materialize.

4 A more intangible reason is the nature of male/female gender identity itself. The two components can undergo changes in

emphasis through relationships, alterations in hormonal functioning, and the vagaries of youth and age. Such changes can have a perplexing effect, and be experienced with anguish.

Many people, conscious of their bi-gender identity, might want to enter into physical relationships with either sex, but do not allow themselves to do so. They introject their unfulfilled desires, dreaming and fantasizing about 'forbidden' feelings, while conforming outwardly to stereotypes. They take on a gender role which is an artefact and incompatible with authentic living.

The fear of isolation and loss of social acceptability can weaken intimate relationships of bisexuals. A woman who participated in my study wrote in a letter to me about this very subject:

> I went to a conference on human sexuality and gave a brief talk on bisexuality as I knew it. The experience . . . helped me to sort things out further in my mind. I wonder if your research is revealing two particular kinds of bisexual experience: there are people who insist that they have a firm gender identity, and who are attracted to both sexes; there are people with an uncertain gender identity who find that the confusion affects their response to others . . . they don't respond to the maleness or femaleness of other people.
>
> This last is my experience: my hetero/homo psyche tends to become asexual in dealings with others.
>
> While talking to a variety of people at the conference, I was impressed with the apparently firm gender identities of firmly hetero- and firmly homosexual people. On the bisexual front, I have not received the same impression, and wonder if there might be a sliding scale of uncertainty as to gender identity.
>
> At the conference I used the term 'boy-girl' to describe my image of myself. I think this caught the interest of many women – not all of whom could see the problems and implications involved . . . I amused myself studying them and their conversations. Two, by way of sharing the problems of mothers, discussed whether they could leave their teenage children to take a part-time job. It was a major problem for them. I was forcibly struck by the difference between us because such a conflict has been unknown to me. It was also interesting to see how a 'conventional' sexual status can imprison intelligent people . . .

The writer expresses the difficulty of certain bisexual women in freeing themselves from a conventional sexual status. Paradoxically, transsexuals are in the same boat. But of all sexual variations, they show the greatest courage in their non-conformity. It would be impossible to fly in the face of convention more than they do. Yet their courage is motivated by a highly conventional idea. It is this: transsexuals want to love men or women in the 'normal' ways of society. Their dislike of homosexuality hides the fear of being outside the accepted man/woman relationship. Although they cannot alter the unpalatable truth that they were born as men or women, they claim to have a predominantly cross-sexed gender identity. The fact that they are so much at odds with their maleness or femaleness produces a dichotomy between the male and female aspects of their personality. They have given many headaches to psychiatrists and research workers because of their psychological complexity. Their situation represents a paradox. A transsexual woman's mind is immersed in her sense of maleness, and a transsexual man's mind in his sense of femaleness. Their condition puts bisexuality into relief through the contrast between sexual and gender identity. I had no opportunity to study female transsexuals and transvestites as none responded to my appeal. I could therefore only deal with the male aspect of both conditions.

Transsexuals aspire to sex-change in order to go along with convention. Male transvestites show a dichotomy between bi-gender identity and sexual orientation, but conform with convention by living heterosexual lives, and not allowing themselves to love men physically. Their sense of femaleness must be overwhelmingly strong because they have a compulsive need to give it full and visible expression. Those who are members of the Beaumont Society meet like-minded men dressed in women's clothes. They shed the burden of being males in coming together as females, talking idly but also seriously discussing their particular situation and its predicaments. Even in their own surroundings, they prefer to take on conventional 'feminine' tasks like cooking, sewing, knitting etc.

The fact that many male transsexuals are made into pseudo-women through surgery and hormonal treatment, has necessitated the legalization of their cross-gender identity. Things have been moving in this direction in the Western world. The American and European governments have recognized that the gender identity in which a person is truly her- or himself and feels most at ease with others, should be accepted as a rightful due and given legal status. There is no doubt, as transsexual participants told me, that they are themselves only when dressed and behaving as women. One mentioned his sexual experience as a female when beaten by a male. He said:

> I learned in later years that many men who paraded their 'masculinity' were, in fact, dominated by their wives. The difference between these men and myself was that they, whilst punished by their wives, are stimulated sexually by an erection of the penis; the bisexual or transsexual (and I

regard myself as a transsexual, predominantly female) when given a spanking on the bottom, becomes basically female. I had the feminine desire of needing the attention of the male as a husband.

The following account illustrates the transsexual position in the extreme, when female gender identity had taken over and maleness was at a minimum.

My mother wanted a girl and up to the age of 4½ years I was dressed as a girl, and everyone took me for a little girl. At school I had no interest in boys' games and always played with the girls. With them I was free, happy. I only wished I could wear dresses, skirts etc. In later schooldays I used to dress in mother's clothes whenever possible. During the war in the Services, my best time was with a concert party where I was asked to be the sixth girl in the troupe as one had to go home pregnant, and another girl could not be found. I was then eighteen years and was treated after a very short time by both sexes as a girl. As in many of the camps, there was only one dressing-room for each sex. I travelled as a girl and shared the girls' dressing-room. Many times after the show we were entertained in the Officers' Mess, and I can't tell you how thrilling it was to be treated as a female, and even be asked for a date!

After the war, I went to Australia where I met a man and lived with him for some time as a woman. Again, it was thrilling to have nice undies, dresses and everything feminine. I did the cooking, housework, and we would go into Sydney for a show or a meal. We also made friends with other couples. Of course, as in every relationship between men and women, sex came into it. I always played the woman's part and he made love to me nearly every night. Sometimes I would fellate him, but mostly he would enter me anally. Many nights when I have felt him spending inside me, I have wished he could make me pregnant. For many years I have wanted to go through pregnancy and give birth to a child. I would not like to be a father, but how I wish I could have been a mother. I think being able to give birth a wonderful thing.

I had to return to this country in 1957. My mother, who died last year, was in poor health. She knew I wanted to be a complete woman, as I always dressed and made-up whenever possible. Since she died, I have tried as far as possible to live as a woman. When I leave work, I change into a dress or skirt, make-up, then do my own cooking, housework etc. I have one or two men friends who take me out for a drink, and then return to the bungalow (I now live alone) with me for sex. All are married. I have not yet found a single man. I have two girl friends, one is heterosexual, the other lesbian.

The other week I had a wonderful three days in London. I know a hotel where I can stay as a woman, and I don't have to wear men's clothes. The other Saturday I wandered round the department stores, looking at clothes and make-up, then had lunch in one with another girl.

I wish I could have hormone treatment to enlarge my breasts and help with skin and hair, but really I would like to change sex, to be a complete woman. There is always something in my mind if I'm dressed as a man and playing his role that makes me – I think uneasy is the word I want. I only relax and take things in, give my whole attention to things about me, when I'm a woman.

It may seem strange that many transsexuals are married and fathers. But this was the case with most of those who participated in this study. And it may be even more surprising to many that three of them had happy marriages. One had been divorced but married again. In their sexual relations with women, these subjects adopted stereotyped female positions in intercourse, but did not find the sex act fulfilling. The following sentence in the autobiography of one of the respondents illustrates this: 'Having sex with a female I feel it is her that has had the satisfaction and not me.'

Genetic or hormonal abnormalities are not usually found in male transsexuals. One of my subjects had been delighted about his breast development in adolescence, though he knew that it was not uncommon in boys at that time of life.

Apart from the comparatively small number of transvestites and transsexuals who reached me through the Beaumont Society, all other subjects were conscious of the fact that their bi-gender identity and their bisexual inclinations went together. They loved both sexes, and by far the greater majority had both hetero- and homosexual relationships. I have dwelt on transsexualism because of the striking evidence it provides for my subject. Most authors believe that male transsexuals are really homosexuals who cannot face living with a man other than as a 'woman'. I am not convinced that this is the case. Homosexual men and women do not depreciate their somatic sex – quite the opposite. The conventionality of transsexuals by no means indicates that they are cowards. How can anybody who is a coward go through the agonies of sex surgery and other forms of treatment, only to be physically more conspicuous at the end than any homosexual could be? It does not make sense.

Whether or not psychoanalysts can provide the answer to this enigma, as Stoller and others suggest, is uncertain. But transsexual people make one realize that to categorize different sexual leanings and behaviour makes little or no sense.

I have already mentioned how uncertainty about the nature of bisexuality led to a semantic confusion similar to that between sexual and gender identity. Freud equated bisexuality with homosexuality, and was not alone in making this mistake. The endocrinologist

Williams, the sociologists Humphreys, Gagnon and Simon as well as other authors, substituted the word ambisexuality for bisexuality. But the two words refer to different syndromes. The word **ambisexuality** means an easy change-over from hetero- to homosexual relationships. It conveys changeability if not instability of psychosexual desire and behaviour. This is by no means the case in bisexuality, where the love for either sex is not interchangeable. Hetero- and homosexual relationships exist side by side. They are of a different nature, and many participants claimed that they complement and strengthen one another.

The question whether bi- and homosexuality are biographically or biologically conditioned, cannot as yet be answered. Only in cases of genetic or hormonal dysfunction can one assume a predisposition to either. Men with Klinefelter's Syndrome, and those whose sex chromosomes have an extra Y (XYY) are frequently homo- or bisexual, But this may be so because society's hold over them is weak, owing to low intelligence and lack of foresight characteristic of the former, and uncontrollable impulsivity in the latter.

The hormonal balance in pregnant women varies individually, which might affect the hormonal balance of the embryo and consequently, his or her constitutional make-up. The level of sex hormones can now be more easily detected at any age through the analysis of blood plasma. Kolodny and co-researchers (1971) tested testosterone levels in bi- and homosexual college students and heterosexual controls. The result was negative in seventy-five per cent, but the remaining twenty-five per cent who were exclusively homosexual, showed a lower level of testosterone than that of the lowest found in the controls. The sperm count was nil in four cases. Money and Erhardt, examining these results, left the issue open. They argued that these findings might point to a new syndrome in primary homosexuals, or, on the other hand, might be due to the effect of negative emotions, particularly depression and anxiety.

Bi- and homosexual people are never fully integrated into present day society, and are quick to make and receive erotic signals. They are easily aroused erotically, and are sexually highly susceptible. They function very well indeed and need no sex therapy, as Dr Kaplan stated in *The New Sex Therapy* (1975): '*The sexual variations* which are also called deviations and perversions are characterized by good and pleasurable functioning. Men who practise variant forms of sexuality may have excellent erections and enjoyable, controlled ejaculations. Or the woman who is sexually "deviant" may be easily aroused, lubricate, and be multiply orgastic' (p. 249). Dörner erred in pronouncing bi- and homosexuality as sexually inferior. The widely held opinion that bi- and homosexuality go with certain character defects cannot be justified either. This accusation has been made particularly against men who prefer passive anal intercourse to other genital activities. But their sexual passivity should not be taken to imply laissez-faire attitudes in other directions and moral laxity in general. There is no reason to assume that any non-conformist sexual behaviour reflects *eo ipso* on a person's ethical code, and no conclusions should therefore be drawn as to their character and personality. I have demonstrated this point through interviews with respondents; and I illustrated that this view was untenable in an example of a man who preferred the insertor position in anal intercourse. He was altogether sexually aggressive, but gentle and balanced in his human relationships. And he was not an isolated case.

In a number of cases, male and female subjects chose heterosexual people as objects of homosexual love. The element of frustration inherent in a heterogeneous choice was obviously no disincentive to them – rather the opposite. One could suspect that masochistic tendencies motivated them, but this could neither be proved nor disproved. A more likely explanation might be their need for self-assertion. Conquest of someone 'on the other side' is an affirmation of powers of seduction and a boost to the ego. The fact that heterosexuals were available to bisexual men and women may seem puzzling unless one realizes that sexual categorization is an artificial exercise. The homosexual side exists in everybody, be it acknowledged, repressed, despised or denied. Highly sexed heterosexuals are inclined to 'try everything' in their pursuit of pleasure. Their sexual versatility includes sensual explorations which are special ingredients in homosexual love-making. In *The Psychoanalytical Theory of Neurosis* (1945), Fenichel pointed to a physiological explanation of men's pleasure in anal intercourse, independent of sexual orientation, when he wrote:

> It is strange how little it is noted in analytic literature that the masculine genital apparatus, corresponding to its 'bisexual' nature . . . possesses two centres. If passive men, in whom passive anal and urethral tendencies are predominant over active phallic ones, are questioned as to where they feel the most intensive sensations, they answer with about equal frequency: at the root of the penis, at the perineum, or in the rectum.

The great majority of 'normal' men and women would decry any possibility of having homosexual affairs, though they might be dimly aware of possessing mental and emotional characteristics of the opposite sex. Some heterosexual men actually boast about a certain 'femininity' in their make-up in the belief that it would enhance their charm and seductive power. But they delude themselves. One must not forget that the notions of 'masculinity' and 'femininity' are artefacts built up by mistaken motives of family and society. Therefore a man who loves women and hopes to be more attractive to them through his 'feminine sensitivity' is deceiving himself about the authenticity of his objective. He is simulating a stereotype which is bound to let him down because it has nothing to do with real femaleness. Unless he is conscious of his male/female gender identity, he cannot be convincing enough to keep up a charade. The same holds good for heterosexual women. In the display of 'masculinity' aimed at adding an extra attraction to their 'femininity', they are only play-acting in simulating a conventional stereotype, which bears little or no relation to real maleness. Their behaviour would be authentic only if they were conscious of their original female/male gender identity.

IV PROCEDURE OF STUDY

A methodical study of bisexuality is a new venture, and I had no model of procedure for my investigation. A number of papers on 'masculinity' and 'femininity' in both sexes, to which I have already referred, were published in the U.S.A. during the last ten years. They dealt with psychological characteristics of androgyny only. The authors used the conventional concepts of masculinity and femininity, which were already many years out of date. They also omitted to investigate a possible correlation between bisexuality (androgyny) and sexual orientation. Nor did their approach include a clear definition of androgyny and its wider implications for *sexual* behaviour. The link between their studies and my investigation is therefore only a tenuous one.

It was a foregone conclusion that I would have to collect ordinary people and not clinical cases for my study. I had therefore to try to reach bisexual people through sexual minority organizations, newspapers and magazines. The realization that we don't really know objectively what we are – and worse, who we are – because of brainwashing processes, determined the way I advertised. Taking note of the subjective nature of psychosexual identity, my advertisements stated that I would be grateful if men and women who *thought* of themselves as bisexual would get in touch with me. At this stage of our mental evolution, the only thing we are able to assess is what we think we are. I realized that I might encounter considerable difficulties in procuring enough subjects for my study. Far more people are used to thinking of themselves as homo- than bisexuals because, in contrast to bisexuality, homosexuality is more easily defined. Bisexuals are not only less conspicuous but more elusive than homosexuals. Some use tactics of mimicry in order to be indistinguishable from 'ordinary' citizens, and I was apprehensive that they might have misgivings about participating in a study of a controversial nature. I knew that the 'gay' press was widely read, not only by homo- but also by bi- and heterosexual people. *Gay News* was my first choice for an advertisement. Through my connections with the Albany Trust, Kenric and Sappho, appeals for suitable subjects were published in the newsletters of the two former, and in the Sappho magazine. The Beaumont Society also published my advertisement in their monthly bulletin. These appeals were meant to reach bisexuals inside minority organizations. The fact that many bisexuals do not join these groups, made me choose, in second place, socially progressive magazines like *Spare Rib* and *Time Out*. The former gave information about my research twice, and produced especially good results, and the latter which has a wide spectrum of people among its readers, also proved very productive. The response to my appeals from all quarters was better than I had expected. Prospective subjects were asked to get in touch with me about questionnaires and arranging an interview. After I had interviewed the first batch of respondents, I received inquiries through personal recommendation, which became a self-propagating method of obtaining subjects. In the end, eighty-two women and eighty-nine men applied to participate in my study. A number of applicants had to be discarded because they did not fulfil the necessary requirements. Four men and three women did not answer the questionnaire, and could not be identified at the address or phone number they had given. Five men and four women did not keep the appointments arranged for them. Five men turned out to be exclusively homosexual, and had to be eliminated from the project for this reason. Transvestites and transsexuals, so important in a study of bisexuality, applied through the bulletin of the Beaumont Society. They fulfilled my request for non-medical subjects because they were neither under psychiatric nor any physical treatment. They had pride of place in punctuality in answering questionnaires and arriving for interviews. It so happened that all of them belonged to older age groups.

I had aimed at an equal distribution of men and women, and arrived at seventy-five for each group. Bisexuality is still regarded as a deviation, if not a perversion, by many professional and lay people. Yet a comparison of bisexual subjects with 'normal' controls would be nonsensical because of their own heterosexual side. The same holds good for homosexual controls as homosexuality is also part of bisexuality. For these reasons, controls could not be used. I soon realized, through questionnaires, autobiographies and interviews, that considerable differences existed between male and female bisexuals. These differences were of great interest, and have been statistically evaluated throughout. As controls could not be used in this study, the male and female respondents were compared as to the differences and similarities of their bisexuality. The choice of subjects was limited through the nature of the study. I was dependent on their initiative in coming forward. I therefore had to deal with self-chosen subjects, which leaves the question open whether those men and women whom I studied were truly representative of bisexual people in general. This is a drawback in any empirical study, even when controls can be used, as numbers of subjects and controls are always limited. Thus valuable information may fall through the net, since it is impossible to do absolute justice to any subject without including everybody in the *entire population* who is connected with the theme of the investigation. It is, however, reasonable to assume that studies of an idiosyncratic nature (and bisexuality is idiosyncratic in the framework of our society) can be done on small numbers. They reveal common characteristics more readily and regularly than people who conform. The standard minimum number for a statistical investigation is fifty, but some researchers regard less than this as valid when each subject is studied in depth. I chose a three-pronged approach consisting of: a questionnaire, an autobiographical sketch, and an interview.

I interviewed all subjects myself, after they had returned the questionnaire and sent an autobiography. The majority returned the questionnaire promptly, and sent the autobiography either with it (when short) or after an interval of about two to four weeks. I came thus into possession of writings, the length of which varied from one to eighty pages. It is common knowledge that answers to questionnaires must be taken with caution where personal and intimate data are concerned. I do not believe that the social acceptability test is of real use in overcoming this difficulty. I paid particular attention to diverging or contradictory statements made in questionnaires and during interviews. Both occurred in a number of cases. In one of these, the interview was instrumental in helping the person concerned to come out into the open, and make him see why he had given some wrong answers in the questionnaire. He assured me in a follow-up letter that he had gained in self-confidence because of our meeting. I considered the questionnaires, for the reasons given, as an illustration rather than an explanation of the material. The meat of the procedure lay in autobiographies and interviews. But questionnaires reveal at a glance the findings communicated at length in the text. The statistics followed the usual pattern, starting with objective information on demographic data, family background, profession and so on. Data on details of family relationships followed. They represented a 'hind-view', and were, of course, subjective estimates. They were of considerable interest just the same, because they indicated how respondents *thought* they had felt. A specially relevant part of the questionnaire asked for information about bisexual feelings and practices at different periods, with reference to lasting relationships and casual contacts. I also inquired whether the subjects considered bisexuality an advantage to them, and what their attitudes were to minority groups. I laid special stress on information about dreams and fantasies in relation to sexual orientation and practices. These are some examples of the questions asked. The statistical items were compiled in thirty-one tables. The way they should be read is explained in an introduction to them.

The subjects came from all over the country, and it must have been a considerable effort and expense for many to visit me in London. To my surprise, only a few who had travelled from such places as Bristol, Bath, Manchester, Leeds wanted their expenses refunded. This attitude might have been due to the hope of finding understanding or even comfort, through the interview. But I know that most people came because they wanted to assist in a project so close to their hearts. Interviews lasted never less than one and a half hours, and some went on for over three hours. The meetings were often followed up by correspondence. The autobiographies had acquainted me with my visitors before we met, and had provided me with some knowledge of their way of life, past and present, their relationships to others and to themselves. While discrepancies between answers to questionnaires could, in most instances, be cleared up during the interview, I regarded the autobiographical sketches as informative vehicles in themselves. They had probably been therapeutic to the writers. The contents were only discussed when the interviewees expressed the wish to do so.

Of the thirty-one statistical tables, one, Table A, was made 'by hand' after discussion with Drs Jonckheere and Caudrey of University College, London. It represents the social background of subjects and their parents. The five social classes used by the Registrar General which reflect superiority and inferiority accorded to mental and physical abilities, do not make sense any more, as we have passed these class barriers. The difference between the former working and middle classes has practically disappeared. We are all working people – except the idle rich. I therefore thought it advisable to classify subjects and parents according to occupation. I did not differentiate between professions and jobs, as I regarded both as occupations. Table A illustrates the broad spectrum of each occupational group.

'Education' comprised university lecturers, teachers and students of any kind.

'Arts' included writers, visual artists, musicians (composers and executives), journalists, actors etc.

'Government employees' with different responsibilities and grading were grouped together, because they work for the same end (or should do so).

The category 'Business' included the self-employed as well as employees of any kind.

'Caring and healing' occupations comprised groups which work for the health of the individual and society: physicians, laboratory assistants, matrons, nurses, social workers, welfare and probation officers, ministers of religion, etc.

'Workers' were divided into skilled and unskilled.

'Housewifery' is a job, if not a vocation, and I therefore classed it as a separate occupation.

The male and female groups exhibited a telling difference in the range of their occupations. Male subjects probably represented a cross-section of society as a whole, while female respondents belonged to a more restricted section. This could be explained by the still limited choice of jobs open to women, and perhaps a spirit of self-limitation which still affects many.

I want to draw attention to Table 1 referring to the age of respondents. It was significantly different in the two groups. This was due to the fact that male subjects who participated through the good offices of the Beaumont Society were all in older age groups. Dr Caudrey took the incongruity of age especially into account in analysing comparable variables according to the same age groups of each sex.

Although the use of the tests applied has been explained in the appendix, Dr David Caudrey supplied the following definitions which might be helpful to the general reader not familiar with statistical terms.

1 *Kendall's S test* is defined as the number calculated from data which express the degree of association between two variables, the

values of which *can be ordered*. The closer S is to zero, the less the association between the variables.

2 *The Chi-square test* (χ^2) is defined as the number calculated from data which express the degree of association between two variables, whose values *cannot be ordered*. The closer Chi-square is to zero the less the association between the variables. The calculated χ^2 statistic has to be compared with a given significance level, found in statistical tables. For example, a significance level of 1% means that χ^2 value would have been obtained less than 1 in 100 times if the hypothesis were true.

The Chi-square is a long-hand way of saying χ^2 (Chi) raised to the power of two, i.e. squared. Thus S and χ^2 are like variables used in algebra. They can have many actual values, but are a shorthand way of getting one number (or variable) out of a veritable maelstrom of raw data.

V EARLY INFLUENCES

Early influences shape later experiences. They play a considerable part in forming the child's sense of identity. Sexual identity, which is its earliest form, lays the foundation of gender identity. It is arguable whether the family or the genetic and endocrine make-up has the greater influence on its development. The family is certainly the determining factor in cases of sexual anomalies. The freedom to find their own sexual and gender identity hardly exists for those with abnormalities of their sexual apparatus. The whole attention of parents and their medical advisers is directed towards 'normalizing' them. They have no chance of finding out who they really are, as they undergo intensive brainwashing, sometimes combined with surgical treatment. But the normal child is also brainwashed to enable him or her to cope with the conventional taboos of stereotyped male and female behaviour prescribed by society. Although strong personalities might find a way to avoid being stereotyped, they can never be absolutely free from early influences. On the other hand, a small minority of parents encourage emotional attitudes out of tune with convention. One need only think of mothers who, because of their own bisexual disposition, treat their boys like girls or their girls like boys. Stoller, Green and others have shown that they might be responsible for transsexualism in their children.

Another point needs careful attention; the fact that the family is *not* an abstract unit, but a group of individuals whose reactions and behaviour may be as different one from the other as the arctic region from the tropics. The mistake of seeing the family as a homogenous entity can lead to false assumptions and generalizations. Families are groupings of individuals whose personalities cannot be calculated.

With this reservation in mind, I tried to find out how the family situation affects the development of lasting bisexuality in the offspring.

The atmosphere in the home permeates the emotional climate of the whole family, and is either a vitalizing or inhibiting element in the process of growing up. Happily married people are bound to be a tonic to each other and their children. The opposite is likely in unhappy marriages, and in cases of separation and divorce. I investigated the marital situation of the subjects' parents. The number of parents who were happily married was practically the same in the case of male and female respondents. It was comparatively high, while that of separations and divorces was comparatively low. A number of subjects did not answer the question. The reason for their silence might have been a feeling of indifference or tension between their parents which defied qualification (Table 7a).

The traumatic experience of a parent's death, particularly that of the mother before the child is eighteen, is an event which has incalculable repercussions on the child's emotional future. There was no significant difference between the two groups in the number of deaths of either parent. Deaths of fathers doubled those of mothers (Table 3).

The number of step-parents did not differ significantly either in the two groups. Stepfathers exceeded stepmothers in number (Table 8). The conventional image of the 'bad' stepfather could not be verified in every case. Some were loving while others were neglectful or directly vicious. I mentioned that parents' happy marriages were likely to give their children a sense of security and joie de vivre. However, two women subjects pointed out that they were made unhappy by the ideal marriage of their parents, who were so engrossed in each other that the children felt left out, deprived and jealous.

The inquiry into the number of siblings and the subject's own position in the family also revealed no significant differences in the two groups. They were most frequently the eldest, the youngest, or an only child. When they were not, they were equally positioned between older and younger siblings (Tables 5, 6).

According to these findings, the structural composition of the family did not appear to deviate from the usual pattern. The question arises whether individual attitudes of either parents or siblings could be a conditioning factor for their sexual behaviour patterns. The answer is both yes and no. It is true that in a number of cases, the character and habits of either parent had encouraged bisexual reactions, but these were exceptions. The majority of parents had the usual stereotyped attitudes towards boys and girls, yet their offspring developed lasting bisexual behaviour.

Not all subjects came from complete families. A considerable number were deprived of a natural family background. This happened through a parent's death, parental divorce or separation, or their own illegitimacy. It seemed appropriate to look at the 'deprived' group, and particularly those who were illegitimate, since one might assume that they would be more vulnerable to sufferings and frustrations than the better protected. Because of their exposed position, they were apt to mature too early and to develop a higher degree of sexual awareness.

Illegitimacy occurred in five of the female, and three of the male subjects. It appeared reasonable to expect that their particular situation would affect their reactions and behaviour. One cannot draw definite conclusions from so few cases, but a link between their 'abnormal' background and unconventional behaviour might be assumed. For this reason I refer to each of the female and two of the male illegitimate subjects individually.

Two of the five women were adopted by well-to-do couples. Both of them happened to be of mixed race. One was half Jewish and half Italian, the other had West Indian blood. One was adopted soon after birth, the other in her second year. Neither knew of her illegitimate birth until late adolescence. The first had reached the age of twenty when she came to see me. Her whole approach had the marks of secretiveness. She was the only respondent who never gave me her name. But she 'unfolded' at our meeting, and told me of her good fortune in having been brought up by people who adored her and were rich. She was a university student, and had 'really nothing to complain about except' that her adopted mother had smothered her with affection. The adopted mother was an intelligent but frustrated woman who disliked her husband and all men. She 'devoured' her daughter. She was interested in literature and the arts, interests which Ruth shared with her. The adopted father, on the other hand, was a materialist who cared for nothing but property and money, although he adored his wife and daughter. He gave them all the worldly goods a tycoon could afford. Ruth disliked him intensely, and identified with the mother. Yet she felt claustrophobic with both, and this unease might have motivated her to find out what men and women were really like. She saw her bisexual tendency as a direct consequence of her unusual situation: 'I had to find out what men were really like. I did not take as gospel truth what my mother told me.'

She embarked on relationships with men at the age of seventeen. It was only during the last year that she had fallen in love with a woman. She had not slept with her, but they did hold hands whenever they met, and she had never been so content with any other person. Ruth realized that she was emotionally disturbed to a degree which needed psychotherapy. It helped her to distance herself from an overpowering mother and an overbearing father. She thought it likely (but was not quite sure) that she had fallen in love with one of the six men she had slept with. She was, however, sure that her feelings for him were quite different from those for her girlfriend. Ruth did not want to find out who her real parents were; life was difficult enough as it was. She had to hide her intimate life from the world of her parents, particularly the lesbian side.

The second adopted subject was Brenda, a middle-aged woman who had been married twice. She had style, elegance and good looks. A few years ago, Brenda had found out about her natural parents. Her mother, a talented painter, had been poor but a spendthrift. She had neglected her as a baby. She fostered her out for a time, then had her adopted when she was two years old. Brenda had been told all this by her adopted mother. Her father was already dead when she traced his whereabouts. He had lived in South Africa and had married there. He never took the trouble to find out about his daughter.

The emotional situation in Brenda's adopted home resembled that of the previous case. She could not bear her 'father', but was devoted to her 'mother', a woman of considerable intelligence who concentrated all her affections on her. The fact that she had been fostered out as an infant perhaps increased her devotion to her mother. A year before she came into the house, her 'parents' had adopted a boy with whom she never made any contact. He was a disappointment all-round, and turned out to be a failure in everything he undertook. Brenda suspected her mother to be a suppressed lesbian. They slept in the same bed until she was fifteen. She related her infatuation with a beautiful married woman soon after to her 'mother complex'. She was attracted by her physical beauty, but never declared her love, which had all the ingredients of the aesthetic delights Sappho described in her poems.

At the age of twenty-one, Brenda fell in love with the man she married, but they were divorced a year later. She married again, a man to whom she was physically and emotionally attracted. But his profession took him away from home too often, which led to her second divorce.

Her early experiences and their consequences had left her with a constant feeling of doom and fear of any commitment. She found sex boring. 'I am a romantic' and 'I hate promiscuity' she told me. She loved men as well as women, but now she would prefer to live with a woman. 'I must have a woman – from choice', she said. But she did not much care for sexual contact with women either. This intuitive and intelligent person, a painter like her natural mother, had gone through many happy and unhappy experiences, but had never got over the memory of her bad beginnings. She believed that her bisexuality was connected with an unending search for 'security' through a relationship with either a man or a woman.

The third subject, Audrey, had, so everybody thought, a 'natural' family, a loving father and a rather cold mother. When she was not quite two years old, her father was taken away because he had a wife in another country. Two years later, her mother married again. Audrey, her elder sister and younger brother were unaware that their stepfather was not their natural father. She discovered the truth by chance. Her stepfather treated her badly, and her mother preferred the brother. The 'good' natural father lingered on as a vague, subconscious memory. She had a close relationship with her two siblings, which was some compensation for the lack of parental care.

Audrey had crushes on girls from the age of twelve. About this time, her stepfather made sexual advances to her and so did two of his friends. In her late teens she fell in and out of love with several boys. She got married in her twenties to a man she much admired and thought she was in love with. At present she loved a woman with a profoundly emotional and sensuous love, but remained faithful to a very understanding husband, with whom she had much in common. He was not jealous of her lesbianism. She did not know whether her early family conditions had influenced her bisexual needs, but she was sure that sexual experiences with her stepfather and his friends had increased her need for a woman's love.

Peggy was born illegitimately, but her parents married when she was seven months old, which makes her case different from the previous ones. She had a natural family, but the stigma of illegitimacy affected the mother-daughter relationship. Her father also seemed biased against her because of the 'mistake'. Both parents treated her indifferently, and her father sometimes cruelly. Two other children born in wedlock had a far better life. Like Audrey, Peggy experienced the unwelcome sexual attentions of her father's best friend, who molested her on excursions in his car on several occasions when she was between nine and twelve years old. She grew to hate him, but when she told her mother about it she did nothing to stop him. Peggy made strong emotional bonds with two women, both of whom were old enough to be her mother. The sensuous and emotional friendship with the first lasted for six years, and the second was still going on. In spite of her early sexual experiences with an older man, she became infatuated with men from the age of fourteen. In her early thirties, she fell deeply in love with a very intelligent man. They lived together, but he left her after one year. She married on the rebound. Neither lover nor husband had interfered with her lesbian friendships. She was convinced that her early experiences and her mother's negligent treatment had contributed to her bisexual needs.

The last woman, Renée, a twenty-two year old, looked like sixteen. She was the unwelcome offspring of her mother's love affair with an alcoholic charmer. Her mother had an unhappy marriage, but was neither separated nor divorced. Renée spent the first four years of her life with her mother's relatives, who treated her as a bastard. When she was three, she was once locked up for disobedience, and has suffered from claustrophobia ever since. Her stepfather loved her and so did her stepbrother who was six years her elder. The whole family slept in one room, and she shared a bed with her brother, who kissed and fondled her. At the age of eighteen, she fell in love with an older French girl who requited her passion. Over the past five years she had lived with a man who did not want to believe in her lesbianism and never mentioned it. Her attachment to him was a mixture of friendship and gratitude. As she suffered from severe attacks of anxiety, she felt too insecure to stand on her own feet. He was able to calm her into a tolerable state of mind. She had always resented her mother, who had tried to instil fear of sex into her since she was a child. At present, she loved another woman who also lived with a man. Although she now wanted women more than men, Renée did not think that this would prevent her from falling in love with a male. She was certain that her mother's negative attitude to sex and her constant nagging, had made her turn to women. 'But there must be something more, something essential about bisexuality,' she told me. 'One is meant to love people not sexes. We are all potential bisexuals.'

A middle-aged man, Charles, married with two children, was the illegitimate son of a domestic servant, and never knew his father. He lived with his mother in a number of bed-sitters until he was five. From that time on, he was sent to several charitable institutions, and landed, aged eleven, in a boarding school as one of 500 boys. There he was unhappy and full of fear. At thirteen, he discovered masturbation which he did not associate with sex, though his sexual curiosity became aroused. When he was fourteen an older boy assaulted him sexually, and shortly afterwards a man of twenty-one performed anal intercourse with him. He was attentive and kind to Charles, who did not resist sex with him because of his need for friendship. From then on, he also had anal sex with other boys, but found the intercourse painful. He endured rather than enjoyed it until he was much older. He had not been able to resist it, because of his dependence on male friendship. At eighteen he joined the Army and became infatuated with a woman whom he married a year later. From that age onwards he became a practising bisexual. He had learned to be a passive homosexual and an active heterosexual. The two forms of sexual love appeared to him to be complementary. He found that one reinforced the other as each followed a different pattern. His extra-marital relationships were most successful and happy. His natural desire and preference was for women, but he did not trust them, while he firmly believed in the friendship of men. His early life was responsible for this difference in attitude, which had resulted in perpetual conflict. He believed in circumstances as releasing factors in active bisexuality, of which his own life seemed to be an example.

Phil, a young man aged twenty-four, a student of philosophy, was born out of wedlock and made legitimate later. He was the only child of well-educated parents who loved and spoiled him. He enjoyed all the advantages of a happy family life, and had never been bothered by the circumstances of his birth. Yet he became a rebel against every form of convention, and did as he pleased without interference from his bourgeois parents. He had been at university for five years, but was now unemployed. He didn't mind this enforced leisure; on the contrary, he rather enjoyed it. Phil was a late developer, who had his first sexual experience with a bisexual woman at the age of twenty-one. Through her he met homosexual men, and had affairs with some of them. At the same time, he also slept with women. He made a definite point of: 'coming out as gay if one is bisexual, is as if one does not come out; one is hiding part of one's personality, which is often disliked.' He stressed that he found it necessary to be open about his heterosexual side to his completely homosexual friends:

'the homosexual disliked the bisexual for his love of women, the heterosexual hated him because of his love for men'. Phil also uttered some wise thoughts about the bisexual in society, in pointing out the truth about attitudes in the two 'sexual camps', and in insisting that one's first duty is to be oneself.

Phil's attitudes emphasized the need for a balanced view about the sexual experiences of the whole 'deprived' group when compared with those of the respondents who came from a normal family background. Among 150 subjects, fifteen men and twenty women had traumatic sexual experiences in childhood, while thirteen men and seventeen women had similar experiences in puberty (Table 9). Twenty-six men and twenty women came from incomplete families. Ten of the former and twelve of the latter had been exposed to sexual traumas in their youth (childhood and adolescence). Eighteen men and twenty-five women who came from a normal family background had similar experiences. *Statistically* the figures show that family circumstances had little to do with the incidence of early sexual trauma. Although both male and female respondents had been subjected to such experiences with almost equal frequency, the women seemed to have been more affected. The molesters had always been older men. Girls were exposed to heterosexual – and boys to homosexual paedophily. Most of the women who had been interfered with felt as if it had somehow been their fault. Yet some admitted a sensation of pleasure mixed with horror. One told me: 'I hated it but went back for more.' The seducers planned procedures carefully. They began, as a rule, with fondling of the breasts and genitals, and finished with masturbation of the clitoris. In some cases, cunnilingus or digital entry of the vagina followed. Some men exhibited themselves and guided the girl's hand onto their penis. Full intercourse was attempted in only one case. Sudden confrontations with exhibitionists were marked as traumatic experiences.

Boys often underwent their first sexual encounter in the form of anal intercourse. In some cases they were assaulted by their teachers; in others they were picked up by men in the street. Masturbatory exploitation between schoolmates was never reported as having been traumatic.

Apart from other possible effects, the boys and girls concerned were made aware of their own sexuality and physical attraction through these experiences. Bisexuality was awakened in girls. Their heterosexual side grew out of conflict between rejection of and desire for the male. Their homosexual side developed through repulsion of the male and a genuine need for a woman's love. *The women subjects' early traumatic sex encounters had always been heterosexual, and those of the men homosexual.* Male subjects described anal intercourse as painful to start with, but they found pleasure in it as time went on. There is little doubt that their homosexual side had developed through anal 'rape'.

Some authors consider women to be more bisexual than men. In *Hormones and Brain Differentiation* (1976) Dörner says: '. . . genetic and gonadal females display physiologically more bisexual behavioural potentials than genetic and gonadal males. This fact may be explained at least in part, by adrenal and ovarian secretion of androgens during the hypothalamic differentiation period and/or the paradoxical organizational effects of oestrogen resulting in a more ambisexual differentiation of the brain' (p. 207).

He saw the cause of female bisexuality in the biological make-up. Most psychologists, on the other hand, think that psychological influences are equally responsible, if not paramount. Social factors are increasingly taken into account to explain why a woman's sexuality is more flexible than that of a man. The findings of this study may add another factor to our understanding.

When sexual awareness in girls was first aroused through a man, both the male and female sides of their nature underwent a shock, which resulted in a division between sexual and emotional preferences. Woman's homosexual side is more readily expressed through sexual acts dictated by emotion than through sex per se, while her heterosexual reactions are physical rather than emotional. Passive anal intercourse enhances the sensitivity of the boy's anal zone, and consequently his female side. Early sexual experiences, be they traumatic or not, open the way to awareness of bi-gender identity, and set the pattern for bisexual behaviour. Boys tend to have a quick and easy response to homosexual pleasures, while girls in the first place usually develop an emotional as well as a sensuous need for women which in no way excludes sexual satisfaction.

Incestuous acts were separately listed in the questionnaire and in the majority of cases were thought of as life enhancing and natural when they occurred between siblings. Incest with a parent, which took place in four cases, had a seriously damaging effect, except in one male subject.

Incest between boys occurred seven times, between girls only once, and between siblings of the opposite sex four times in both groups. Sexual curiosity had led to sexual exploration, and in some cases to a lasting bond (Table 10a, b). One of the women had experienced physical love with her brother only in fantasies, but was affected by her imaginative longings for good. She believed that the desire for her brother had a great deal to do with her bisexuality.

Two women had been sexually used by their fathers; both hated him, were bound to secrecy, and lived in constant anguish and guilt. One man had intercourse with his mother with the opposite result (Table 10c, d). He thought that it had increased his confidence in his attractiveness to both sexes. He believed in his erotic omniscience, and was sure that his experience had released him from all sexual inhibitions. The unusual incest between father and son happened once. The person concerned communicated only the bare fact in his autobiographical sketch, and no further information was forthcoming during the interview. Incestuous acts with other boys were thought of by the respondents concerned as natural and highly pleasurable. Only one, who had been used anally at the age of six by two elder brothers, had found the intercourse painful and disturbing. Yet later in life he wanted the experience, and always remained a passive partner in homosexual encounters. But in heterosexual relationships he became active and aggressive. It should be understood that early homosexuality in male subjects went side by side with heterosexual feelings. Their reactions to both sexes were well illustrated in their response to the question: did you think of yourself as bisexual before the age of fifteen? Female subjects were, of course, asked the same (Table 14). Both male and female subjects became aware of their bisexuality in almost equal numbers at an early age, before they were fifteen. Any difference was statistically not significant. The dramatic onset of homosexuality in male subjects, released through anal seduction, overshadowed the fact that they also reacted sexually to girls. These early sensations had a strong emotional flavour for both sexes, whether there had been physical contact or not. They dwelt on them nostalgically in their autobiographies and during interviews.

Early sexual contacts between siblings had an effect on their sexual orientation. But neither close nor antagonistic feelings between them influenced their later emotional life, in spite of the fact that girls often had a close relationship with their younger sisters (Tables 18, 19). Apart from other similarities, the number of older and younger siblings did not differ much in the two groups (Table 16).

In studying parental influence on bisexuality, it became clear that female subjects were in many instances the favourite child of both parents. Male subjects had a great advantage when they were the eldest, compared with the females who were often burdened with early responsibility for younger children when they were the firstborn. Women, even when they were their mother's favourite, find themselves in a paradoxical situation because of a nagging suspicion that she would have preferred them to be male. This was probably the reason for the wish of many in the female group to be boys when they were children (Table 12). Yet a considerable number of mothers had wanted their boys to be of the opposite sex, which, however, could explain the inclusion of transsexuals and transvestites in this study. But the men were less influenced by their mother's wishes than the women, who had to cope with another paradox. Fathers preferred them to their brothers, but at the same time would have liked them to be boys even more frequently than their mothers did (Table 12). Ambiguous attitudes of parents to their children's sex, gave the latter an 'instinctive' realization of their own bisexuality.

Money and Erhardt as well as Dörner, have fallen into the trap of assuming that tomboyishness is 'masculine' and characteristic of bisexuality and lesbianism. This is far from the truth. 'Masculine' behaviour in girls is, in many cases, a protest against privileges given to the male. Helene Deutsch, Karen Horney and others have already shown that ambition and rivalry can induce girls and women to emulate the male in order to prove that they are as good as them. Male behaviour in the female does not indicate her sexual orientation. It is well known that bi- and homosexual women cannot be singled out in appearance and behaviour from other women. Many of their male counterparts, on the other hand, can be recognized by idiosyncratic gestures and postures, which is a protest against stereotyping and may express the desire to be themselves. But this expression of protest can become a danger and create a homosexual stereotype.

A mother's love tends to strengthen her children's sense of personal and gender identity, unless she projects her emotional or sexual problems onto them. But the lack of maternal love need not necessarily weaken it. Most mothers gave respondents loving care, but had a slight bias in favour of the male. Nineteen female subjects had been treated either indifferently or negligently by their mothers, compared with only fifteen male respondents. Fathers' attitudes were reversed. They were more often loving towards their female than their male children, and treated them less often with indifference. But the difference in parents' attitudes towards either sex was too small to have statistical significance (Table 21).

Emotional constellations between people escape objective assessment, especially when they are recalled through hindsight. As I have already mentioned, I was not concerned with the reality of the subjects' experiences, but what they remembered and thought about them. The way they recalled parental attitudes was inevitably coloured by the detours of memory and their own emotional bias.

Male and female subjects alike who answered the question 'Who was your mother's favourite child?' most often reported that they themselves were preferred to their siblings. They believed that their position had strengthened their sense of personal and gender identity. As could be expected, there was a general tendency of mothers to make favourites of boys rather than girls (Table 22a).

Fathers' favouritism lay in the opposite direction, and ran true to heterosexual stereotype. They preferred their female children, who had been conscious of the situation as well as their brothers (Table 22b).

A mother's favouritism for a son is on a different plane from that for a daughter. A special closeness and unconscious magnetism draws mother and son together. In extreme cases their bond leads to complete identification which, under circumstances, makes the boy a transsexual. A girl rarely enjoys a comparable closeness, even when she is the favourite child. But her need to be the only one who matters might overshadow her whole life, and prevent her from outgrowing her dependence on the mother. She will try to establish later a similar position, either with husband or lover, or with another woman. Alternatively, she might take an opposite position, and protest against the maternal image through a show of independence and rebellion in personal relationships and social behaviour. Women like these may become highly ambitious and fiendishly anti-homosexual.

The following sketches are examples of relationships between mothers and favourite sons.

John, aged nineteen and one of the youngest participants, came from a working-class family. He had three sisters, and it was not surprising that he was his mother's favourite child. His father preferred a sister and hardly ever spoke to him. He was an alcoholic, beset by attacks of jealousy which he vented on the boy, whom he often treated with physical violence. The mother was an intelligent woman who had no outside job. She gave much time to her children, and read to John from as far back as he could remember. He grew up, spoiled by her and his sisters whom he loved. He was completely identified with the female members of the family, and this closeness influenced all his later relationships. He loathed his father and tried to disregard him. He became infatuated with girls before he was fifteen, but was also attracted to older boys. He reacted emotionally to both sexes with equal intensity. 'I love people, regardless of their gender,' he told me.

Herbert had been the apple of his mother's eye ever since he could remember. She preferred him to his brother and two elder sisters. He was her youngest, and she treated him like a doll. She enhanced his girlish looks by letting his curly hair grow long and dressing him daintily. He remained her baby until she died when he was forty-three. He could have become a transsexual, he told me, but his early infatuation with one of his sisters probably prevented this. They had an incestuous relationship when he was fourteen and she sixteen. When he was about twelve years old, two teachers performed anal intercourse on him. He dared not resist though he felt considerable pain. But, as happened with other youths, repetition of the 'exercise' made it, in the end, a desirable experience. His bisexuality had been established in puberty, but he felt that he was more hetero- than homosexual as he preferred intercourse with women to sex with men. Yet he found men's bodies more exciting than the female physique. He still identified with women, and at times wished that he were a beautiful lady. But most of all he would feel happiest to be a baby again, looked after by a loving mother. In other words, he had never got away from her. He was married to a woman eighteen years his senior. Although his psychological past appeared to be the root cause of Herbert's bisexuality, his general appearance and his hands suggested an endocrine factor, probably dysfunction of the pituitary. He was of small build, baby-faced, and fat.

Roy, a young dancer of twenty-three, son of an old mother (she was over 40 at his birth) had been her darling, and the beloved 'baby brother' of three sisters. They all spoiled him, but his robust father, a factory worker, resented the cissy boy. He was less intelligent than the mother who over-shadowed him in every way. She wanted her son to be well educated, and went herself to evening classes. Roy modelled himself on her, but unfortunately he had not the intellectual capacity his mother thought he had, and left school at fifteen. His interests were ballet and the theatre, and he had a talent for dancing, but human relationships were his priority. He belonged to 'Men against Sexism', and described himself as a religious and idealistic person. He adored and loved women, and could perform coitus with them, but preferred sensuous pleasures and cuddling. 'Sex is too much hard work', were his words. He was, and is, afraid of homosexuality. His homosexual contacts were always with heterosexual men. Roy had the looks of a strong youth, but the graceful, rather languid gestures and postures of an androgynous male. He told me that he had learned more in his childhood about being a woman than a man, and that he had suffered ever since from conflicting emotions.

The two following examples of a mother's favouritism for a daughter highlight the difference in her preference for a son and a daughter.

Carmen, a woman of forty-nine, was brought up in unusual circumstances. Her mother had been married before and already had two sons. Carmen had been a much wanted child, and became her mother's favourite. One might have assumed that this preference over two step brothers, six and seven years her seniors, would have assured her of her worth, and dispelled the thought of rivalry with the male, particularly as her father was also devoted to her. But this was not so, probably because of an unfortunate remark of her mother's. She wrote in her autobiography: 'Although I was a much wanted child, I am sure that, being a girl, I was a disappointment. I once overheard my mother remark that she would have preferred a boy.' The family moved to different places while she was still very young, because of her father's profession. He was a naval officer of high rank. They were well off, and a nanny took charge of her while her mother was engaged in war work. But she gave all her free time to her daughter. The family was united and Carmen never thought of her brothers as step brothers. She was vivacious, adventurous and intelligent, and felt emotionally suffocated in her conventional surroundings. Yet she clung to her mother with an almost desperate love, never feeling secure in spite of her favouritism. She wrote: 'Often I would fling my arms round her, demanding: "You *do* love me, don't you Mummy?"' Then she felt remorse for hurting her mother's feelings by having doubted her.

She went to a co-educational grammar school, and had the usual crushes on women teachers. Her first sexual experience at about fourteen was with a boy of sixteen. At the same time, she loved emotionally and sensuously, a beautiful girl of her own age. Carmen thought of herself as a rebel, who would not build her future on the ideas and values of her aristocratic family. She grew restless at the end of her schooldays, and during her time at university she became a communist. At the same time she discovered her lesbian side which she openly declared.

Hermione, a student of twenty-one, came from a liberal and somewhat unconventional family. She had an older brother, but had always been her mother's favourite. Her mother absolutely adored her, and there was no question of any feeling of insecurity about her love, or rivalry with a male, whether brother or father. Her mother's emotional fervour was balanced by the quiet fondness her father showed her. Hermione was 'master' in the house; she was never criticized and was thoroughly spoilt by her mother. She was unusually intelligent with an I.Q. of around 150, but her nervous state had always given cause for anxiety. She was highly strung, and had no clear idea what to do with her life. Her first sexual experiences were with two girls, but at sixteen she fell in love with a young man and they slept together. She considered herself a bisexual woman from this time onwards. Her precarious nervous balance led to a breakdown, necessitating psychiatric treatment. Her feelings towards her mother were ambivalent. She was entirely dependent on her, but terrified of being devoured by her. She always returned the moment 'life' seemed too much for her.

In two other cases where mothers preferred daughters to sons, conflict arose because of the children's fear of intruding into the blissfully happy marriage of their parents. A dislocation of conflict might have been the real cause of their unease: the subconscious fear that their mother would have loved them even more if they had been of the opposite sex. The sense of female inferiority is so deeply rooted that it persists in spite of outward demonstrations to the contrary.

The last two examples are of female respondents whose parents did not prefer any of their children.

Jane's parents treated her and a younger brother with undivided love and affection, and showed no preference for either. She wrote in her autobiographical sketch: 'We were both wanted children, and had the enormous good fortune to grow up in a very loving, stable home. My parents were the example of what a good marriage should be. They were the sort of people to whom others turn for help, comfort and companionship.' Jane and her brother were told the full facts of life by their parents at an early age. There were several homosexuals among the family's friends, who were regarded by all of them as normal. Jane had romantic affairs with girls during early adolescence, and the usual crush on a mistress at school which she considered to be more than 'calf-love' as it lasted for five years. She looked on men as brothers, an attitude which only changed after she had left home for university. There she fell in love with a fellow student and went to bed with him. The affair lasted a year. Jane struck me as one of those fortunate people who had undergone the least possible brainwashing by her parents, and had remained as natural as a human being of our time can be. Bisexuality was, in her eyes, not a problem but a natural condition.

Patricia's background was similar to Jane's. Her brother was two years her junior, and both were wanted and much loved children, with no preference shown for either. The only, but considerable, difference in her early surroundings was the rather narrow-minded social attitudes of her parents. This might explain why Patricia followed their pattern until she was seventeen, and thought of herself as heterosexual. But, having left home for college, she discovered her bisexuality, and found little difficulty in accepting her lesbian side. She thought that her parents whose love and confidence she had enjoyed since childhood, had given her the freedom to accept herself as she was, even when she could not comply with their conventional code.

The last two cases were exceptions, in that both parents had been equally instrumental in their children's freedom to be themselves.

As a rule, an intimate bond with the mother was not equalled in the relationship with the father. Apart from the *natural* predominance of the maternal figure, social conditions in a male-dominated society are averse to a comparable closeness between father and child. It is not true that a man does not possess the potentiality for 'maternal' care and tenderness towards the young, but he has not the opportunity to develop it as long as all of life's activities are not fully shared between the sexes. Only then can maternal and paternal influences overlap, which will give the father a much closer relationship with his child. Some of the younger male participants had already achieved this goal. (See VIII, autobiography 7)

In any case, early parental attitudes and environmental conditions exert a decisive influence on the conduct of later relationships.

VI LATER RELATIONSHIPS

Freud made infantile eroticism respectable. But he did not make it clear that the child's 'libido' for the parents is but a safeguard against fears of being damaged by them: a device of ingratiation and a sign of gratitude for services rendered. The first 'erotic' stirrings are screams of 'help me, feed me, protect me'. The supposed sexual expressions of the infant are the poisoned fruit of anxiety. Freud's 'Oedipus complex' illustrates, in fact, the child's anxiety at seeing his anchor of safety – the mother – removed, which he tries to prevent through displays of love and desire. Not libido, but prostitution is the hallmark of early relationships. While our emotional life starts with prostitution, our sexual life starts with masturbation, the ABC of sexual knowledge on which much of later love-making is based. The infant's autistic gestures discover the pleasure-giving genitals, the erotogenous zone par excellence. This is a time when sexual satisfaction happens without the burden of ulterior motives. But the 'Garden of Eden' is soon abandoned when the child learns how to use masturbation for healing purposes. Auto-sexual activity begins as early as the first two years of life. The use of masturbation as a 'drug' follows suit at about three years of age. It acts as a tranquillizer in relieving tension and anxiety, and an anti-depressant in relieving frustration and disappointment. Masturbation can also replace hypnotics in stimulating pituitary action, the GH hormones (growth hormones) of which induce sleep. It is well known that women of so-called 'primitive' cultures masturbate their infants to sleep.

Self-discovery leads to sex-discovery which, in its turn, leads to self-help.

A child is mother- and ego-centred, and the boundaries between the two are blurred. This symbiosis remains, though less obviously, with human beings for good. Psychoanalysts who call ego-centred people narcissistic, have misunderstood the famous Greek legend, in spite of Melanie Klein's fascinating interpretation which put the record straight. Jung described the bisexual nature of man in his 'animus' and 'anima'. He revealed an essential truth about the nature of love: the search for the other-sexed aspect of oneself in the love-object, which illustrates that all love is self-love. The child's masturbation is not a chrysalis which develops into the butterfly of heterosexuality, after passing through a homo- or bisexual phase. The real situation is different. Masturbation remains with us throughout life as an essential part of erotic relationships. Only through the experience of the pleasurable and exciting 'spots' of one's own body can one find those which arouse similar reactions in others. Masturbatory acts occupy the greater part of a person's love-life, even when successful and fulfilling relationships have been established in adulthood. Masturbation is the path-finder in the exploration of the erotogenous zones. Tactile contact between people is both an end in itself and a preliminary to full orgastic satisfaction. The delight of touching and being touched finds an echo in the emotions, which is expressed in words like: 'how I am touched by you', and 'how happy I am that I am able to touch your heart'. The art of love has its roots in tactile sensuousness, which is the playground for bi- and homosexual pleasures. Heterosexual people might regard these solely as an *hors d'œuvre*, but no love-making worth its salt can do without them. Boredom and dissatisfaction would follow at the heel of stereotyped sexual techniques. The art of loving would become a mechanical exercise, if the imagination did not make every erotic experience a new one. Curiosity, which attempts to discover the unknown and conquer the unfamiliar, stimulates the imagination and is its helpmate in intimate relationships with both sexes. Curiosity is a good teacher, but no learning would be successful if the brain had not the capacity of pre-structured knowledge, as Chomsky taught us. I believe in his theory, and hold the view that all knowledge depends on innate pre-knowledge, not only in the mental but also the emotional sphere. We can be everybody and everything in our imagination, which has a fine ear for subliminal memories, and the unconscious stirrings of our prenatal past. The difference between bi- and heterosexuality is the repression of the homosexual component in the latter. The difference between bi- and homosexuality lies in the exclusion of the heterosexual component, for biographical and/or endocrine reasons. Bisexuality makes otherness come close to sameness, and puts the androgynous nature of human beings into relief. Homo- and heterosexuality follow essentially the same pattern, and differ from bisexuality only in emphasizing exclusive practices. All sexuality comes from the same source and uses similar means of expression. To categorize psychosexual behaviour blurs the issue. In the last resort we do not add much to the child's sexual discoveries. We remain infants, not only at heart but also at 'sex'. The child uses sex as a drug and so does the adult. Sex is a method of escape and a measure to relieve tension and induce sleep at any time of life. Adults use sex more often as means to an end than spontaneous communication of desire and love. The will to power, the wish to conquer and to hold on to the conquered, makes human beings prostitutes in adulthood for the very same reason as it did in childhood. 'Keep me', 'hold me', and 'behold me', are the emotional cries of adults and children alike. The people for whom these cries are meant are not different from the love-objects of the child either. Men cry out for the mother in the beloved, and women do the same, even when the loved object has the face of a male.

The concept of intimate relationships suggests different things to different people. Many will associate it with sex, others with love and some with friendship, but the common denominator is emotional involvement. Behind every relationship stands the past: the experiences of childhood and youth. Those who give sexual intimacy pride of place in a close relationship, make it a mirror image of self-love and masturbation. Those who think that emotional love links two people intimately, repeat either the active or passive role of the mother-child bond. Whether intimate relationships are ego- or mother-centred, they always regress to childhood. Its shadow makes or mars them for good. The paternal image is generally perceived only dimly, as through a glass darkly. The way in which people experience their intimate feelings for either sex is a matter of emphasis. Emotional and sexual attachments do not necessarily go together, which has particular relevance for bisexual people. Love for the same sex has different ingredients from that for the opposite sex, and intimate relationships of both male and female respondents followed different patterns. The men were emotionally attached to women and dependent on them (Table 11). They also loved them sexually, but the emphasis was on their maternal concern. The women often felt an overwhelming emotional need for other women, which was different from the way they felt for men. The bond with their male lovers and spouses was, in most cases, founded on maternal love and companionship. But they did fall in love with men, which distinguished them from lesbians. Some were sexually more attracted to their male than their female lovers. Such a complex situation tended to create difficulties in relationships with either sex. This might have contributed to psychological disturbances (Table 21). In their youth, male respondents had indulged in homosexual incest far more often than female subjects. Easy arousal through homosexual signals persisted into adulthood, and made sex with men irresistible. Their homoemotional attachments, on the other hand, were less highly pitched, and often lacked stability. This was, however, not so with some sophisticated intellectuals who rejected homosexual promiscuity, and wished for a durable bond with another man alongside their marriage or marriage-like relationships. The feelings and emotions of male respondents for their female lovers were, on the whole, solid, a bedrock of security. Any idea of separation aroused anxiety, if not panic in them. Men's dependence on women equalled women's independence from men, which reflected the early ties of both sexes with the mother. As a rule, the male had felt safe in her protective love, while the female had been unable to get over a sense of insecurity with her. She had to fight for her love, and in the process, developed self-sufficiency. The early mother-child bond was, in my view, responsible for the different approach to love and marriage in male and female respondents. Women were not afraid for themselves if the bond with the husband should break, but they feared *for him*, and could not bear the thought of abandoning their children. They had outgrown their early feeling of rivalry with the male, and with it the wish to be of the opposite sex (Table 13). They had given up the struggle to be what they were not, demonstrating the need of all human beings to feel well under their own skin, which is nature's greatest gift. They were assisted in their struggle for personal freedom by the fight for collective freedom of the Women's Liberation Movement. While they accepted themselves as females, and emphatically so, they were at the same time conscious of their bi-gender identity, and their need to love women as well as men. Their reactions demonstrated the psychological and social impact on bisexuality, and is a valid argument against a purely genetic theory. Individual life experiences might have helped them to accept their femaleness wholeheartedly. While they differed from lesbians in their capacity to fall in love with men, they shared with them the homoemotionality of intimate attachments. This might be the reason why they have not been accorded a status of their own, but have been identified with homosexual women.

Most of the women were homoemotional, while most of the men were bi-emotional. Few male participants had an emotional preference for either sex. But women's emotional attachments to, and emotional preoccupation with, other women was a striking feature of the investigation and contrasted with the results found in the male participants (Table 11a, b).

I had asked every subject how they understood the meaning of 'falling in love'. Not all of them were articulate about it, but those who were gave the same answer: one thinks of the person day and night, one wants them to be there and wants to know what they feel about one, and what they are occupied with at any time of the day or night. They had got hold of the meaning of emotional preoccupation as I understand it myself. Although the women could fall in love with men physically and emotionally, their homoemotional preoccupation exceeded by far the feelings they had for the male. *Bisexual women love other women rather than men emotionally.* Their preference is rooted in the early mother-daughter relationship and intensified by a sense of sexual inferiority, for which they make the mother, consciously or unconsciously, responsible. Female respondents did not reject men emotionally, but they were less profoundly moved by them than by their own sex.

One must remember that the word emotion has suffered the same fate as that of love and many others. They have become vague denominations, having different meanings for different people. Emotion is a moving force which stirs body and mind. The 'stirrings' can be gentle or fierce, leading to calm or tumultous feelings. Emotion has many faces, as many as, if not more than, love. It can be shallow or deep, but nothing which alters life for one moment happens without an inner movement. Even the most perfunctory sexual appetite has an emotional ingredient. Not all relationships have a sexual connotation, but they always have an emotional one. Differences in emotional attachments and preoccupations in the male and female groups were matched by differences in their attitudes to sex. But there were male and female respondents who 'changed places', in accordance with their individuality and their particular quality of mental and emotional androgyny. In this sense one could perhaps class certain homosexual men as lesbians and their female counterparts as 'queens'. The same holds good for bisexual people.

Male and female respondents were asked whether they thought bisexuality an advantage emotionally or not. The opinion of the majority in both groups was in the affirmative (Table 23). The relevant table correlates this question with another one on the number of male and female lovers the subjects had. Their answers were not related to the number of lovers, whether of the same or the opposite sex. Statistics also correlated the age of respondents with the number of lovers of either sex. Male subjects had significantly more homosexual lovers than female subjects, and women more heterosexual lovers than the men (Tables 16, 17).

An unexpected finding of this investigation was the fact that over half of both groups were married. Marriages of male subjects were mostly happy. Those of female respondents were less often so. Their separation and divorce rate was higher than that of the male group (Table 7b). Males had taken marriage vows more often than females, which could have been due to the higher number of older men in the sample. Their emotional dependence on women might explain why they adapted themselves well to marriage. They needed the anchor of a 'settled' life with a maternal figure in the background. Many longed for bourgeois respectability as an antidote to their social insecurity. Marriage served as a hideout from the outer world and a balancing factor in their inner world. Female subjects were more adjusted to solitude. They also wanted independence because they felt the need to stand on their own feet. The influence of the Women's Liberation Movement made them less conventional, and more independent of other people's opinions. Both groups were united in their attitude to parenthood and love for their children. None of the women and only two of the men felt indifferent towards them (Table 7c). They conformed to the structure of the nuclear family as much as their parents did. No generation gap existed in this respect (Table 7a). But there must have been a considerable difference in life style between the two generations. It was readily discernible among the women who differed from their mothers in their attitude to marriage. According to their own impressions they were less often happily married.

CONFLICTS ABOUT BISEXUALITY

It was a matter of routine to ask about attitudes of married men to their spouses. Autobiographies of the older ones often referred to their wives rather condescendingly. When I asked whether their partners had bisexual or lesbian leanings, I usually got startled looks and: 'Oh no, she does not understand women like that, but she is a bit more tolerant of male homosexuality.' These men regarded their wives as a combination of mother and housekeeper. An old-fashioned attitude to the women chosen as life partners left one in no doubt that many bisexual men of the older generation adhere to the female ideal of yesteryear. And not all the younger men took a different line. No wonder that many tried to keep their homosexual inclinations secret from their wives. Some did not want them to know that they were participating in my research, and did not give me their home address. They pursued their homosexual ventures with cunning and a certain bravado, and appeared to have no sense of guilt towards their family, Only a very small number of older respondents lived in an atmosphere of understanding and openness with their wives. They were generally married to women older than themselves. On the face of it, all these men appeared to be well adjusted, leading ordinary lives. They did not seem to fear losing either jobs or friends should their homosexual side be discovered. They lived a double life, wearing the mask of bourgeois respectability. But what would the face look like if one tore off the mask? When they were relaxed and became more themselves during the interview, they confessed to being constantly afraid of being found out. Some admitted a sense of guilt, more towards their children than their wife; others denied guilt feelings but said that they never felt really 'safe' inside or outside their home. Their denial of guilt feelings could not cover up the truth; it showed itself in the exaggerated care they took of wife and family (Table 20).

Conflicts of this kind were even more pronounced in the transvestites and transsexuals who participated in this research. The condition has a compulsive character, and the sufferings of the subjects concerned were caused in the first place through a dichotomy between sexual and gender identity. As they were predominantly introvert, conflicts concerned their relationships with themselves rather than with others. All transvestites I interviewed had conflicts about their homosexual side. They confessed, without exception, to wanting sexual relationships with men.

A number of younger respondents had a different mentality from that of the older men. Three had bisexual wives who were members of the Women's Liberation Movement. Six young couples who lived in marriage-like relationships, regarded bisexuality as a bonus because of the understanding of each other's reactions. They were people in search of new ways in personal and collective contacts. Three other non-married couples enjoyed group sex, and experimented in unorthodox psychological methods like consciousness raising and bioenergetics. Four male respondents, two of them married, belonged to Men Against Sexism. A generation gap really existed between older and younger male subjects, with the proviso that biological age did not always coincide with psychological age. But the younger men were not without conflicts about bisexuality either. Apart from a few exceptions, they did not reveal their sexual orientation, except to close friends and colleagues. In some, the more serious conflict came from anxiety about their manliness in general and a fear of impotence with women in particular. But others were convinced that their homosexual relationships made heterosexual ones stronger and more enjoyable. Both older and younger respondents saw themselves as footloose in our society, being afraid of being found out as 'queers'. Some felt guilty, some did not, but all were very apprehensive of being stigmatized.

Feelings of guilt about the homosexual aspect of bisexuality were higher in male than female respondents. A number of subjects in both groups experienced a sense of guilt about all sexuality, inside or outside marriage (Table 20). The fact that some bisexual women and men were tormented in this way could perhaps be explained by their upbringing. In some cases, a schizoid temperament might have led them into this cul-de-sac.

It appeared that the women were more often stronger than the men in having the courage of their convictions in sexual matters. They were more independent of public opinion. This made their lives less complicated. It would be easy to attribute their greater freedom to their exemption from the law against homosexuality. It is as well to remember that bisexual people are generally classed with homosexuals. A clear differentiation between the two has not been made hitherto. Bisexual (and homosexual) women have never suffered the humiliation which legal persecution has dealt out to men. But subtle, and often not so subtle, mental, social and even physical maltreatment to which lesbians are exposed, were known to many of the subjects. However, the mimicry of a normal family life, more plausible in bi- than homosexual women, afforded some of them a certain protection from being singled out as 'undesirables'. Their intimate relationships with men, legalized or not, provided a safety valve. Their love for women was less exposed to public view because they kept a certain balance between hetero- and homosexuality, with no obvious preference for either. Some of them lived in a 'no-man's land', where their lesbian relationships were hidden from attack and often from view. Radical lesbians had reproached them for 'copping out' of their homosexual responsibilities by letting the side down. Actually, the women I dealt with had done nothing of the sort. They declared their loyalty to homosexual women at least as strongly as their commitment to men. I have already mentioned that their emotional love for and preoccupation with other women generally exceeded their feelings for men, and it seemed paradoxical that conflicts about their bisexuality came from their insecurity with lesbians rather than male lovers or husbands. One respondent, who was part of a commune, had fallen in love with a man. She dared not have an affair with him for fear of disapproval by a radical lesbian friend with whom she shared rooms. Bisexual men suffered both ways, by displeasing homosexual as well as heterosexual partners. Bisexual women had it easier because they had less fear of being outcasts, and were frequently more independent of their marriage partners or male lovers. No wonder that their conflicts differed in character from those of the male respondents. They did not attempt to hide their love for women from husbands, who, on the whole, accepted the situation, and, in a number of cases, encouraged it. They welcomed their wives' lesbian loves into the house, and sometimes into bed. They desired an affair à trois because they did not want to be excluded from their wives' 'other' love and loved the sensation. No doubt they never believed that they could be replaced when it came to a decision. But threesome sex never worked for any length of time, and the husband had to beat a dignified retreat. While in some cases conflicts of jealousy did arise, it was not uncommon for husbands to make real friends of their spouses' homosexual lovers. Such a happy outcome was illustrated in a recent letter from one of the women. She gave me permission to quote from it: 'I found myself much attracted to a woman in the lesbian group to which I belong, and by the end of December we were lovers. It has been a wonderful relationship for us both. It is a deeply caring relationship, full of great friendship and mutual delight. My husband has taken to this turn of events with good humour. He and she are good friends and seem to enjoy each other's company. We often do things as a threesome, and I am pleased that they get along well together.' An air of 'laissez-faire' prevailed, and the acceptance of the partner's homosexual side was a model of tolerance.

The idea of male superiority is deeply ingrained in the minds of most men, which might have influenced their attitude to their wives' lesbianism. Not many could believe that another woman could drive them out of the marriage bed, except those who actually experienced it. How male arrogance can lead to a false sense of security was illustrated in three autobiographies. The husbands had no idea that their marriage only survived because of their wives' loyalty and love for their children, which made them resist separation or divorce. None of them had objected to their wives' lesbianism. One of the women concerned told me that she had married for reasons of convenience. But she had grown to love her husband, and both adored their three children. After ten years of marriage she fell in love with another woman, and not for the first time in her life. Her husband's disinclination for sexual intercourse and his altogether withdrawn behaviour, made her want to get away from him and live with her friend. But she was unable to make the jump because of her love for the children and concern for him. 'He is such a lonely person. I cannot do it to him,' she said to me during the interview. Early influences played their part in her decision to stay. While still at school, her mother had discovered her kissing another girl; she reprimanded her severely. Because of this incident, she never grew free from guilt feelings about her lesbian inclination. She was worried that it might overshadow her capacity to love a man, but she kept on reassuring herself that she was bisexual and not a lesbian, as she had been in love with two men before her marriage. I agreed with her because her husband was apparently not only undersexed, but also a bad lover. He had been a virgin when they married.

Conflict in another woman concerned her heterosexual – and not her lesbian – relationships. She had been sexually assaulted as a child, and was badly treated by her father who despised women. Her mother lived in terror of her husband, and never came to her aid when he ill-treated her. She was good-looking and attractive to men, and learned to use her female charms as a weapon of conquest and revenge. She had many lovers and took pleasure in betraying them, preferably with their friends. In her early teens, she had loved girls older than herself, but she became so engrossed in the exercise of punishing the male, that she did not even think of her past attachments to women. After two broken marriages, she had definitely had enough of men. She told me with glee how unfaithful she had been to her two husbands. She was now visiting lesbian clubs because she wanted to find a woman to live with. 'I could only be faithful to another woman,' she said. And: 'I could love a woman, if I am able to love at all.'

More often than not, conflicts in relationships of female subjects were with other women. Bisexual women arouse insecurity and jealousy in lesbian partners, who fear they will be let down because of their lover's commitment to children and husband. This is so even if there is no real ground for jealousy. The fear that a bisexual woman might prefer a man is at the root of the trouble.

Love for both her husband and a lesbian led, in another case, to confusion about gender identity. This woman was not sure whether

her husband was right in insisting that she was heterosexual, or her lesbian lover who declared that she was a homosexual at heart. She had always thought of herself as bisexual, but when these two battered her with arguments and passion, she was no longer sure.

The difference between male and female respondents in intimate relationships was unquestionable, and so was the difference in their conflicts. One wonders whether the divide was caused by environmental or constitutional conditions. Had they undergone brainwashing processes which produced different qualities for the task to cope with themselves and others? Or were sex differences of temperament the cause? I do not believe that these exist, but think that early environmental influences, particularly of parents, shape reactions through false instructions. The male respondents' emotional dependence on women, and their greater sense of guilt about homosexuality, arose from their close relationship with their mothers who favoured them. The female respondents' less fortunate position in family and society had the opposite effect. It produced a sense of independence, and rarely guilt feelings about homosexuality.

Casual sexual contacts were of particular interest because of a striking divergence between male and female respondents. I have mentioned before that their age groups could not be matched because of the particular circumstances of the investigation. This discrepancy had to be taken into account when age could be an important factor in the number of homo- or heterosexual experiences. According to the statistical tables, age had no relevance to the numerical incidences of these encounters in either group (Tables 27, 28).

Male subjects had far more casual homosexual than heterosexual encounters, women subjects had more hetero- than homosexual casual encounters. These findings might suggest that women are by nature more bisexual than men. But I wonder how much early conditioning contributed to the situation, which might be different in a society free from male dominance and its psychological consequences. Both groups had a fairly equal share of casual encounters with the opposite sex. But the difference in their homosexual chance meetings was indeed dramatic.

Casual homosexual encounters are 'prostitution' with a difference, a *l'art pour l'art* performance, without barter or money exchange. Anonymous sexual contacts can be as habit-forming as drug-addiction. On the other hand, they may be transient acts without after-effects. Why did these women and men indulge in them at all? The reasons were very different in each of the two groups.

In the first place, I want to treat the less dramatic situation of female respondents. None of them had more than twenty homosexual 'one night stands', and, as far as I know, none of these occurred in public places, which were (and are) the usual venue for male respondents. Why was there such a difference between the two groups? Firstly, immediacy of sexual gratification depends on speed of arousal and accessibility of the genitals. Women's clothes can be a hindrance. Men have the edge over them in this respect. But the sense of privacy and (to utter an almost unutterable word) modesty, has been instilled into women as profoundly as their sense of sexual inferiority. This might explain their reluctance to make a public exhibition of their private parts.

Women's sexual desire is as strong and easily aroused as that of men. But they are conditioned to adopt a more passive role in coital positions with the male, which might reflect on their sexual attitudes as a whole. However, this pattern loses much of its significance in bi- and homosexual women who are particularly highly sexed. They are in many cases inclined to take the initiative in sexual contacts on the spur of the moment. Some of the women explained their desire for casual sex with a lesbian through loneliness, or disappointments in love either with another woman or a man. Others did it for kicks, or to prove their sexual freedom. While their homosexual 'brief encounters' were comparatively few, their heterosexual ones reached much higher numbers. Two reported over eighty, another over 300. The latter, an American woman of remarkable beauty and intelligence, had given her profession as 'call girl' (see VIII, autobiography 1).

The need for anonymous heterosexual contacts was practically the same in the two groups. The males' lesser desire for casual sex with women than men might have been due to the greater difficulty of 'getting going' with a girl. A different campaign had to be applied in sex with women, whether casual or not, as one respondent remarked. According to information given in interviews and autobiographies, other reasons for casual homosexuality played a more important part. Quick sexual encounters with men are easier than with women because of the anatomy of the male genitals, but the principal causes lie in the physio-psychological make-up of the male.

Society and its laws make it necessary that casual homosexuality be pursued in places where its possible discovery can be avoided through dissimulation. Opportunities are available in urinals and lavatories. The latter are generally divided by low partitions, which make anal intercourse 'over the wall' a possibility. Fellatio and mutual masturbation can be quickly and discreetly performed at the urinal. These gratifications, solicited by furtive signals, are a modern version of an old phenomenon: male prostitution. Its roots go back to orgiastic rituals of ancient religious ceremonies. It already figured in the earliest times of Judaism, as Klimmer has shown in *Die Homosexualität* (p. 286). Religion and sex are bedfellows which heighten the zest for life. In those early days, male prostitution was not the forbidden fruit it later became, but was accepted as natural and desirable. It had a touch of inspiration all its own. Sexual acts were carried out in an atmosphere of ecstasy and hypnotic trance inherent in ancient forms of worship. It is a long jump in time from the temples of early religions to the venues in public places which serve the purpose of anonymous sex between males today. There are obvious differences between such intimate meetings then and now. In our day, homosexual acts between men in public places are considered indecent. They are disreputable and distasteful to the great majority of the population. They must be performed with the skill, secrecy and cunning of delinquents. A sense of danger, the dread of being apprehended by the police, make them scaring adventures. The fact that not only bi- and homosexuals but also 'normal' males indulge in them, is proof of their tremendous attraction, and also of the error of dividing unorthodox sexual practices from 'ordinary' ones. Kinsey has shown that fifty per cent of *all* men react physically to their own sex. Laud Humphreys made a similar observation in *The Tearoom Trade* (1970). His study of the subject was carried out in lavatories and other public places. He called himself 'a research worker as voyeur'. He saw all manner of men in the acts of fellatio, anal intercourse, and mutual masturbation. The number of visitors to lavatories and urinals ran into millions. The conditions he described were the same in all major American cities and, as male respondents told me, resemble closely the situation in this country. What drives men of all classes to take risks which could damage them personally and professionally? Anonymous homosexual acts in public places are punishable by law throughout Europe and America. In view of such hazards, powerful motives must be at work to engage men in these daring activities. I have mentioned that easy access to venues presents a temptation in itself, and also that the really compelling causes are of a physio-psychological nature.

I have already quoted (see chapter II) Fenichel's physiological explanation of men's predisposition to anal intercourse with other men. Laud Humphreys reported that one should not take it for granted that there are definite passive and active roles in anal intercourse. He observed that 'insertors' became 'insertees' and vice versa, which shows the variability of sexual roles, and the particular sensitivity of the anal erotogenous zone in men. The German author, Redhardt (1952), mentioned a number of male prostitutes who claimed that anal intercourse was practised mainly by bisexual – and mutual masturbation by homosexual – men. This statement was not confirmed by male respondents of this study. Homosexual practices other than anal coitus were just as well favoured.

The oral zone is an erotogenous region par excellence. It is undeniable that a primitive connection exists between sucking, feeding and oral eroticism. The latter might be the result of the former two. Fellatio is a combination of the three, if we accept the claim of a number of male respondents that they wanted to be fed by the semen they ingested. For them, sucking the penis or 'blowing' it was the most desirable sex thrill. Some were active, some passive partners. Others had it both ways.

The frequency of anal intercourse performed in lavatories might surprise 'uninitiated' readers, but it came second to fellatio according to the written and verbal statements of male subjects. Mutual masturbation did not produce, on the whole, the same thrill as the other two practices, and was mostly used as foreplay to them. It served as the 'full meal' only in a minority of cases. Time being of the essence, sex in public places acquired the momentum of an emergency. Partners had to look over their shoulders unless they had a reliable watchman like Laud Humphreys to give them warning signals. There was hardly a moment between signals of invitation and acts. Many never heard the voice of their partner, and some did not even see him when they were insertees in anal intercourse.

Psychological causes for the pursuit of anonymous sex can be the result of personal idiosyncrasies or individual experiences. It would be impossible to discuss those here. I am referring therefore only to the collective drive of a compulsive need for sexual gratification with unknown people. These activities are adventures fraught with danger, which provide stolen pleasures redolent of children's exploits. Perhaps danger shared loses its sting, perhaps the mystique of a 'common' secret makes it all the more exciting. From childhood onwards, those who have a secret, excite curiosity and are singled out because of the interest and disquiet they arouse in others. The element of sensation which makes adventure the life blood of the young, does not lose its power over the adult. The excitement of stealing sexual pleasures can be out of proportion to the actual experience, when life is dreary, full of frustrations and altogether against the grain. 'Going underground' is an excitement in itself, but there is a practical reason: a sexual need in search of a suitable place to satisfy it. Society has driven 'unorthodox' sex underground, and protest against the heavy hand of the law gives verve to an adventure which hits back at conventional codes. Nobody can gauge how deeply collective injustice, persistent over centuries, lingers on in the minds of bi- and homosexual people, in spite of a somewhat better understanding of their sexual needs among socially progressive people. Men have never been punished for visiting female prostitutes; many have boasted of their exploits. But men with the desire for homosexual gratification must meet like conspirators, under the Damocles sword of the law. They had to invent a sign language to make themselves known to the like-minded. The sense of their secret fraternity bears a resemblance to the brotherhood of Free Masons. But there the comparison ends. Their communal spirit remains without an organized community. Their fleeting unions are over in minutes, without leaving visible traces. Yet it is society which has produced their sexual furtiveness.

Although fleeting homosexual acts are often performed in cars, hotels, or private rooms, they take place mainly in 'dangerous' surroundings. Apart from public lavatories, sauna baths, parks and quiet streets are used. The 'mystique' of the goings on described is by now known in the market place. But curiosity mixed with hate and envy keeps constant watch, and policemen, assisted by philistines, are ready to pounce. If the threat of legal proceedings no longer played a part, would the desire for anonymous sex decrease? I don't believe it would, so long as bi- and homosexual men are made to feel insecure. If they could dispense with public places, they would probably pursue their adventures both more openly and more discreetly.

Male respondents in the older age groups were more hooked on 'public' sex than the younger men, because they lived on the whole bourgeois lives with wives hostile to their homosexuality. A number of younger respondents expressed the wish to be free of furtive sex in public places. They wanted the same status and opportunities for homo- and heterosexual love.

Casual sex encounters of male and female subjects showed similarity in hetero- and dissimilarity in homosexual behaviour. But their astounding difference in the homosexual variety indicated the greater sexual restlessness and daring of the male. Legal and social conditions partly account for it, but the degree of difference remains puzzling. Sixteen men counted up to eighty experiences, seven up to 300, and three over 300. Several respondents mentioned that it was impossible to count them at all, as they came to many hundreds, and two declared that they had been involved in such acts over 3000 times. The highest number of casual homosexual encounters in women was twenty. It might be well to remember that thirty-seven women compared with thirteen men never indulged in them at all. Those women who did, had no need to use public places. Their 'one night stands' usually happened in private surroundings, free from the sneaking eye of voyeurs. They risked less than men in every respect.

One would have expected the bisexual male to suffer from emotional difficulties more frequently and intensely than the female. But this was not the case.

Psychological disturbances were not uncommon among the subjects. Psychoanalysis claims that parental attitudes play a major part in their etiology. I therefore investigated whether parents had an influence on emotional disturbances in the respondents. States of anxiety and depression were the prevalent forms in both groups. They occurred more often in women subjects who, however, underwent psychotherapy less frequently than the men. According to statistics, parental attitudes were not at the root of the conditions (Table 21a).

Ten women and eight men had needed hospitalization because of more serious complaints, but none had suffered from psychosis. They were confined to a special hospital ward either for observation after a suicide attempt, or a 'nervous breakdown'. The parent-child relationship had apparently no bearing on the situation where the women were concerned, but the men had suffered from severe psychological disturbances somewhat less frequently than the women. It appeared that the mother's more loving attitude towards the male had a beneficial effect (Table 21b). Fathers had no influence on the situation. The fact that parental attitudes played no part in the milder and only a minor one in more severe conditions, pointed to problems of adaptation or perhaps early sexual traumas as possible causes. Adaptation to society is not an easy matter for bisexual people. They need great faith in themselves and considerable courage to 'swim against the stream'. It was therefore not surprising that some became disturbed in the process. Difficulties in adult relationships might have been a contributory factor.

Recent brain research has brought the interpretation of dreams into disrepute. Dream images are now supposed to be without rhyme or reason. The brain, drowned in sleep, picks them up in a haphazard fashion. This demotion of our dream world makes Freud, Jung and their followers resemble croupiers who preside over games of chance. But scientific theory cannot as yet explain why certain dreams are remembered, nor why there are recurrent ones with a high emotional charge. Dreams of a sexual nature are a case in point. It seemed sensible to compare sex dreams with sexual fantasies. Both groups dreamed most frequently of both sexes, which was to be expected. With male subjects, sexual orientation in dreams accorded with objects of sexual fantasies in two respects. The more often they made love to women in dreams, the more often they fantasized heterosexual coitus and cunnilingus. Women subjects whose dream objects were women and men, day-dreamed most often of cunnilingus, which was not surprising. No connection was found in either group between imaginings of mutual masturbation and sexual dream objects (Table 29). The close link between male subjects' heterosexual dreams and fantasies of coitus illustrated, in my view, their strong emotional rather than sexual need for women. It is of particular interest that female and male respondents were much alike in their sexual dreams about women and fantasies of cunnilingus. Day-dreams of anal intercourse and fellatio in relation to 'dream lovers' were as different in the two groups as could be expected. But the women imagined fellatio comparatively often, which was in line with their bisexuality. They desired men as well as women in their dreams (Table 29). Fellatio is enjoyed by many heterosexual women also, proving once more the basic unity of human sexuality.

Another statistical investigation referred to a possible correlation between love objects in dreams and fantasies about people with whom the respondents were infatuated, casual acquaintances, and 'dream people'. In neither group were sexual dreams and fantasies concerned with casual acquaintances and 'dream people', but women fantasized significantly more often than men about people they were infatuated with (Table 30). The conventional view that women's romanticism is the cause of their imaginative preoccupation when in love was not confirmed by my subjects. The fundamental cause of their need to invest imaginative and emotional longings in those they fancied, went back to early childhood, when the little girl was made to feel less loved by her mother than her father or brother. In a recent radio programme on the mother-child relationship, Dr Miriam Rosenthal of the Hebrew University, Jerusalem, reported on an experimental study which confirms my view that certain sex differences originate in the mother's different treatment of infant boys and girls. Contrary to certain American studies which proclaimed that many sexual differences are innate, Dr Rosenthal showed how much they are the result of the mother's different relationships with her male and female children. To quote her own words: 'We found that 80% of mothers of boys expressed extreme enjoyment in breast-feeding, 10% were neutral, and 10% did not like it too much. While among the mothers of girls, only 45% expressed extreme enjoyment, and 39% expressed more neutral feelings. I think it is the first time that it has been documented that mothers regard their boy infants of only three days old as a sexual entity.' (*Listener*, 18 November 1976)

I have already mentioned male respondents' pronounced guilt feelings about homosexuality, and their emotional dependence on women. The psychoanalytical view that both are rooted in an early mother-son bond seems a valid explanation. Male subjects dreamed more often of heterosexual lovers than female respondents, which could suggest that bisexual men have a stronger heterosexual side than bisexual women. But this is contrary to documentary and statistical evidence of this investigation. It should be interpreted as symbolic of men's emotional vulnerability, and consequent dependence on the stronger female sex. The history of persecution of unorthodox sexual behaviour accentuates their insecurity. Bisexual men find themselves between the devil and the deep blue sea, and look to women for solace and protection.

Both personal and collective relationships depend to a great extent on one's relationship with oneself. Bisexual people tend to be shunned by 'normal' citizens, and often despised by homosexuals. How did respondents see their own situation in relation to themselves, to other people, and to society? Did their self-esteem depend on approval and confirmation by others, their female or male partners in particular? Did the number of lovers of either sex weigh for or against the possibility that bisexuality was advantageous to them? All respondents were unanimous in their view that bisexuality was not a social advantage. But the men were convinced that their social prestige grew in direct proportion to the number of their heterosexual lovers (Table 26).

I asked all interviewees whether they felt their emotional life was enriched through their love for either sex. Many of them were uncertain, but the general feeling seemed to be positive. The majority in favour was around sixty per cent. The number of hetero- or homosexual lovers did not influence the verdict in either group (Table 23).

It might be assumed that a broadening of perceptivity and human understanding would be the natural consequence of bisexuality. It need hardly be mentioned that male domination limits the understanding of human beings and distorts attitudes towards them. It stultifies ideas because they are perceived with a mental squint. A similar threat to balanced behaviour and judgement would follow in the wake of female domination. A bisexual society with no exclusive claims made for either sex, would be best suited to free humanity from the evils of the world we live in.

I had hoped that my interviewees would wholeheartedly express this view, and the majority did. Apart from this general concensus, both women and men respondents believed that they had gained mentally in direct proportion to the number of their female lovers (Table 24).

The question whether bisexuality had a creative advantage was positively answered by both groups, but with a significantly stronger emphasis by the women. The number of female lovers did influence the verdict in the female group. The women felt that their love for other women greatly enhanced their own creative urges and achievements. This demonstrated strikingly that they had an altogether closer link with women than with men (Table 25). Their mutual comradeship, their intellectual and artistic inspiration united them in a world apart. They saw their lesbian side as a definite advantage in this and most other aspects of their lives.

Bisexuals live in a twilight world. Heterosexual people blame them for eating their cake and having it. Homosexuals accuse them of hypocrisy in not belonging to *them*, and so avoiding being true to themselves and 'copping out'. This attitude makes it difficult to understand why homosexual groups invite them to join at all. The fact is that they accept them grudgingly, and tolerate them in the hope of converting them. However, this does not apply to all members of such organizations, which gives bisexuals a tenuous hold on community life inside them. They know that they cannot expect ever to be fully integrated. Anyone belonging to a sexual variation resents not being regarded as a first class citizen who fulfils his duties to society like anybody else. Because of their anxiety to prove that mistrust of them is ill-founded, bisexual people might even be a step or two ahead of others. They can easily avoid being conspicuous, especially when they are married. They have an advantage over other sexual variations in that their natural mimicry can be of considerable assistance to them in the ways of the world. But this does not ease their inner conflicts, which are aggravated rather than helped by their superficially normal situation. They have to use subterfuges to satisfy their homosexual needs, and are in danger of greater condemnation than those who are open about them. The majority of male and female respondents gave me to understand that they felt at home neither in the conventional world of society, nor in the unconventional one of sexual minority groups. They were always between two stools, thrown back on personal relationships. Yet many tried against all odds to find consolation in the C.H.E. or the Gay Liberation Front. A number of female respondents also belonged to these organizations, but most of them had joined the two lesbian groups, Sappho and Kenric, which gave them a more congenial milieu. Membership of sexual minority groups and frequency of integration into them were recorded in the following table:

	Membership		*Integrated*		
	Yes	No	Yes	No	No answer
Men 75	41	34	15	23	3
Women 75	34	41	16	15	3

I have no doubt that Sappho and Kenric are tolerant of their bisexual members. I know of their attitude from the inside as I belong to both. Fewer women than men joined sexual minority organizations, and more women than men found a niche in them. Apart from the main groups, Integroup and Friend deserve a special mention. The first provides a link between sexual variations and heterosexuals, the second has a counselling and befriending service for homo- and bisexual women and men. The Albany Trust provides counselling for individuals of every sexual orientation. The C.H.E., Friend and Sappho have branches all over the country, and have created a gay community without becoming a ghetto. Gay switchboards, which offer friendship and help, also operate nationally. The Swindon branch of Sappho declares itself a gay/bisexual group, which shows an exemplary sense of what minority groups should be about. The C.H.E. has made great strides in gathering members into its fold, and providing services in many fields. It is particularly active in improving communications within its own membership and with society. The Scottish Minority Group works in close collaboration with the C.H.E., and has branches for women in Edinburgh and Glasgow. The principal aim of all these groups is to combat the isolation of sexual non-conformers by creating a homogeneous collective where their members can relax and be themselves.

Disharmony within the ranks of sexual variations is against their own interest, and indeed destructive. The situation is as regrettable as it is understandable in the present climate of society. Human beings have the same sense of territory as other mammals; they get aggressive, and wildly so, when another species invades their sacred ground. Possessiveness and jealousy are the natural consequences of territorial claims. In fighting for territory, invader and defender can destroy each other, but collective identity would be at risk if its integrity was not constantly watched. Such is the dilemma which the need for self-preservation can bring about. But a fatal error arises when the real frontiers of the territory are either not known or disregarded. This is the situation between bi- and homosexuals. Obviously, the need of homosexuals to define and to defend their ground is far greater than that of bisexuals. Homosexuals demand a clear-cut differentiation from those who are not completely identified with them. They either become aggressive or withdraw from those who might question their 'territorial' claims. And they won't look favourably at anyone whose identification reaches beyond their own domain into the heterosexual world, which, to them, smacks of the enemy. The bisexual, on the other hand, has more affinity with them than with heterosexuals, because he too is of an unorthodox psychosexual persuasion. He/she is often accused of using the device of mimicry to guard his/her identity, but rejects such a suggestion as unjustified and insulting. Bisexuals believe that the frontiers of psychosexual territories have been wrongly cast, and that they must be designed anew. This was the prevailing opinion of male and female participants; the women were particularly emphatic about it. Many homosexuals who have thought the matter through with detachment, have come to the same conclusion. I had occasion to verify this when, as a Trustee of the Albany Trust, I was tutor at some courses in which a number of homosexuals participated.

During the last six years, the gay press has served as a liaison between people of unorthodox sexual persuasions who might not see eye to eye in direct contact. *Gay News* is a newspaper which appears fortnightly. It provides a link between sexual variations, helping to ease their sense of isolation. It carries personal advertisements, notices of counselling services and other useful information. It has a progressive and aggressive policy, and includes in its pages contributions from our foremost writers and commentators. The magazine *Sappho* unites lesbians and bisexual women on an international scale. It advertises important occasions, meetings and discussions. *Sappho* not only provides information about questions of sexuality, but is also an active feminist organ. Kenric is a lesbian organization which is devoted mainly to promoting social contact between them. It counts now about 500 members. A monthly newsletter gives notices of social events, play readings and discussions on homosexual topics. All these publications are designed to bring people together, and give them a sense of 'belonging'. Their service lies in strengthening the sense of collective identity in individuals whose situation in society is uneasy or worse.

Society has categorized people according to their sexual orientation, and has never understood that there is only *human sexuality* with manifold expressions. It has given heterosexuality pride of place, and has made other sexual orientations look ugly. Society does not realize that its very continuation might well depend on those whom it tries to diminish in the eyes of their fellow citizens. I am convinced that the atom bomb will destroy us all if we do not in time achieve an alternative, that is, a bisexual society. Heterosexual people, conforming to conventional dictate, are pillars of the society with which they are identified. Bisexuals and homosexuals, on the other hand, make valiant efforts to free themselves from the fetters of its conditioning power, and therefore come nearer to authentic behaviour. By reason of their rebellion, they are inclined to reject second-hand living as laid down by social conventions. It is not surprising that one finds many of them in the forefront of the fight for a new society, a society where authenticity is the guiding principle. But others are so much caught up in defensive behaviour that they neglect the pursuit of individual freedom in preference for collective regimentation, which ensures a more successful battle against the cruel and subtle persecution by 'normal' people. Nevertheless they are, by virtue of their still precarious position, well endowed to realize that the assignment of roles which rules every aspect of behaviour, permeates society like an infectious disease, that there is a social sickness about which leads via hypocrisy and falsity to alienation. Their own fringe position makes them particularly sensitive to the schizoid shortcomings of our society where nobody knows what the other thinks or feels, and where relationships lose their essential qualities – solidity and trust. Needless to say, it is not the privilege of bisexual and homosexual people alone to be aware of this predicament, but their particular make-up encourages a greater flexibility of approach towards new ventures, because they have less to lose and are less afraid of change. Only in a bisexual society can human beings get rid of the sexual compartments in which they are entrenched, and understand that we are all in the same boat, only in different attire.

VII INTERVIEWS

          Opening the door to a stranger and seeing a face for the first time, is a mild shock experience. One never knows how one is going to be affected by the visitor, and vice versa. First meetings of importance affect me like a *caresse* or a blow. First impressions can be decisive for the outcome of an interview, and the fear of failure is always at the back of one's mind. The following three interviews are much shortened versions of my conversations with two men and one woman.

1

A meticulously dressed man entered. His eyes looked tired, and he hardly gave me a glance. His air of indifference probably hid his apprehension about the interview which he had tried to avoid for a long time. He had put off several appointments before he finally managed to face me (or – himself?). He walked with small, inhibited steps, and his first question, after having divested himself of an elegant overcoat with fur collar, was: 'May I use your lavatory?' I was familiar with this start to a meeting. It happened more frequently with men than women. Was it, in this instance, acute anxiety or just failure to find a convenience on the way? I settled for anxiety.

    I kept well in the shadow of silent expectancy until he started: 'It took me a long time to answer your questionnaire, and to arrange this visit. But I could manage it at last today.'

Q: How did you manage? I know that you had to take a train.
A: A woman friend invited me to stay with her for the week-end in Highbury, and I can combine the two visits. Perhaps I hope to find some encouragement for my visit from you? You see, I am at a cross-roads. It is possible that my friend is going to influence my future.
Q: Can you tell me how?
A: I might ask her to marry me. It will depend on how we get on – three days under the same roof. I must marry now or I never shall. I am nearly fifty.
Q: Did you not think of marriage before?
A: I was frightened of women, although my first love was a girl. I was twelve and she fourteen. I wanted to marry her. But two years later I started homosexual contacts which I could not resist, but did not find emotionally satisfactory. I never got on with my sisters until I was about eighteen.
Q: Tell me about them and your mother.
A: My mother is a neurotic who spoiled me. I must have been in love with her as I wanted to marry her when I was about six. [He hesitated] I even made preparations for a wedding ceremony. Isn't it rather odd for a boy of six to behave like this?
Q: Now you are asking me a question. I think that the timing of such behaviour depends on the complexities of family relationships and perhaps certain imponderabilities. Did your mother prefer you to your sisters because you were her only son?
A: She rather did the opposite, if you know what I mean, but probably you don't. She treated me like a girl, as if she wanted me to be one. Yet she preferred me to my sisters. I was the youngest, her baby, which might have had something to do with it. And I have often thought that she was a suppressed lesbian, which could explain her treatment of me. My eldest sister is eight years and the second four years older than I. I felt hostile to them both when I was a child. But later on I loved my eldest sister. She was the first woman I really got to know. As a child I needed my mother, but I did not feel secure with her because she was insecure. Yet I loved her.
Q: Do you still love her and your eldest sister?
A: My mother died four years ago. My sister and I are close friends. She is good-looking and intelligent. Perhaps she opened my eyes to the grace and beauty of women. I could fall in love with a woman.
Q: Well, have you?

111

A: Yes and no. I don't know really. I certainly have not been in love with a man, although I find men sexually attractive. My mother could have made me a homosexual.

Q: Why do you think that you are not?

A: I know that I am bisexual. I had three successful physical relations with women, one of which lasted over three years, and my feelings for them were stronger than those I have for men. I am closer to women. I think that one really loves 'people', whether they are male or female. Sex takes only what it takes. [He now folded his hands tightly and appeared to be under considerable strain. He stared at the carpet.]

Q: But am I right to conclude from what you just said, that you could also love a man? Aren't you contradicting yourself?

A: I really don't know. Theoretically I could, but I don't think I ever will.

Q: Do you feel guilty about homosexuality?

A: No, I don't, but I feel uncomfortable about it. I had many contacts, but mostly with emotionally unsuitable people.

Q: I know that you belong to the C.H.E. You also told me that you remained rather on the fringes, but appreciated the organization and want to further its aims. What then is the difficulty about your 'homo' side?

A: I think it is a disadvantage emotionally. But perhaps I think so because I never found a suitable partner, a man I could live with. I just don't know. But I am sure that I am able to love a woman. Can you explain the difficulty I have about my two 'sides'?

Q: I wouldn't dare to give you an answer, even if I knew it. I wonder though, how much your social position and your profession might affect your choice of friends and lovers?

A: A good question. [For the first time, he looked straight at me.] I am ambitious and depend much on public opinion. I don't think I am a coward, but I am influenced by conventions of society. I would 'look' right with a wife at my side. I would feel more secure. I am an artist, I love women's movements, their poise and grace. No, I do love women and not men. I am a romantic, and love is more important to me than gratification of any kind.

Q: Do you think you could love from a distance, unrequitedly?

A: No doubt I could. I have dreamt about it, and once fell in love with a photograph of a girl one of my students showed me. She was his girl friend. And what is love for one person? [He now looked down again, hands folded, probably really relaxed, although it might have been a pose.] The real thing is universal love. Most individuals are really not worth much. Idiots.

Q: You don't think much of people! Have you turned to religion because of dissatisfaction with what you have observed of human beings?

A: It may have something to do with it. In the last years, I have found more comfort and 'love' in groups who learn about transcendental meditation and believe in the tenets of Eastern religion, rather than in personal relationships. I believe in change of consciousness through which one experiences the timelessness of the state of being. I believe in the silent level of communication. It is mind-blowing. It changes perceptions and relationships.

Q: If you have found all that, you can't be lonely whatever happens?

A: I am not sure of that. I live on different planes, in two worlds or more.

Q: Does your friend with whom you are going to stay this week-end, share your faith?

A: She does. She is a spiritual person. I met her abroad on one of the courses on transcendental meditation.

Q: Can you tell me about her?

A: She is a sportswoman and a writer. She plays tennis very well and she won a competition in show jumping. She struck me as masculine when I met her, but I discovered later that she was also a tender and maternal person. She does not like domesticity. I do. I am good at cooking and gardening. I like to do jobs about the house. These things relax me after the effort of my teaching job. Sometimes I go on working the whole week-end. I want things to be perfect.

Q: Tell me, how can you combine your spirituality with your professional dedication and your sensuousness?

[He got up abruptly, walked up and down, looked at me with eyes wide open.]

A: Yes, I try to combine the three sources of life. I can devote myself to each one without falling short of the others. I recharge my batteries of nervous vitality through transcendental meditation. The strength which I need for my work comes from nervous energy; my physical powers are revived through domestic work and gardening. I am sensuous by nature and because I am an artist. Sensuousness heightens spiritual awareness you know.

Q: I would like you to tell me in what ways your bisexuality affects your attitudes to other people and your personal relationships?

A: All human beings are bisexual. Heterosexuals are people who suppress their homosexuality. I love *people*, not men or women, as I told you. But there are differences in response, I mean in my response. My immediate reaction to men is stronger than that to women, partly because I have greater experience of men, and am in a habit to respond. Women are holistic. They are lost in the actual physical act. With men, sex needs no effort. It is more visual and sex movements are similar. Not so with women. They are different. They are more compelling. They are soft; they give me a 'floating away' sensation. And they are very soothing, which makes sex satisfactory. But the peripheral erotic activity is not so good with them as with men. I now absolutely want sex with women. And I want their friendship.

He didn't wait for another question, but asked to go to the bathroom. I shall never know whether I had 'met' him or not. He didn't shake hands, nor did he make any other sign of personal contact. But I think he was glad to have come, because he walked away with an expression of ease.

2

When Mrs B. stood at my doorstep, her eyes and lips smiled at me, testifying to her pleasurable anticipation of the visit. We shook hands; her's was warm, and firmly grasped mine with the grip of an outgoing personality who wants to be involved in everything that comes her way. An overall impression which is intuitive goes beyond conscious awareness. It can be compared to a portrait which reveals simultaneously the whole of a person, while description in words can only be piecemeal, in the sequence of time. Mrs B. struck me as an athletic beauty, a woman of remarkable vitality, who radiated a zest for life under a thin veil of shyness, due to modesty and regard for others.

Her reaction towards me must have been positive also, because she appeared to relax at once and seemed eager to answer my questions.

Q: You look so healthy and 'sportive'. Are you an outdoor person, though I know you have an indoor job?

A: You are right. My life is tuned to physical activity. I have been a racing driver since I was seventeen years old. I told you in my autobiographical sketch that I had a bad motor accident when I was twenty-seven, which forced me to abandon racing as a career.

Q: Are you still driving, or has the injury altered your life and your tastes?

A: Oh no, I love driving and do a lot of it, but am not allowed to go back to motor racing. I have a satisfactory job, which gives me some chance of travelling abroad. But it is, in the main, an office job.

Q: What are the compensations you have found in your life during the last ten years?

A: So many. I have a super boss; he is very intelligent and a lovely human being, and I am in charge of a number of other people with whom I get on well. The work I am doing brings me in contact with foreigners. I learn much from them, and I like them. I found my husband probably because of the accident. When I had sufficiently recovered, my doctor recommended me to play golf, and I met him on the golf course.

Q: I know that you have a good marriage, though with considerable problems. Can you tell me more about this and your husband? I only know that he is a brilliant mathematician and an understanding human being.

A: Yes, I shall be glad to talk to you about it. I think my first reaction to him was protective. He seemed lonely and scared of everybody. He fell in love with me, perhaps because we are such opposites. I did fall for him too, but only after marriage. He was spoilt, being the only son in a family of five. He knows he is an egoist, but his love for me makes him considerate and understanding, partly, I think, because of fear of losing me. I am no longer in love with him, but I enjoy sex with him now just as much as in the beginning. And I feel free to live my own life.

Q: Do you mean that he does not resent either your women friends or your profession?

A: Yes. He knows that I love women and he appears not to be jealous. But I don't know what is underneath; he is reserved and secretive. Pride? I don't really want to probe into that.

Q: Have you opportunities to meet women? Perhaps you will tell me how you discovered your lesbian side.

A: I fell in love with a girl friend at the age of twelve. I also had numerous boy friends from that age on until I met my husband. During this time I got infatuated with a number of females, but nothing physical ever happened until I was twenty-one, when I had an affair with a married woman which lasted over two years. I got engaged while that went on. But the engagement was broken off soon after, when I realized that we were not suited. After that I went out with many men and had four serious heterosexual affairs before I married. At the same time I loved three women, and went to bed with them. But it was the emotional tie which bound me to them; I don't *really* enjoy sex with a female. But I love them emotionally more than I could love a man.

Q: I would like to know about your early background, your mother in particular. What was your relationship with her?

A: I adored my mother and idealized her before I was eighteen. She is intelligent and was very good-looking. But when I realized that she suppressed me and resented any relationship I had outside, I despised her. She was so possessive.

Q: Was your parents' marriage unhappy? You mentioned that they quarrelled a lot, but you also said that they were both happily and unhappily married. Can you explain?

A: They are both strong personalities, which clashed at times. They are happy now. I feel that my mother had a strong homo-emotional side; she is unconscious of it of course. She dislikes men, and tried to put me off the male sex. I certainly was her favourite, while my father probably preferred my younger sister. But I'm not sure about this because he was always remote, and never demonstrative in his affections, if he had any. I could never be myself with either my father or my mother for different reasons.

Q: How did this affect your relationships in later life, if at all? Have you any ideas about this?

A: I can only guess; I don't really know. My mother's antagonism to men made me curious about them. My father was distant, but he is a tolerant person who understood, I suspect, that I was bemused by my mother's possessiveness and emotionalism. Perhaps the change in my feelings for her made me conscious of my bisexuality. Perhaps I looked for a woman, an older one, with whom I could be at peace, but I wanted to know men also.

Q: Did you fall in love with men *and* women?

A: Yes, but in a different way. I could be emotional about both sexes, but it never lasted for long with males (except my husband), while I went on to love my women friends emotionally after the 'thrill' was over. It is so different. I can feel at peace with women in a way I never could with a male. But perhaps most women feel that way?

Q: You may be right, although many women might not admit it. The desire to be oneself in the presence of someone else is surely common to most people. It is the wish for wholeness and inner harmony.

A: You put it so clearly. Yes, that is my real longing in any relationship. My women lovers were mostly artists. They are so much freer than others. Although I am over thirty and rather close to middle age, I want more new experiences.

Q: Emotional and sexual ones?

A: Not only – I want to travel all over the world – India, Australia, the Continent, everywhere.

Q: What would happen to your marriage if you did?

A: My husband would perhaps suffer in silence, but he is too tolerant to stop me. Anyway, he couldn't. At the moment, I want to be in London. Only two years ago I discovered Sappho, and broke into the 'gay' scene. I think they are doing a great service to women's liberation. They are, in any case, a natural lesbian and bisexual community. I go to their meetings of married women. It means a lot to me.

Q: Do you feel really integrated there, as it is primarily a lesbian organization?

A: Yes, I do. They are aware of what you, Dr Wolff, termed 'homoemotionality', in your book *Love Between Women*, and that makes the difference between them and mixed gay groups. Married or not, bisexual or homosexual, they accept you if you have that deep emotional love for women.

Q: Do you feel guilty about sex, homosexuality in particular?

A: Not about my love for women. But I am religious and gave my marriage vow to be faithful. I do feel guilty about extra-marital sex and unfaithfulness to one's husband – with another man. Anyway, mine does not regard the love for my own sex as a threat to him, nor as unfaithfulness. And nor do I. The two loves are different and don't clash.

Q: To which religious denomination do you belong?

A: I believe in the basic teachings, not denominations. I belong nominally to the Church of England, but am not a practising churchgoer.

Q: But what about your desire to see the world? When, do you think, could you do something about that?

A: I am quite fatalistic and wait for the answer to come of its own accord. I go on short journeys to the Continent already. Only a few weeks ago, I went to Amsterdam. And if that wasn't an adventure!...

Q: Do tell me please.

A: With pleasure. I was curious about the C.O.C. of Amsterdam, and so I went there for a week-end. I went on my own. I like to go by myself, because it leaves everything open. On the first day, a Sunday, I lost my handbag with everything in it – passport, money, etc. I had absolutely nothing. I went to the Women's House of the C.O.C. and they took me on completely. They looked after everything for me. A beautiful Dutch girl invited me to stay in her flat and we shared all she had. She was a really liberated woman, intelligent, and generous to a fault. She accompanied me to the Embassy and I got the necessary papers. She insisted on giving me the money for my journey back. It was a wonderful experience to be with her.

Q: Were you frightened when you discovered the loss of your belongings?

A: No, I was not frightened, I rather enjoyed the challenge. I like the unexpected to happen, to try to get out of a difficulty by my own wits. And I have faith in luck. You see, I managed, and had a wonderful experience on top of it.

After this highlight in her revelations, I asked Mrs B. if she would like to ask me any questions, and she said:

'Yes, I would much like to know what made you do this research, and much more.'

'I felt that a study of this kind was necessary, and it linked up with my research on female homosexuality. It was another step on the road to a broader knowledge of human emotional and sexual possibilities. I have no doubt that these are to some extent still hidden because even liberated women and men cannot completely free themselves from the shadows of convention. But what else do you want me to tell you?'

'Tell me about yourself, just something.'

'A difficult question to answer. I came to England before the war, and have the history of someone who had to leave her own country. In any case it turned out to be a blessing.'

We talked for some time longer, now freely exchanging what came into our minds. She had been with me for about two hours, when she suddenly got up, came towards me with open arms, and, gripping my shoulders, said:

'You must be tired out. I shall go now, but I would love to see you again.'

3

The young man who entered had the open face and directness of speech of a child. He shook hands vigorously, and said, before sitting down:

'I have been looking forward to this, Dr Wolff.'

We had 'met' at sight. His trendy clothes and jewellery would have been suitable for a fashion advertisement – for the modern young man. But he was so much at ease in his conspicuous garb that, in his case, clothes did not 'make the man'.

Alan told me of his job as a personnel officer in a large industrial concern, a job which he enjoyed because he met many men and women whom he liked and whom he could sometimes help.

Q: Do you feel personally involved with those whom you have to vet for their suitability?
A: Yes, I do. I am a personal person and try to help, but of course not against the interests of the firm. Sometimes I come into conflict because I am left-wing and hate the whole capitalist set-up. I guess from your question that you anticipated something like that.
Q: I had the impression that you liked people, that you were outgoing and warm. Is this due to your temperament, or has your family background something to do with it?
A: I was my mother's favourite. I have two brothers but no sisters. We were a united family, and both parents always showed us love and understanding, but there was no open display of emotion. The closeness with my mother made me self-confident, and gave me faith in the fundamental decency of people. A rather dangerous proposition which I already had to unlearn at school.
Q: What happened?
A: I was brought up to keep myself to myself and feel responsible for what I said or did. I did not find it easy to adapt to the boisterous kids in my school. They boasted of their sexual knowledge and exploits. We never discussed sexual matters at

home, and I felt like a fish out of water with them. I also disliked their accounts of real or imaginary affairs with girls. I felt inadequate, and they looked on me as an outsider to be teased and despised.

Q: Without exception?

A: One boy, a sensitive lad, made friends with me when we were about fourteen. We didn't 'do' anything then, perhaps because I was infatuated with a girl a year older than me, with whom I had sex. [He did not tell me of what kind.] But it only lasted a year, and after it was over my boy friend and I had sex, but not anal intercourse.

Q: Did you think of yourself as bisexual at that time?

A: I don't quite know. I never thought about it; it seemed natural to have sex with males and females. But I do know that I preferred to be with girls. I still do. I went steady with a lovely girl when I was sixteen, after leaving school. We never discussed homosexuality, but I read a good deal about it. Two years later I fell deeply in love with a girl whom I had known as a child.

Q: Had men faded out of the picture?

A: Yes. At that time I wanted to be normal and to marry. I found another girl friend who was highly intelligent and who seemed to return my love. Yet I often dreamt of a male lover in a masochistic way. I wanted him to beat and kick me. On the other hand, I fancied being a sadistic lover of women.

Q: You wrote to me that you went to university to read sociology. What did life hold for you there?

A: It changed everything. I loved being a student and became overtly bisexual. I did not mind anybody knowing, apart from my parents. They had many problems at the time, and I did not wish to add to them. They would never have objected to my way of life, but they would probably have been afraid for me. I went cottaging and enjoyed anal intercourse. I had many one-night stands with men.

Q: Could you reconcile your homosexuality with your love for a woman?

A: I found one who fully understood me and was, by all appearances, not jealous. I wanted to marry her after I got my degree, but she could not commit herself. She did not believe in making love a legal business. I still love her.

Q: Is there a type of woman or man you are especially attracted to?

A: I dislike butch men and female women. I love intelligent people of either sex. No, I am not attracted by types. I love people, not their sex.

Q: I am interested to know in what ways you think relationships with either sex are similar or different.

A: I did not tell you because it slipped my mind, that several men tied me up and had anal intercourse with me when I was fifteen. I hated and enjoyed it.

Q: Was this rape or did you want it?

A: It was rape, but I must have provoked it unconsciously. This incident might have been the reason why I came late to bisexuality. But I went all out in both directions when I was a student ... You asked me about differences in my reactions to men and women. I find it easier to love a woman than a man, but more laborious to have sexual relations with her. My contacts with men are short and mostly impersonal. But my ideal is to love one woman and one man, and to be faithful. Perhaps I have found them. I find men sexually, and women emotionally, more exciting.

Q: Do you come into conflict about the two different kinds of love?

A: Not so far. But I must be sure that my lovers are not jealous of each other. I cannot stand rows. I despise emotional and any other possessiveness.

Q: Do the two people you love come up to this?

A: They do, so far. My friend and I belong to Men Against Sexism, and we see eye to eye about possessiveness. He likes her immensely, and she feels the same. There is no question of jealousy.

Q: What do you feel about homophile organizations? I know that you belong to the C.H.E. and the G.L.F.

A: Both did a great deal for me in the past, before I came out. But things have changed. I think the C.H.E. is too male-dominated, and the G.L.F. too chauvinistic. I joined Men Against Sexism as a reaction.

Q: You have not mentioned your brothers during the whole conversation. Why?

A: I come from a working-class family, and we lived in narrow circumstances. My brothers are younger than I. They still live at home. We have been brought up to respect each other's privacy, and to keep our feelings to ourselves. I never had a close relationship with either of my brothers, but we would help each other if need be. I never thought of involving them in my ideas about sex. I told you that I didn't want my parents to be bothered with my problems, which would have affected the boys also.

Q: Are you open about your bisexuality with people outside the family?

A: Yes, I am. Nobody has treated me differently because of it. People in our firm know. They are tolerant, and many are politically progressive like me.

Q: Do you think that attitudes towards bi- and homosexuality have changed?

A: In certain circles, yes. Progressive people are generally progressive all round. I know that this is so with many of my colleagues at work.

Q: Do you believe in a bisexual society?

A: Indeed I do. It is the right way to get a better life for everybody.

He got up and said:
'I am glad you are doing this work. Could I come again one day?'
'Yes.'

VIII AUTOBIOGRAPHICAL DOCUMENTS: AS THEY SAW THEMSELVES

The following autobiographical reports of five women and four men are for the most part unedited, but 'Ingrid's' had to be shortened. They concern people from different walks of life and of different ages, who speak of the various aspects of bisexuality from the inside. An American couple who visited me while on holiday here, sent me extracts from their diaries after their return home. These are of particular interest as the writers are lovers. The woman's contribution is unique because she is not only a great lover of men and women, but has a special knowledge of 'sex' through her profession as a call girl. All other contributors wrote their autobiographies in the solitude of self-reflection before they met me. They participated in this study for different reasons. Their main motive was the wish to talk about their own bisexuality, which had directed their life style, emotions and sex drive. But self-interest coincided with social and educational interest. Every one of them was concerned about the second-class citizenship accorded to sexual variations, and wanted to assist research which could help 'normal' people to understand them better. The reports, varying in length, speak for themselves through personal experiences and reflections.

1   FROM THE DIARIES OF INGRID

11 August 1974
God – it's been three weeks, three weeks exactly to this night. I keep waiting for the passion to start melting – waiting for it to evaporate

into nothing. Yet, that's not happening – the passion's still there and I'm not sure whether it's just a desire of my heart, but I really believe that the passion has not yet reached its fire. I feel that it's going on its way there and that soon – very very soon something explosive is going to happen . . . at least that's my hope. Oh God, I couldn't stand it if everything just ended here – now. My mind says it won't but my emotions aren't as trusting.

Three weeks ago tonight – as though it were minutes ago. And the night before that – candles/dimness – four of us seated in anticipation – chicken and wine, and all the other things disappearing into us as formalities. I drank my last glass of sherry with a physical awareness of a body very close to me – the sherry slipped down my throat and in my drunken imagination it became sperm . . . and I closed my eyes briefly and when I opened them I stole a quick glance at his left hand.

Where were these feelings coming from? It had been so long. I couldn't remember . . .

Ruby in a long blue dress – words kept coming from her – forming phrases, creating sentences, breeding stories – endless. Words – just fluttering – tongue flapping. In my ears I heard sighs, groans, and screams of pleasure. They came from within. Within me – deep within my body. My body writhing in loneliness – seeking a new, familiar but untouched other.

Ben – Ben to my left – hands moving, eyes closing, mouth speaking – but none of it remembered. I can't recall how he moved his hands or how he closed his eyes – only that he did. There is no remembrance of his words. Did he speak at all? All I can bring to mind are his open eyes staring at me with seductiveness – blatant. Memories of men in *el parque el Mexico* – their dark eyes saying 'Okay baby, it's all over – here I come. Every inch of me – right into you' . . . and Ben's eyes said that, for one fleeting second. I blinked, and perhaps I shouldn't have, for when my eyes focused again, there looked at me the frightened eyes of a little boy.

The candles burnt lower. We smoked a good-night joint. My shoulders were quivering and I avoided looking to my right. Ben stood up – his yawns had been shaking the room for hours – he now took them away to the bedroom.

I went in to say good night to him. All I heard were apologies. They weren't what I needed to hear. My ears were seeking something much different. Back in the dining-room – I gently pushed Ruby towards the bedroom and mumbled something about Ben.

She turned and so did I – right into the arms I had been wanting all evening. My body wanted to take this other body and just disappear. I wanted Adrian's arms around me tighter, I wanted his sperm in my throat instead of the sherry that I was still tasting.

Suddenly he was saying it – tomorrow night – tomorrow night. I said something very prim but my body was rejoicing.

How long had we wanted each other?

Downstairs in my bedroom Ruby and I fell drunkenly into bed. I started to do Ruby but my head began to spin and I couldn't continue. She wanted to do me but I persuaded her to fall asleep. I wanted to be alone with my fantasies.

The next morning with Ruby still asleep, I was off to the store. I ran into him there. We spoke briefly of the evening before and even more briefly of the evening to come. I couldn't understand it. We had run into each other in the store before, also in the street; in the hallway. Why *now*? What was happening?

And all day long at the beach I thought about how it would happen. Ruby lay close to me on the beach blanket. The sun was hot; the sky very blue. Every once in a while Ruby's toe would touch mine. It felt nice. Sometimes I'd run my foot up the length of her leg. We'd look at each other and smile . . . It was nice.

But, when Ruby drifted off into a sort of half-sleep as people do when they sunbathe, I shut my eyes and the images started coming.

My heels braced themselves in the sand. I saw him above me, coming down slowly. His tongue came first and I took it in my mouth, sucking it way back in my throat. His stomach came down and placed itself on mine. Sharp sensations came shooting up inside me. He raised his body once again and I widened my legs and lifted up my hips a bit in anticipation . . .

I opened my eyes. The brilliant blue of the sea was there with thousands of sailboats on a horizon that was dominated by a large cargo ship making its way out to the open sea. Beside me a tiny towheaded child dug in the sand with his shovel. His pale, obese grandmother sat on a folding chair and spoke to him in senseless words.

I turned to Ruby. She was stretched out in her glory with my tiny pink bikini barely covering her. Her eyes were closed and her thoughts were quiet.

'Ruby,' I said, on our way home. We were walking down Chandler Street about to turn the corner of Berkeley. 'Ruby, I want to tell you something. I know it's going to upset you. I know you're going to feel left out. But I want to be honest with you. I want you to know what's going on. Ruby, I'm going to be with Adrian to-night.'

She was very breezy about it. Why should she be upset? She

intellectualized the whole thing and smiled and told me to have a nice time. We walked into Gray Street. There was a note at my door. I knew that she knew it was from Adrian . . . and she hasn't been breezy since.

I showered and dressed with a feeling of pleased contentment. My body was under control. I felt calm and any anticipation that was riding in the undercurrent must have been assuaged by my calmness. I felt rested and loving.

Adrian knocked on the door. He was dressed, looking spiffy in tight white pants. He asked me if I wanted to go out for drinks. I told him that no, I was tired, we'd have drinks upstairs. What I meant, however, and what I should have said, was: 'Uh-uh Baby. You're all mine tonight. No sharing you with the general public. I want you all to *myself*. I want to be alone with you.'

We sat upstairs and talked. The drinks kept coming. One after another. One drink was barely finished when it was whisked away to be replaced by another. Adrian got up to go into the bathroom.

'Do you want another drink?' he asked. I replied in the negative.

'Well, if you do, why don't you make another one and we can bring our drinks to bed with us.'

I sat on the loveseat and smiled. What a nice way to say it! And I smiled all through the night and Adrian kept on saying nice things. We made love twice and I fell asleep in his arms . . .

31 August 1974

The overwhelming feeling of sadness that I've felt with Adrian so many times came back and I began to cry. I'd never cried with Adrian before and it felt strange. I was torn between wanting to be somewhere else, comfortable and asleep, and wanting Adrian to wake up and comfort me.

It was quite a while before Adrian awoke to do that. And when he did, I could tell I was punishing him. He immediately thought it was something he had done wrong and wanted to know what. How could I explain why I was crying? Yes, indirectly it had something to do with drinking, but not specifically. So, I told him, we'd talk about it in the morning.

It's just that I'm afraid for him. I look at him sometimes and he reminds me of a senile old man. How do you tell someone *that*? How do you say: 'Sometimes I see you on the brink of disaster and I feel helpless.' I remember the summer I was twelve years old and my father was having a nervous breakdown. I look at Adrian sometimes, in certain situations, and I am reminded of that same summer.

I don't think things are going to get worse, but there are so many things to be straightened out in Adrian's life. In many ways I think I can help and I feel things will be better for Adrian from here on. But there are times such as when I was lying in that bed last night, that I wonder what I can really do.

Adrian was talking – I can't even remember how it came about and he said: 'Or are you going to go away like everything else in my life?' I said, 'Stop it', and I said it very softly. But I felt like screaming it. I told him he said that too often. But how can he help not saying it if that is what he constantly feels?

And even before he mentioned it this morning, I knew he was worried about the erection problem. I feel I can only reassure him so much. I know that there is a chance that the problem is physiological. But seeing the circumstances are what they are, I imagine the problems are more psychological. And there are so many of them! When I begin to think about it . . . and I'm sure they all contribute. I am positive that drinking is a big part of it – as are general nervous problems, worries and work pressures. But there are so many more complex things – such as being hurt so much by Peggy – even though it took place a long time ago now, I can tell it's still a hurt. Then not being with women sexually for a while and the whole gay trip. I even feel that myself now once in a while when I sit and wonder what I'm doing in a heterosexual relationship. I also feel that Adrian wants very much to make our relationship work, and that feeling in itself is enough to cause many problems. Then, of course, there's the whole male ego thing – an idea that can't be just flushed out. And I am not the best woman to start thinking along these lines since I can be quite intimidating. Not intimidating as a person but as a sexual creature. Men sometimes worry when they go to bed with me since they know that I have had lots of cocks to compare them with. Even when they don't know what's wrong, that often is the subconscious answer.

I want to help Adrian so much, but sometimes I feel drained. Verbal communication has often been one of my problems and I am determined that we won't have communication problems between us. I've been thinking what Gordon asked me the other night: 'Are you writing the kind of journal you're going to let someone read?' I hadn't really thought of it before, but now that I think about it, I can remember letting people read my journals months or years after the time in which they were written. And they would always be interesting, but letting someone read them after that much time had expired didn't help much. Perhaps I shall let Adrian read this now.

4 September 1974 – Maine

... and now I really am alone but it's all right now. Up here in the middle of an empty black valley in the midst of an equally empty black night. A household asleep – even at this early evening hour. (Folks always bed down early at night in the country.) There's not a sound here – complete stillness. And the temperature has dropped too low now for the crickets and frogs to make their summer noises.

I would only desire that there be arms here to hold me, but there's only the night – the night with its quiet ebony arms. And tonight, it will be my own fingers trailing down over my body making promises to my flesh that perhaps they cannot keep.

And my mind rings with memories of many other times over many years when nights like this were part of my life and this valley part of my heart. Now I feel that the valley and its nights have nothing to do with me. I am just a temporary visitor ... and these fingers on my breast are restless as they move downward over my body feeling as foreign to me as this night. But the more my body feels, the more it welcomes them. They are a strange sort of comfort.

The nagging feeling of aloneness from the weekend has passed. My body has stopped trembling now and no longer feels isolated from my mind. A sort of restfulness came to me last night when I climbed into Adrian's bed in his new apartment.

Some broken pieces inside me suddenly came together. The circle of air around my head that had been pushing in on me, lifted and disappeared. There was something reassuring in last night that makes me able to be alone tonight in this dark countryside with my own hands on my own breasts.

It all has to do with arms – and being held. I miss those arms around me; I feel in place in that embrace – but when I am outside of it all, I no longer feel alone. Since now, I know where I stand.

5 September 1974

It was hard to rise this morning. The fog had settled in and surrounded us during the night, and the house had a sharp dampness about it. The radio gave the temperature as being thirty-eight degrees and I almost believe it.

This afternoon, however, the fog has burnt off and the temperature has climbed up to seventy degrees – typically whimsy Maine autumn.

I've felt good today. Came up to Rutland with Christina and she did my hair at the Academy. A very changed image for sure – short and curly. An ash-blond Afro!

I took her out to lunch and bought her some perfume as a thank-you. I felt good about being with Christina and having her do my hair. She obviously enjoyed it too and it helped us to feel closer.

I've always wished for a sister I could be really close to. The twins and I were never very close due to age differences and differing mental capacities, personalities, etc. It hasn't been until the past year that Christina and I have gotten to the point where we can talk fairly openly. I've told Christina a lot about my life in the past month. She knows about how I've been making a living and we've discussed the bisexual thing quite thoroughly.

9 September 1974

The time in Maine passed quickly and quietly – the kind of relaxation that lulls one into nothingness. I am glad to be back again, hassling the world.

It seems as though I waited days to get back to Adrian's embrace. We haven't made love in a week (one week to the day – but that was a strange lovemaking. I was having my period, and for some reason, no matter how horny I was, I didn't feel sensual).

The night before I left for Maine I spent with Adrian at his new apartment. We didn't make love, but that seemed of no significance. I found complete satisfaction in falling asleep in his bed while he worked on his art in the next room. It gave me a great deal of pleasure to wake up, briefly, when he came to bed – to be aware of his body next to mine. And I loved when the morning came, and he kept disappearing and appearing again as he rushed about on errands. I lay in bed drifting in and out of a beautiful sleep. When I arose, we drank tea and coffee and talked until it was time for me to catch the bus to Maine.

And I fantasized a lot while I was up country. But the only real person in my fantasies was Adrian. All of my sexual fantasies are of women – unknown, sensuous women seeking to be discovered.

Adrian has mentioned several times how he hates to be rejected. Of course, so do I and a thousand others. But I never really thought too much about it until Adrian spoke of it in a sexual content. He was speaking of the pain (and the fury) he felt when being denied sexual pleasure with Peggy.

I suddenly felt fear. What will happen when I become turned off to sex in one of my 'too-many-tricks blues' periods? What will happen then? How will Adrian feel when I make it clear that the thought or sight of a cock makes me nauseous? Or how will he feel when I turn my back on him in bed? I hope it never happens, but I know that this spurt of horniness I've been feeling for the past two months won't last forever.

And I'm concerned because I know how I am. I know Adrian will try to understand but I know it will be hard for both of us.

I also came to the realization last week that my relationship with Adrian is bound to affect my capability to turn tricks sanely. It was all right – my near platonic relationship with Nanita never had any effect on the way I thought of or treated customers. And being with Ruby was all right too. Even though Ruby and I didn't have a 'marathon' sex life, we did get it on and I dug it (even more towards the end) and my trick life and personal life remained separate. When I didn't want to have sex with Ruby, it was due to my own low sex drive and not because I'd been fucked too much by customers. It was okay. I could keep them separate because my tricks were male and my lovers female.

I had a woman trick once and vowed I'd never have another. I never made a vow not to have another male lover but perhaps I should have.

Somewhere I hope I can find the strength to separate Adrian from all the other cocks. I think I will be able to; however, his being a male is a threat nevertheless.

10 September 1974

Now that I'm back from Maine and have turned five tricks in forty-eight hours, I feel much better. I'm always happy when I'm making money. The only thing I regret is that I've had five men in my body and Adrian was not one of them. I'm not hung up on his being the first before the others, I just want to fit him in somewhere. Any time . . .

Sometimes I wonder why Adrian speaks so often in pronouns. When he is speaking to me about his thoughts of me, he never directly says 'you', nor does he use my name. It's always 'her' and 'she'. When he speaks of Peggy, he uses her name occasionally, but more often than not, she's a pronoun too.

I must speak with Adrian and tell him how I feel about being ignored. I know he is busy and has things he must do and people he must see, but despite all of that, I feel left out. I feel now as though I'm able to cope with the issue of being alone. What I cannot cope with is Adrian spending time with other people when he should be working or sleeping. It infuriates me that he cannot kick these people out. I want to go to see him and he suggests that I don't because he has too much work to concentrate on. Then I make the mistake of calling him later (to say good night or whatever) and he tells me somebody or other is there visiting him. I'm not jealous of the 'whomever' but I do wonder why that particular person(s) has the right to disturb Adrian while he's working and I don't have that privilege.

17 September 1974

I told Adrian I was having trouble separating him from all the other cocks. That's not entirely true. I usually don't have too much trouble keeping my tricks from messing up my personal life because of the way I am. But, *I am changing*, and I don't want to admit that I'm becoming softer and that I feel myself giving in to vulnerability. What I wanted Adrian to understand was my *fear* of not being able to keep him separate. I am afraid that problem will come about and I won't be able to cope with it. I am afraid of hurting Adrian. I don't *want* to reject him sexually. Despite what I told him about how the sex part of it isn't important to me, I realize now that it *has* to be important if we bother doing it at all.

Adrian is afraid of hurting me too. He explained to me how he hesitates calling me at night after he's seen a trick(s) for fear I'll want to get together and make love and he won't be able to get it up. It's funny now that I think of it. Yesterday, I told Adrian I'd rather be involved with a woman – that much is true – at least, I'd like to have a woman to be involved with *also*. After all Adrian has Brian and I feel that gives him a more equal balance than what I have now . . . And Adrian talked about how he likes men. We both know where the other stands. *But*, I neglected to realize how close our fears are.

I am afraid of saying: 'No, no more cock. I've had enough for today – get that thing away from me.' I would be afraid of hurting Adrian through rejection. Adrian's afraid to be in bed with me thinking that he won't be able to perform and that that will seem like a rejection to me and I will be hurt. And in that way we would both be rejecting each other which is what neither of us wants.

I think we both feel more comfortable now knowing that it's all right to just hold each other and be close and not have to worry about sex. However, Adrian has really enjoyed some, maybe all, of our lovemakings and I have to be truthful and say that Adrian really turns me on. I believe that there's a desire in *each* of us to want to make love to the other and for it to be *all right*. And there's times it has been for me and there's times it has been for Adrian, but it's not always going to be good.

I really feel as though we must talk about it and establish what we desire from each other sexually and what we can do about the situation when neither of us can supply what the other wants. I know, and have written before, that if I feel loving and feel a lot of affection from the man, I can enjoy intercourse very much. If I'm getting the right kind of affection, orgasms are very unimportant. I'll only seek orgasm, or feel frustrated about not having one, if I'm feeling ill at ease about my relationship with that person.

20 September 1974
Went to pick up my tickets at the airline office. Everything is becoming more and more a reality. I think of my fantasies about being with Nanita and I wonder what will happen to me if all the fantasies don't fall into the right places. I do feel reassured, however, that I am doing the right thing, at least for Nanita's sake. When she called me Wednesday afternoon, she was ecstatic. There's no other way to define her reaction.

Last night I re-read all of the letters Nanita has written me since her departure just before Christmas. There aren't that many of them – but each one is very long and very loving.

'. . . I guess I really am finding out now, that love has no sex or colour. Love is love and when one offers the most precious thing there is to give, it shouldn't be taken so lightly. I guess I've never really had too many people who seriously loved me – not even my own parents. And I guess that sort of puts a person on guard. I've run around for so long looking for something to fill that emptiness that I don't even know the real thing when it hits me in the face. I just know things will be different the next time we're together. I promise you that . . .'

Dear Nanita – in all of her honest simplicity. Strange, I never told Nanita that I loved her. I've never told anyone that – not even James, and if ever I loved anyone, it was him. I never mentioned love to Nanita, but she saw through me. She saw that there was love there and she acknowledged it.

I only hope that she's right. I only hope that this time when we're together, things will be different. I really don't see how they can be anything but, since I'm going there for the purpose of *being with her*. When we were together on Gray Street, there were too many circumstances confusing the situation. She was with me because she needed a place to live, and the entire time she was with me, she had 'leaving' as her ultimate goal. It wasn't that she didn't want to be with me, it's just that that was her goal even before she came to stay with me. It was all so hard . . .

I realize now that there's only one way for me to deal with my situation with Adrian. I have been frightened of falling in love, of creating a dependency, of needing and of being without. I want to be able to enjoy a relationship with Adrian without the danger of any of those things occurring. But I know that that is impossible. If I feel those things now, then they exist and I must deal with them. I have only had to deal with feelings like that once before in my life – and I dealt with them poorly. I will not deal with them badly this time. I will be very upfront about everything and I will try very hard not to hurt either myself or Adrian.

22 September 1974

Celestine came to me last night. Perhaps that is why I feel stronger today within myself – and mildly bitter with Adrian although it's something I can cope with now. But it began with Celestine the same way it began with Adrian: 'How long had we both desired each other?'

I thought I would have a delicate job with Celestine but that was not at all the case. She wanted me – and had wanted me – that was clear from the beginning.

It was a tired night. My body and face – in fact, my entire being, felt that what it really wanted to do was to hide itself. Hide away and rest for a long, long night. Celestine called and didn't come right out and say what she wanted. When I ventured forward with the hint of an invitation, she came alive. When I confirmed it, she became vague. However, in the end, she came through.

I asked her what she wanted to drink and she couldn't decide. I suggested champagne and she became very excited. 'That's what I was thinking of bringing! Oh, do you really have some?' I brought out a bottle of Asti Spumante. It turned out to be her favourite.

Many things continued to delight her throughout the evening. We sat on the floor and drank Asti and talked – talked of many things. Conversation was easy and there was much to say.

I asked Celestine whether she was going home that night. She said it was still early enough for her to do that. I moved very close to her and told her that I very much wanted her to stay with me. My arms moved out and placed themselves around her. That was all Celestine needed. Her arms came around my shoulders and we were in each others arms – squeezing gently, touching, hugging, and feeling our way into each other's desires.

She seemed a bit hesitant as though she were waiting to be reassured. I knew of no other way to assure her but to take her upstairs . . .

I lay on the bed taking small hits off the joint Celestine had brought. She was in the bathroom doing something. When I looked up again, she came into the room – dungarees gone and replaced by a long black piece of material dotted with thousands of miniscule stars.

Outside, lightning flashed, again and again. Inside, candles burned above us on the mantel. We were on the floor in front of the fireplace. I put my hands on her shoulders and pulled her back towards me. The rain began. Right outside my bedroom door, the rain drummed heavily on the skylight. Harder and harder – it sounded as though it were pounding to get in. Pounding wildly as Celestine's heart . . .

All I could hear was the heaviness of the rain and the lightness of Celestine's giggles. 'Have you ever taken a bath in Vita-Bath?' she asked. 'No', I answered, not believing any of the evening was happening. Was *Celestine* asking *me* to take a bath? I realized then that I did not have to go easy with her any longer. Her passions were harder and wilder than the rain.

I ran a warm-hot bath and Celestine added the bubbles. Lightning still flashed. I could still hear the thunder – the rain still fell on the skylight. I felt intensity everywhere.

The bathroom candle flickered above our faces – casting some calmness on our passions. We reached out for each other – our bodies and arms coming together with soap bubbles squeezed between us. I turned and snuggled myself in between Celestine's legs and lay my head back on her breast.

'Oh Ingrid, I'm not good enough for you.' Celestine's soft, hushed voice – almost broken.

'Celestine, why do you feel that way? That's a horrible way for you to feel. I'm going to make that feeling go away.'

I turned and bent over to kiss her breasts, to take the tip of her nipple in my mouth. 'Celestine, Celestine,' I gasped, 'Let's get out of this tub.'

'No – no first I want you to lie on top of me.' She lay with her back against the back wall of the tub, her legs spread slightly.

'Oh!' I came down on top of her. My stomach first atop her and then our breasts touching each other. Water splashed up everywhere. Celestine moaned and writhed and we splashed down together – our hair and faces becoming as wet as the rest of our bodies.

Celestine was grabbing me excitedly, arousing something in me that had too long been dormant. 'Celestine,' I said, 'we have to get out of this tub!' I pulled the water release lever and the water and bubbles began to disappear down around us.

I stood up and stepped from the tub. I handed Celestine a towel, but before either of us could properly dry off, Celestine gave a cry and was down on her knees kissing and licking me all over. I shut my eyes and leaned against the bathroom door.

I got out a bottle of moisturizing lotion and we rubbed it into each other's skin. 'Hey,' I said, 'You have a black and blue mark in the same place I do!' We each had a good sized bruise above our left knees.

'Oh!' Celestine laughed, 'I saw yours and thought it was mine! I remember thinking that I should hide it from you!'

'You silly, silly girl.' I kissed her beneath her ear. We blew out the candle and went into the bedroom where other candles still burned and where rain still hit against the windowpanes.

'Have you been with other women?' I asked her. Before then I thought Celestine had never had a woman. But now I knew better. 'One other,' she answered me.

It could have been a million others. I didn't care. All I was concerned with was this overwhelming passion that was confronting me. I was seeing in Celestine more passion and more desire than I had seen in a long time. More than in Nanita or in Ruby – more than in any of my dozens of tricks – more than in Adrian. And it wasn't just a desire of the flesh. I felt as though Celestine were desirous of many things – of knowledge (self-knowledge of her desires and more knowledge of mine). I felt as though she were filled with a passion for sharing and affection. And, on top of all these things, I felt that she was seeking to tear me open so she could come inside – and be a part of me.

We made love to each other for a long, long time. Everything I did seemed to make Celestine quiver. She is, truly, a lady of passion. I felt as though she could never tire – that she could float, from one peak to the next, through the night till morning came.

But it was not that way with me. Something was wrong. Every inch of my body desired Celestine. I longed for her tongue against mine, her nipples gently tickling my nipples. Something in my body demanded recognition, and, suddenly, orgasm became *very very* important.

But it was impossible. My body remained dry and unresponsive to Celestine's beautiful efforts. Why? Why, when I wanted it more than I had with anyone in a long time? I strained toward what I thought would eventually happen. It was frustration. Celestine began feeling it was her own fault which was the last thing I wanted to have happen.

We talked about it a little. Celestine is the first woman I've ever been with who has asked me point blank: 'Can you come?' 'Do you *want* to come?' I was so happy that she asked me – that she was so open about it all.

She was very determined, and I gave in and let her do what she wanted. Finally, between the two of us, we had success. I had never in my life taken so long to come.

'Celestine,' I said, taking her in my arms, 'I've discovered lately that there are things much more important to me than orgasms...'

Her wide eyes looked into mine. 'I know,' she said, 'but orgasms are really nice!' We both giggled and she curled around on her side, her back and her buttocks pressing tightly against me. I reached over her and my hand cupped her breast. We fell asleep... Outside the window, the sky had become a very white-grey and parading across it were dark blue-grey clouds in the form of dinosaurs.

We woke early, and outside the sun was very strong. Celestine got out of bed and dressed. She wanted to leave right away. I was filled with very mixed feelings. In a way I wanted her to stay...

22 October 1974

Adrian showed me a portrait he'd done of Brian. 'Although I know you don't want to see it...' he said.

I grew quite exasperated. I did want to see it! I don't hate Brian, despite what Adrian thinks. The portrait was one of the best Adrian has ever done – better than mine. It's because of Adrian's feelings toward Brian. I saw the same in the picture of Michael that Adrian never finished. Even if Adrian had been feeling bitter about Michael when he painted it, one could easily tell that this was someone Adrian had known well... maybe even loved. I saw the same thing happen when Adrian started to paint Ben. I always thought of Ben's portrait as potentially being one of Adrian's best... but Adrian's feelings for Ben went away and so did the painting.

But here was Brian – complete on canvas. I told Adrian I liked it. (I did.) I felt it wasn't really necessary to tell him that it was the best thing he'd done in a long time. He knows it. I know he does.

The two of us were each harbouring a certain bitterness toward the other. When we spoke there was a certain remoteness in each of our voices. With new physical strength coming back into my body, the cynicism and toughness were again appearing. I felt like I could handle whatever arose.

Adrian had prepped himself for a real 'going-over' by me, so he was feeling the same way. Unfortunately, with both of our shields out there so far, not much could be accomplished. Neither one of us broke down the way we should have. Neither one of us wanted to be the weak one in the game any more.

When I finally left Adrian's, I was aware of one thing and one thing only – that my love for Adrian is going to continue to exist no matter how cruel or remote Adrian becomes. I also knew (or have finally had confirmed) what I had been fearing for quite a while – that my love is not returned, at least not in the way I desire it. And I feel the chances of it ever existing are very slim.

25 October 1974

I'm finally feeling as though my body belongs to me again. It's taken so long and even now, I don't quite feel as well as I should. A lot of it has to do with my depressed state of mind. The forever nagging feeling that something is wrong – something in my life that I may never discover.

It's been a long time since my body has refused to function properly. It's been a couple of years, maybe even longer, since I've had an illness that's lasted longer than a couple of days. And it has been quite a few years since I've felt any confusion in my living.

Confusion has just never been a word in my life. There are times now when I think back on many parts of my life (especially the past five and a half years) and I *know* there were times when I was very confused. But I never *felt* confused. I have never been enveloped by feelings of not knowing what I wanted.

I do not feel confused now, either. I know what I want, but there is a confusion in my life pattern (as opposed to a confusion in my mind). I am used to having a fairly well ordered life that I can expect certain things from.

19 November 1974

I am feeling better about almost everything in my life these days. Most all of that has to do with Adrian, of course, and being here on Waltham Street, and not feeling alone any more.

I still do feel alone at times, however. It has to do with my overwhelming desire to be with Adrian all of the time. The other night when Joe came over, or last night when Michael was visiting, both times I heard Adrian leave to go out with them, and I felt a bit of jealousy arising. Not hard-core jealousy, just a slight feeling of remorse. I would have liked Adrian's guests to leave and Adrian to come downstairs to be with me.

I am not always lonely when Adrian isn't with me. I adapt well to being by myself, but I am becoming less and less a singular being. I realize now that it's others who bring out the parts of me I like best. I miss the good feeling I have about myself when Adrian isn't around . . .

On the other hand, I am afraid. Afraid that living on Waltham Street and being so much a part of each other's lives will soon bring everything good we have to an end. I never think of the relationship (or any relationship) as being permanent. The best things in my life have been ephemeral.

I am delighted that Adrian and I will be having Thanksgiving dinner together. I am looking forward to a quiet day with Adrian or perhaps Adrian and a few of his friends. Invitations to eat dinner with Lu and her kids or with Edward, Donald et al didn't appeal to me in any way.

I remember last year – Thanksgiving with Nanita and Alan. Two people that, at different times in my life, meant a lot to me. Two people I cared about and sacrificed for. Now Alan is dead and Nanita is becoming more remote as the days go on.

I wrote to Nanita this week though. I felt I owed it to her, and to myself, to tell her just how badly I was affected by my week in Maine. I don't think I'll ever give in to my whims again as I did when I travelled all the way to Nanita this fall to be treated like such shit. I told her very plainly this time: 'Nani, you hurt me.' I also wrote to tell her about Alan's death. I thought she'd want to know.

21 November 1974

Monday afternoon so strange. In bed with Adrian and a trick. Finally, after so long, bringing my two worlds together ... I was very remote from the situation as though I were on the outside looking in. I went through my smiling and laughing, sucking and pleasing, groaning, fucking, moaning, writhing. I went through it all as though I was in a play that had been running successfully for quite a while. I couldn't forget a line; miss a beat because I was so familiar with it all.

I kept on thinking I'd have to carry the show – that was my job. I couldn't lie back and watch Adrian take this man's cock in his mouth and move up and down on it. I couldn't remove myself that much. And it was all such a farce. Everyone pretending they were enjoying it – even the trick – playing make-believe.

And while this alien cock was nestling inside me, making itself a bit *too* comfortable, the owner said: 'I have this fantasy about a hard cock up my ass. Think you can manage that, Adrian?'

Adrian said yes in a hard, assertive way, but when I reached around to touch him, he was shrivelled up, tinier than I had ever felt him before. The trick never got it rammed up inside him – Adrian never got an erection. And I never stopped pretending that I was the most lustful, insatiable woman on earth.

We got paid, even though I know the trick didn't come off. I couldn't have cared whether he did anyway.

When he left, I wanted Adrian back in bed with me. There had been weird feelings throughout . . . I wanted to make love – just to make everything 'all right'.

But – nothing happened. I thought for sure when Adrian was alone with me, things would be different. The whole situation with the trick had been bringing it too close to home. The emotional ties between Adrian and myself had made themselves known. Too many feelings in the air. It would never work.

And it didn't . . . even after the trick left, we couldn't make love. Adrian had to go upstairs and draw T.Vs. There were too many pressures, he couldn't relax at all.

While he was upstairs at his desk drawing televisions, I was lying with my back flat against the watery blue of my bathroom floor – my legs spread – masturbating, because, at that moment orgasm was extremely important.

I stopped in The Turnabout, a fashion design boutique near here run by a black couple. I stopped in to see if, by chance, they might have something I could wear to my party. Peter was there, alone. I really don't know either of them (Peter or Linda) very well. But we chatted a while and I invited them to my housewarming party.

In the course of the conversation, Peter asked me what I did, and I told him: 'I'm a hooker.' He seemed quite surprised. Later in the conversation he asked if I had a boyfriend. I said: 'No, I have a girlfriend.' Perhaps all of that should have confused him, or at least put him off, but it didn't.

There was a pile of black chiffon on the table. I picked some of it up. 'What's this?'

'It's a dress I'm making. You'd look great in it,' Peter said. I held it up to my body; even through sweater and blue jeans I loved the image it brought to mind!

'Try it on,' Peter urged.

Into the dressing-room – actually not a room at all but just a curtained off section of the store. Hat boxes, signs, material, junk everywhere. Peter moves things out of the way so I can undress. The dress is difficult to put on by myself. Peter assists.

Step out into the store, in front of the mirror. I love it. See through black chiffon whirling about me – exposing my nipples on top and allowing my black panties to show through below.

I prance around in the store, swirling the skirt out around me.

Really getting off on my own image. I am becoming turned on by *my* body in the black chiffon dress.

'Oh Ingrid,' Peter said. He locked the door and before I could speak or move, the two of us were both in the dressing-room. Peter was removing the black chiffon. I was standing still but everything suddenly became very dizzy. I was standing naked in that little closet filled with junk. Through the light blue cloth curtain I could dimly see the traffic go by, people on the street. I knew that, in a few more seconds, everything outside would be very, very remote.

In front of me was the nearly nude body of a handsome black man. His cock was straight and large, and I knelt down to take it in my mouth. It grew in my mouth and I began to gag trying to take it all in. Suddenly, I was pulled up, lifted and placed on this cock. We were both standing, and then I was sitting on this black prick – riding up and down with my legs wrapped around this strong man's waist.

It was too difficult to maintain that position. I slithered down to the floor. I couldn't stand up, my body kept giving out. I leaned against the wall. He squatted on the floor in front of me, and began using his tongue wildly.

The blue cloth curtain was jerking back and forth – moving in every direction as our bodies hit up against it. I turned and knelt a bit, leaning forward, reaching behind me as I did so to guide this man's cock inside me.

He came up behind me and slid it in doggie style. My knees, weak since the beginning of the whole episode, began to fall to the floor. I held on to the wall for support. It had been a very long time since I'd felt a cock like that – going in and out of me with such hardness and force.

I cried out several times, not even bothering to think who might hear me. And then it was over. I tried to stand up and couldn't. My body, incredibly weak all over. Peter held me up until my balance returned. He dressed, grinned and disappeared outside the curtain. A few moments later I, too, was dressed – outside the curtain, outside the door, down the street – walking home wondering what it was all about.

4 January 1975

Stayed home New Year's Eve which was what I wanted to do. Had Adrian and Gordon here for an Italian casserole dinner and a fire in the fireplace. It was snowing outside – a rather traditional New Year's Eve. After a while, Gordon left and Adrian and I went to bed early (even before the midnight hour).

I felt sick most of the next day. Not hangover, but a variety of annoying minor ailments – being bothered by my asthma, upset stomach, a slight urinary tract infection – all put together tended to make me feel wiped out.

Upstairs, a roast beef dinner, Patrick and Joe as guests. I watched Patrick closely. There have been times when I've felt sexually attracted to Patrick (perhaps *sexually* is a bad choice of word; *sensually* might be better). I could imagine being naked with Patrick, touching him, holding him, but I can't actually imagine having sex with him.

Adrian and I have discussed my feelings for Patrick. Adrian watched me watching Patrick through dinner. Soon it became a game in my head. I got bored.

I came downstairs feeling tired and ill. Everyone upstairs was very stoned and merry. For something to do, I got into writing a short story for stoned people. I was pleased with it. It was the first thing I'd written in a long time, and it had some value. When I had finished it, I called Adrian and asked him to come down and get it.

He called me back a bit later and said he was too stoned to read anything, so he wasn't coming down to get the story. I was hurt. But then, I had felt a bit strange toward Adrian all evening anyway, and I thought that he had been in a particularly bitchy mood.

I felt a bit shunned and rejected. I felt angry and I didn't know why. I called Adrian back and told him I thought he was being a bastard. That did it! He became extremely defensive and threw my words back at me. A minorly destructive conversation. We both hung up.

Suddenly, everything reached me, all at once, with such an overwhelming rush that I became hysterical without fully knowing why. All my breath became caught up, and only tiny, strangled gasps were coming from my throat. I was crying and rivulets of mascara-streaked tears were rolling down my cheeks. I couldn't stop crying. I was really hysterical.

I kept thinking I could stop the tears, get myself together, and go to sleep. But I didn't want that. Now that the hysteria was there, so surface-close, I should let it out; let it go all the way.

And I did. But I knew I shouldn't be alone. I kept thinking of people I could call to come and stay with me, but they were all lost in a blur of sobs. I finally called Adrian back. He came to me immediately. 'Baby! What's wrong?' and he took me in his arms and as he did so, I let go even more, and whimpers turned to wails.

I don't even know how long Adrian was with me. I was unconscious of time, and only became aware of it when it occurred to me that Joe was still upstairs at Adrian's, and that Adrian should probably be up there rather than downstairs with me. I had Adrian get me some Butisol, and after a bit, I began to calm down. Adrian had become very quiet and finally left me without saying a word.

After the Butisol took hold, the sobs subsided, and my body stopped shaking, I took out paper and pen and wrote a long note to Adrian. I spoke of fear of dependence primarily, but I covered other things too. When I finished it, I felt much better. I went upstairs and put it under his door.

When I awoke the next morning, there was a note from Adrian under my door (note enclosed in journal, clipped to back cover). He also called me.

I felt better. My volcano had erupted.

25 October 1975

Reading Rosamond Lehmann's *Dusty Answer*. Never would have picked it off the shelf amongst all those books in Lauriat's, if I hadn't recognized it from 'Carrington'. Rosamond Lehmann had been one of the focal points of Carrington's correspondence, especially in the latter part of her life. Since some of Carrington's letters to R. Lehmann were quite intriguing, I swooped upon this novel and bought it, knowing I would probably enjoy it considerably.

I *am* enjoying it. Am in the middle of it now and am feeling quite wrapped up in Judith and Jennifer's relationship. 'You could not do without Jennifer now.' That sentence struck me bluntly. I wonder what it would be like to be that tied up with another woman – so involved with her that you could not do without her . . .

I am thinking tonight of all the women I have known; but the special three – the three that I have allowed myself to be vulnerable with, Nanita, Ruby and Celestine – are most on my mind.

I think of women that I have been close to but wasn't allowed to have feelings of sex towards: Brenda from Springfield, darling Alice, now in Newburyport. I regret that I never had the opportunity to hold them, in some warm bed, somewhere.

I am overwhelmed with my feelings towards women tonight. Perhaps it's because I don't have one now in my life, or perhaps it's because Adrian's downstairs in bed with some guy – but whatever it is, it is tearing at my heart.

And it couldn't be just anyone. I know that now. It would have to be someone special. And where, I ask myself, where is she going to come from?

. . . A bit later now, another day. I don't even know the date. Everything going a bit more smoothly in my life now. Phone ringing with a fair amount of regularity, bringing in the desired bits of money, here and there, in small sums and large.

Peace between Adrian and me. Very much in love, rather out of touch physically, but mentally not at all. Each day I grow to appreciate, more and more, our life together.

And then . . . and then there's Sarah. Beginning, if even just slightly, to satisfy my desires for having a woman in my life. I'm enjoying our talks more and more, and her company (we went out to dinner together and it was as though no-one else existed) is delightful.

There has been no desire to touch, however. Not yet. Perhaps there will be later, or perhaps, not at all. I think I am in the dawn of a realization about myself (and my desires for women). I know now that I love to share . . . thoughts, secrets, worries, or wine, food and affection – but not, necessarily, bodies.

2   FROM THE DIARIES OF ADRIAN

7 June 1975 – Barcelona

Life! But, alas! I have a woman that loves me now – Ingrid. She is in my heart, my life and my work. She, I will paint, sketch, draw, mould, produce into my work from my hand. While she is with me, I shall be intelligent enough to take heed of this portion of life, my life with her. But more than *all* that I have just mentioned, is the over-all substance of my whole life – my painting!

13 June 1975

While walking around the beautiful park here in Barcelona called El Parque de la Ciudadela, I painted a fountain that has sculptured children flowing from it. After I had spent enough effort on this piece of work, I went to a nearby men's room and got screwed. There was a guy in there with his cock out, and he looked at me with eyes that said: 'I want to get sucked off.' The room was small and we could hear footsteps just outside on the gravel which made it sound as if each moment, someone would come in. I haven't had a man since leaving Boston on 27 May. I became so excited at the sight of his erect cock, I just wanted to get down on him and feel his load shoot off inside my mouth – to look at his pubic hair and fat, long hard shaft while my lips were on his cock, feeling the strength of the male. However, the uncertainty of sounds and the strange surroundings said 'No' to me. At least for today, until I familiarize myself with the park and its routine. Perhaps tomorrow! In the meantime I left there to go outside and walk away with Ingrid, frustrated, trembling and horny. I told Ingrid all about it and turned her on.

Ingrid fell asleep upon our arrival back, or shortly after we fucked. I didn't feel sleepy, but I *did* feel like drawing. I did a good charcoal drawing of the rear view of Ingrid sleeping – nice ass! I love to draw ass!

25 June – Preston, England 1975
I wasn't in the mood to cope with her tears, and she had started to have them. I felt my patience running short so I left out of the house for some drinks as arranged. All the time I was away, I was feeling Ingrid's presence with me and my presence back at the house in the bedroom. It made me feel extremely sad. I let her know when I returned that my love for her is real and becomes more so every day. I am frightened of returning to Boston. I am afraid for our relationship. The thought of all those tricks fucking her, and some of them making her suck them off, tears at me. I realize now it *is* because I love her. Yet – I wouldn't want her to feel jealous or upset about my having sex with a man. The only difference, and a great one, is that there is no threat to our relationship. Although if Ingrid meets another woman she really likes, she could easily leave me for that woman. Here again – I've been through that once already. I wonder how I'll manage it again if it happens?

Ingrid has become the same to me as the women in Pablo Picasso's life. I don't claim any greatness as compared to Picasso, but I understand his life now after having read his feelings, his words, the way he lived and worked. It's wonderful to know and experience an identity that I have now which was similar when I read about Matisse. She helps me paint. I have gone leaps and bounds and I intend going on to more. I have so much to do. So much drawing and painting now that I have found myself *in* my work. It took 3,500 miles of travelling in one direction to find it all – and Ingrid has been with me – another reason for love for her! I only hope the Spirit of God will give me a long life to finish it all.

Have been thinking of my sons – Walter, Benjamin and Joseph. I have felt tears welling up inside and have felt them rolling down the one side of my face late at night – missing them, thinking and seeing their little faces, hoping they never forget their Dad. Lately, I have felt so much like a worthless and empty father to them. The only way I can get to them is to paint them a lot more. Here again, I must trust the Spirit of God to keep it together. Picasso suffered when his wife took his child and left. I admired the way he handled it all. If I had only been able to read something like that when I lost my family. I am making better preparations this time for when Ingrid leaves me. Even then – when it happens it's always a shock.

My body... When I am with Ingrid I feel a 'total man and woman'. How can a man feel like a woman too? I cannot answer that, but again, I am much more aware of my male body now than in past years. I look down and am pleased to see my cock hanging over my balls, and to see my pubic hairs. I love to feel my cock roll over to the side when I turn in bed to fuck Ingrid. Her body and her presence makes me and my body feel that way. I love to feel her breasts and yet I love it when she feels mine. I love her hand to gently touch my cock and balls.

I love to masturbate in bed with Ingrid. I love to have her see me ejaculate and see the sperm shoot on my stomach. I adore it when we masturbate together.

12 August 1975

A guy picked me up and I brought him here. I closed the large door at the bottom inside hall and had him blow me and suck my balls and ass, and treated him as if he were an S. and M. trick. He loved it and I hated *it* and *him*! I had to take *it* all out on someone. I was screaming inside with desire to treat Ingrid with gentleness, with soft kisses on her breast, to kiss her soft, sweet cunt and lick her until she reached her beautiful orgasm, to feel my big hard cock inside her and let me explode inside her. But it all disappeared before it could begin. I don't mean to make sex an emphasis, but it is *so very much* the total expression of love for me with her. I have never felt such expression in sex before. Perhaps that's why I feel the way I do.

I understand the same of Ingrid's tricks. When I am ready to make love to her, she has been fucked twice in one day – therefore she doesn't want to. I have to sacrifice a love that is *real* for something that is very *unreal* and temporary! How long can I last?

30 October 1975

This afternoon I had my usual class on Thursday with the seniors.

The only difference was that Brian (one of my students) was quitting and he was coming to get his things. I dreaded it because I had felt such magnetism and strong vibrations of immense sexuality that drives me mad – his eyes staring into mine – wanting to touch each other, wanting to feel him all over. I know all these things would be the wind (or like the wind). It would come and go, for Brian is married to a beautiful girl, and so am I, in essence. I would do *nothing* to jeopardize this relationship with Ingrid and me.

Brian and I made love tonight. It was a moment that we had both felt for two years, two years in coming. Finally, in bed we really touched each other. We kissed in passionate rage for each other. I slipped myself down to his erect cock and big balls and sucked on him as he did with me.

4 November 1975

As I approached the school steps today, I felt a very strange feeling, and it was the presence of another human being with whom I had a strong intimacy. It was Brian!

My heart took on an extra beat and I wanted to reach out and embrace him and put my cheek against his lips and feel his hair in my hands and say: 'Come back!'

He was back! He is back!

We talked about Angela, the baby, his newborn son. He's silently proud. I love him so much for that.

His eyes shot out towards me in fires of blues, greens, hazels, and a mist of love and need – telling me not to forsake him; that he needs me for what I am. He has it. The day was beautiful, he looked beautiful, and he made me feel beautiful.

When he left class at the end of the day, he lingered as long as he could, and then touched my arm as he said: 'See you.'

3 RUTH

My parents married during the last war. My father was forty-nine, my mother twenty years younger. He died from tuberculosis ten years later when I was just four. Sometimes I think I remember him, but am never quite sure whether I fabricate these images from old photographs and from what people have told me about him. He was a very intelligent man, well read, and I think, like me, rather moody. He was brought up in a poor immigrant family in the East End. He became a musician, a singer, with a beautiful voice. I still have some records he made. But because he had a bad leg, had to walk with a stick and limped, he never did opera or became successful. Instead he worked for H.M.V. as an artist and recording manager. I still remember vaguely the singers who used to come to our house in Highbury. It was a huge place with a front staircase and a back for servants (apparently my father was once a Communist but it seems like so many others he didn't live up to those ideals when the money came along). That was due to my mother who never worked and still lives on her private income as a widow. Her family were successful builders from Derbyshire, very 'county'. Though I had a lot of contact with my relatives when I was small I never see them now, we have nothing in common at all. Perhaps one or two are O.K. but mostly it's hunt balls, the races and coming out (debutantes, not dykes). My mother's not really like that and was kind of an odd one out in the family. She, like my father, was a singer. She has performed in public a few times and given lessons. In fact she teaches a bit at the moment, but it's hardly 'breadwinning'. She also studies Russian.

Most of what I know about my father I have had to learn from relations; my mother hardly ever volunteers information or even shows any obvious grief about his death . . . though as I was only four at the time she would have hidden it from me I guess. She's typically British about that, very phlegmatic on the surface. Once when I asked her about him for quite a while she broke down crying and ran out of the room. I remember feeling very warm towards her and wanting to comfort her, though because we never discussed anything at all intense I think I was a bit embarrassed. I never saw her cry again (I was thirteen at the time) and since then the strongest emotion I seem to feel towards her is a vague anxiety. I feel really confused about this. When I was little I remember looking up to her as a kind of ideal, she seemed terribly beautiful, sort of unattainable. It's true I was brought up mainly by nannies. When I was at boarding school from nine to thirteen I missed her terribly (though it was I that asked to be sent there) but now I not only don't miss her . . . I find her terribly annoying and feel really aggressive towards her if I'm with her for any length of time.

I could go on for ages talking about my mother. We are hardly close now, nor ever have been but I seem to be beset by conflicting emotions about her. Mike (I'll talk about him later) once said he thought she was manipulating, double binding and unloving and I was really relieved on one level because all my friends had always said how charming she was and that left me terribly guilty about not loving her. On another level I felt angry he should make those judgements about her and defended her. At the moment she seems to be rather obsessed with my brother's new family. He and his wife (called Ros) have a new baby boy and my mother is the doting gran. I am very fond of Simon (my brother) and we have been quite close at times but not so now. He seems totally preoccupied with his work and the house and Ros and the baby (I don't get on with Ros at all). He knows I'm bisexual but doesn't seem very keen to discuss it. I think it embarrasses him. My mother's the same. I once told her I was going to a lesbian disco. She'd been surprised when, on asking me where I was going I said a disco because she knows I don't usually go to them. When she said what sort of disco, I just didn't want to tell lies. It's not that I wanted to shock her. I think she was pretty taken aback but kept her cool and asked me politely about my 'inclinations' and whether I still had 'feminine instincts'. I said I didn't know what she meant. 'Oh, having children.' I said I'd never been very keen. Since then she's always been extra nice to any men I bring home, even if they don't look terribly reputable. But she avoids a scene and if the subject of homosexuality ever arises she tries to switch to something else. I'm not much better because I'm really quite inhibited about talking to her about anything important to me.

I had a very 'liberal' upbringing. There was never much fuss about me staying out the night or coming home late and I started to do all those things very young. I was rather advanced at school, did my O levels at thirteen and then moved on to a London grammar school. That was a shock. I struggled to keep up academically, but I could hardly keep up socially. I think the desire to keep up to be acceptable was so overwhelming I hardly questioned my sexuality. I had had intense 'crushes' on women teachers at my previous school and felt emotionally drawn to women. But at my new school all the talk seemed to be about boys and you had to have a boyfriend and if possible sleep with him in order to be 'in'. As a result I did all those things and found it quite heavy going until I was about sixteen. By then I looked rather more attractive, had lost a lot of weight and gained some confidence. Perhaps I was beginning to enjoy what power I had over men and I didn't have many women friends. But I did have one best friend, Leni, who had 'adopted' me in earlier, lonelier times. She was two years older than me and at a time when no one spoke to me (I later found out this was partly because I had the reputation of being frighteningly clever, or perhaps just a swot, but in any case something of a freak) she took me over. I was her protégé, the child she showed off to her friends at parties. That was her power trip and she had a lot of control over me. It was that which broke up our relationship about two years ago. I was fed up with being patronized. Though we slept together quite a lot I guess we were too selfconscious ever to touch. I was surprised to hear she had been having gay scenes recently. I doubt whether she'll give up easily the power of being heterosexual. Because I do think heterosexual women have power. Relating sexually to other women has shown me what games they play. It is perhaps rather ironical that the Women's Movement, which brought me closer to women in so many ways has also given me a new insight and sympathy into the problems of men. I went through school and university with a series of not very satisfactory relationships. My first lover, Charles, and I were friends for about five years on and off. In fact we still are friends though we never sleep together. I did get bored with him sexually quite early on in the relationship though I still enjoyed the warmth and intimacy of our fucks. My next big affair was Tim. Not bright and witty like Charles . . . rather ponderous in many ways, devoted to me and unlike Charles who always laughed at me, he treated me with great respect. I was a cow and treated him very badly. We lived together at Oxford, sharing the house with a very graceful girl from West Pakistan, Nilly. Later when I had left Oxford I tried to write a novel and it was all about Nilly. Though I had never had any sexual contact with a woman at that stage in the book I fell in love with her and we slept together. The other main character in my 'novel' was my father. I decided that the only reason I was writing a lesbian novel was that lesbianism was something I knew nothing about and that I was too inhibited to write about my immediate experiences with men which were of course more important to me. (In fact Tim was not very important to me at all except that he was always boosting my ego by his admiration. I did give him a bad time.) The fact that the other main character was my father seemed almost conclusive proof that I was unable to write about what I had experienced. Now that I am older and wiser I see rather clearly that I was mistaken in my interpretation. In fact the relationship with my father in the book is in many ways similar to my relationship with Mike who is a lot older than me and has been my friend for about eighteen months. My attitude to Nilly, slave-like, adoring, is frighteningly like a foolish scene I got myself into over the last few months. I should have listened to Mike who is my best friend and guide: 'Don't allow yourself to become vulnerable'. But while I have almost never done that with men, with women I seem to act like a kid of fourteen. I forget to play the waiting games, I place all my trust in them. But I'd better go back to what was perhaps the crucial event in realizing my homosexuality and the subsequent virtual transformation of my life, which was when I met Mike in January 1974.

I had in fact met him on and off before that date as he'd been going out with the sister of my first boyfriend, Charles. I hadn't liked him, found him very aggressive and rude. When, some time later I was working on a newspaper in the North and not enjoying life much, there wasn't a lot of variety in the small town in which I lived, Charles invited me over to Bradford where he was staying with his sister and it was then that I got to know Mike and I suppose I fell in love with him. I'm not sure about using that expression. I am still very fond of Mike but I wonder whether at that time I didn't fall in love with an image . . . exotic, bisexual, Mike wandering about his flat in his silk kimono. He was also very left wing and I was amazed and delighted to find a socialist who had so little of the Puritan in him. That had put me off revolutionary politics at university and later the terrible humourlessness of the left. 'But we're the bent left,' Mike told me. It was he that first spoke to me about homosexuality and the first time I slept with a woman Mike was there too, and Rosa's boyfriend. I didn't much enjoy fucking him and did get a bit jealous of Mike and Rosa, but not very. Mostly I was just amazed and excited at the sensations of kissing, caressing and being close to another woman. I had never been particularly friendly with Rosa before that and nothing much developed afterwards, nor was I particularly upset. I suppose making love to three people at once is kind of a momentous event but it wasn't *love* and I felt rather numb about it. Mike and I had this fantasy of finding Ms Right and all living together happily ever after. We didn't find her of course and I was gradually becoming more interested in keeping my gay affairs to myself. I think perhaps Mike gets less jealous of me sleeping with other women than of sleeping with men because it's less directly competitive, which is not to say he isn't affected.

A few months ago I met Lucy. When I first met her (at a gay conference) I didn't think she was gay. She seemed sort of innocent, but interested in a sympathetic heterosexual way. She works for a women's magazine. I was reporting the conference for them but she said she'd be interested to come up anyway as she'd never been to that sort of thing. Later I wrote a couple of other things for them and we sort of drifted into a correspondence that became quite intense . . . more intense than our relationship would apparently seem to merit . . . in that we'd only met once. As a result when I saw her again in London I was quite wrought up about it (Mike looms up again here . . . I showed him the first letter Lucy had written to me which to me seemed quite innocent and he'd said 'that's a love letter'). I remember sitting in my mother's sitting-room not knowing quite what to say to her (Lucy) and her saying 'I think there's sex in the air'. It stayed in the air for a couple of months because I had to go away. When we did eventually sleep together it was wonderful, very gentle, and loving. The next morning I went out in the park, dancing on air, in love with the trees and the bunny rabbits and the grass and the whole world. We would have a wonderful affair I thought and I had fantasies of moving back to London in a year and living with her for ever and ever. Just to be with her made me feel happy. I had never felt quite like that about a woman . . . except perhaps Leni at first and Kate, a woman I became involved with, but, though there was some of that magic in the air then, we had little in common. Lucy and I could talk for hours. I felt quite protective towards her because she had all sorts of phobias about being in strange houses and going out in cars. But gradually I started to get the brush off. I'd ring her up and she'd be terribly busy or feeling ill or whatever. And I know I was very heavy, kept telling her the only reason I'd stayed in London was to see her. (I was at my mother's house as I had nowhere else to live at the time. I could have gone to be with Mike which would have been much nicer, but I just wanted to see Lucy.) I kept telling her how upset I was at not seeing her, all that sort of thing, things I'd never say to a man, I'd have been much more cool. Now I know you have to play the same games with women. Because Lucy and I had talked so long about so many things I'd placed this huge trust in her. I'll try not to do that again. Of course I frightened her off though I'm glad to say things hadn't gone on long enough for me to be irreparably hurt. My affair with Kate had had a similar outcome.

I'm warier now. I've never been deeply hurt or deserted by a man and never sufficiently involved with a woman to feel that either. Perhaps I don't give a lot in a relationship, but I do know when I see friends tied together by guilt, property and hysteria I just feel I don't want any of that. Things have changed a bit now with Mike. In the beginning I simply barged into his life, arriving at his house one day with my furniture and the news that I'd given up my job in Yorkshire to come and live in London. He wasn't tough enough to throw me out . . . I don't say that disparagingly because the best thing about Mike is that he has never made decisions for me. He just said to me 'Please don't move in, I can't deal with it.' There's a lot more to the whole business than I feel like putting down now, but he did say if I moved in he'd grow fond of me and then I'd leave him. Well, that did happen, though on the surface I only left him because he had a job in Kent and I had to move to Hull . . . but I guess I'd have left anyway . . . it was easier this way. We are still very close in spirit though we don't fuck very often. He is my best friend and the only person I could talk to when Lucy had made me unhappy and he told me all the bad luck he'd had with his affairs and we had a good cry together. He seemed rather sad when I said I didn't think I could live with him . . . but I'm not sure how he'd feel if I turned up with my furniture again. I'm terribly impulsive and always rush into everything.

I do think it's hard being bisexual. That seems to be a strange thing to say because I think, and I think you agree with me, that we're all bisexual. What is hard is to live that way. After being het for most of my life I would like now to live without being emotionally involved with men, though the idea frightens me because I'm sure I'll get hurt by women as I never have by men . . . but marriage or any settled heterosexual relationship fills me with horror . . . a settled lesbian relationship? Well I do think the possibilities of a truly equal and sharing partnership are infinitely greater. More and more I think of myself as a lesbian and yet I'm writing to you as a bisexual partly in an effort to sort these things out and because I guess someone who can feel as close to a man as I have felt to Mike can't be a lesbian. I find the whole business very confusing, especially as it ought not to be even a matter of importance . . . but given the way society is, it does matter, it's crucial. I find myself moving more and more among lesbians because I can't bear being the object of a man's heterosexual assumptions.

While I lived with Mike I did go along to the lesbian group but sometimes I'd withdraw for a while because I'd feel like a humbug. Now he's far away it's kind of easier, but I'd feel just as dishonest if I denied my heterosexual feelings . . . well they're not very sexual, I don't think I've desired another man for about two years. Mostly I call myself a lesbian because that's the side of me that's oppressed and I don't think I shall have much more to do with men. I think you won't find many bisexual people who don't live either a homosexual or a heterosexual life . . . that is who don't inwardly define themselves as one or the other. I work with Women's Liberation and Gay Liberation in the hopes that one day we, or our nieces, nephews and children's children, can live in a society where names like homo and hetero are irrelevant, where you just sleep with whom you love.

I've missed out lots of things but perhaps they'll come up when we meet. I suppose however I should tell you that I took an overdose almost exactly a year ago, in the midst of a terrible depression. It lasted about three months during which time I gave up going to the group and just stayed with Mike who was tremendously supportive. I couldn't bear going out or seeing anyone. I did go to see a psychotherapist three times but I felt sure he didn't like me or disapproved of me. I didn't like him either, though I was never sure if that wasn't simply through fear of what he might say to me, fear of opening myself up. I guess that's partly why I'm writing to you . . . you're asking for help, and maybe this will help you . . . but I guess I'm sort of asking you for help too.

If we are all bisexual, and even the most reactionary among psychologists seem prepared to accept that, why do they never spend any time asking why most people seem to be so oppressively heterosexual? That seems to be the role of the sociologists. I enjoyed reading your book about lesbians but I can't help feeling that a lot of the stress on masculinity among lesbians is the result of social pressures on women. If we don't want to be frail, 'feminine', emotional, instinctive creatures, but strong, intellectual, independent, what can we be but manly? There's no other model for us. I felt very lost when I was young and did want to be a boy when I was small and perhaps even in my teens. Now however I am committed to Women's Liberation and see that we can retain a woman's gentleness and be strong if we can only scramble through the heavy trips society lays on us. Hopefully the Movement will one day be much more than a few scattered groups. I wear masculine type clothes because they're comfortable . . . but I am a woman and I'm proud of it. When I first came out and went to a gay disco I was so unsure how to behave, I immediately put on masculine airs in the hope of meeting a nice girl. Our culture as lesbians is so underground, so secondary that we seem to have to take on the games of the heterosexual world. Well, I don't do this any more but I still find myself acting and feeling like a man sometimes and I'm sure this is because there is no other role for me to emulate. If there were more lesbian films I wouldn't have to always identify with the male hero. I enjoyed your book and found it very sympathetic, but it did leave me with the feeling that perhaps I was a bit 'queer' . . . too many male hormones or something. Does it really matter? Anyhow I look forward to meeting you. Writing this reminds me of something Lucy said. When she first met me she found me very 'right on' politically; it's easy for me to stand on a platform and tell the crowd I'm a lesbian and I love women. Personally and in private I'm not so suave and I find the whole business quite freaking. Perhaps I should add that I never have orgasms except masturbating, though I seem to come quite close to it with women. I don't think there's any kind of psychological block however, rather something to do with my physical construction, very small clitoris. I say this now because I'll probably be too shy to talk about it when we meet.

4 PENELOPE

I suppose it was not until I fell in love with my room-mate at college that I learned that my sexuality differed from that of others, and even then it did not strike me in a very forceful way.

As a child I was what everyone patronizingly called a 'tomboy'. I was a very active child, delighting in climbing trees and playing rough games with my older brother. I preferred live cats and dogs to dolls. My parents were divorced when I was three, and I lived with my mother. As a pre-school child I spent a great deal of time with my maternal grandparents, particularly my grandfather, who was a carpenter. I spent all available time with him in his carpentry shop and announced that I intended to be a carpenter when I grew up. This was met with good-humoured acceptance by the adults around me, and the occasional mild objection that women weren't carpenters. In general, my elders never seriously deterred me from any ambition because of my being a girl. I disliked dresses and was not forced to wear them. (I suspect that children do not identify with adults as much as adults suppose. All grown-ups are so strange to children that the difference between men and women is a secondary difference. As a small child I don't believe it ever occurred to me that I would grow up to resemble the older women in my family; I could just as easily grow up to be like my grandfather, who at least wore overalls very like mine. I thought I would grow up to be *me*, but larger.)

When I was eight, I had a somewhat traumatic sexual experience, which I feel is irrelevant to my sexual development but which seems to be the mainstay of statistics about people with unconventional sexual preferences. A man invited me into his car on the pretext of taking me home. He took me into the country near our town, and as he drove he massaged his erect penis, which protruded from his clothing. I had never seen one before, but was not unduly alarmed. He stopped the car and insisted on touching my genitals and on my kissing his penis. With great reluctance I finally did this and was taken home. He was apparently harmless, although I might have been in great danger. I was uneasy about the experience for some time afterwards, but not really frightened. I told my mother about it immediately and urged her to call the police (I had noted the number of the car), but she did not.

At about eleven I decided to become a veterinary surgeon because of my love of animals and because of an enthralling book, *All About Cats* by Whitney. The section on genetics I found absorbing, and the detailed chapter on reproduction was my introduction to the mechanics of sex. I watched with great interest as my cats mated. I felt no anthropomorphic prurience about it.

By puberty my liking for physical activity was being channelled into disciplined sports. I had learned to swim and play tennis. At school I played basketball, softball and volleyball. At twelve or so I had a boy friend, probably because of a social need to pair off rather than any genuine affection. I belonged to a clique of girls and had several close friends. As a teenager my main interests were English, foreign languages, swimming and tennis. I was devoted to certain of my friends, but I think only mildly interested in boys. I had 'gone steady' with boys twice during this period; both times I must have thought I was in love. I can't help but feel now that my feelings then were a conventional response to the society of my high school. I don't think my heart was quite in it. At the same time there were other girls whom I liked very much. I think now there was an unrecognized sexual content in my feelings for them. I had crushes on girls older than I and a few of about my own age. I wished for excuses to touch them, although in a general way I was not, and am not, very demonstrative.

Some relationships inside the family were changing. My older brother had become a black sheep. Although intelligent, he made poor marks at school and eventually quit before graduation. His interests seemed to be mainly cars and disreputable companions. By the time I was eighteen or twenty we had nothing in common except our parentage. We disagreed radically in every possible way. I hear of him from time to time through my mother, but I have not seen him for several years. When I was sixteen my mother remarried. Her husband was older than she and fifty-six years older than I. He was an avuncular figure and we did not try to become particularly close.

At seventeen I entered college, where I lived in a dormitory and made a number of friends. I enjoyed going to plays and concerts, but most of my time was taken up with studies. In my first year I met another young woman who shared some of my intellectual interests and we became close friends. We played chess together, listened to Beethoven's piano sonatas, and discussed politics. The next year we roomed together and continued to be devoted friends. The following summer we went on a guided tour of Europe together.

However, that spring of my second year, the spring of 1963, something began to happen. I met a young woman who lived down the hall, Janet. Gradually I became very fond of her. By the end of May, when classes ended, we had agreed to room together the next year, when my other room-mate would be studying abroad. Janet was infinitely fascinating. She had a quick mind and a delicious sense of humour. Since I was away for the summer, I did not see her again until the following September, although I wrote her several letters. On the way back I imagined our meeting – I would hug her. Young women of our age often hugged each other, I reasoned, and so it would be the natural thing to do. And besides, I just wanted to embrace her. Our first meeting was nothing like that, of course. We met in a public place in the hubbub of the first day at college, with people around us shouting and carrying boxes of clothing and books.

I was never happier than when I was near Janet; it was as though she carried with her a bracing aura of ozone. I cannot even remember how our first physical intimacy came about. I do remember vividly, however, that I had a sense of gradualness and discovery. I think that in ordinary heterosexual relationships the partners act out what they already know to be the usual behaviour for two people in their position. We knew nothing about our relationship before we experienced it and therefore had nothing to 'act out'. Neither of us was more than dimly aware of the existence of lesbianism, and it never dawned on us that we might be lesbians. Our relationship was supremely natural. At some points we were a little startled to discover feelings in ourselves that we did not know could exist. We knew, of course, that our relationship must be kept private at all costs. We took precautions in locking our doors and not holding hands in public. We made love together with great tenderness and joy. The physical side of our love was a natural outgrowth of our friendship, our affection for each other, our spiritual and intellectual unity. It is this experience that convinces me of the silliness of sex manuals. I discovered that, for me, when love exists first, the expression of it follows naturally. It therefore seems to me that 'technique' and the avid pursuit of it suggests the absence of a genuine, deep feeling. The possibility of this discovery – based *entirely* on experience – seems to me the great advantage, the gift even, of lesbianism in the days before all the popular studies, essays, and cover stories in *Time* magazine. I regret that it is harder and harder for women to make the same discovery now.

In the years that followed Janet and I were able to see each other only intermittently. We wrote regularly to each other, but for three years I felt a gnawing need for her companionship and for our old intimacy. She, in the meantime, began to fear the consequences of being a lesbian and therefore 'abnormal'. By 1967 she wished to extract herself from our relationship and resist any further attraction she might feel toward other women. By this time we were both in graduate school, and I went abroad to finish my doctorate.

In despair over the final break-up of my love affair, I found welcome companionship among new friends. I knew several pleasant young men. One of them was very companionable and seemed to pursue me. I eventually fell in love with him and we became engaged. I thought that my affair with Janet must have been some sort of passing phase after all. My love for Andrew was quite genuine and our physical relationship was unforced and satisfying. Meanwhile, Janet had become engaged to a man at her graduate school. During all this time, Janet and I exchanged friendly letters and worked single-mindedly on our respective degrees. My marriage with Andrew has always been a happy, loving one.

After we had been married for four or five years, Andrew and I visited Janet and Arthur. It was the first time I had seen Janet for six years. I wondered idly if I would be capable of such a relationship again as the one we had shared in college. I hadn't imagined in my wildest dreams that she still felt a sense of loss for our old love. I felt a little awkward with her at first, but the awkwardness soon passed and I recognized my old friend again. Every movement and gesture seemed familiar. We had never stopped being affectionate friends. But then one night she told me that she regretted that our intimacy had ended as it had. She needed my friendship and the reassurance that I was not angry with her for what had gone before. I assured her that I had never been angry with her and that I liked her very much. We visited the seashore, and one evening we walked along the deserted autumnal beach together, our arms around each other. We walked perfectly in step, and talked about our lives since we had parted. We promised to renew our old friendship, which we both felt had been, and should be, an important part of our lives. We both felt, when I held her in my arms one day, a sense of rightness and, as Janet expressed it, a sense of having regained one's home.

After that we wrote to one another almost every day. A few months later she came, alone this time, to visit me. We went off for a week together. Before she came I didn't know whether we would decide to make love, and I couldn't even have said whether I wanted to. But when she came I threw myself into her arms and later we made love again with all the old tenderness and delight. Since then we have arranged other protracted visits together. We have never thought seriously of leaving our husbands, for we both value our marriages and we are happy for the other to have the advantages of a married home life. It has become necessary to explain this turn of events to our husbands. Andrew has been remarkably understanding about it all, and even Arthur has come to accept it. Andrew has taken a keen interest in sexual variations and is very sympathetic toward lesbians and the problems they face in society. He told me once that, upon hearing a colleague lamenting her lack of a boyfriend, he wished he could tell her not to ignore the possibility of an emotional relationship with one of her women friends! Since my love for Janet has re-awakened I have taken a gradually diminishing pleasure in physical relations with my husband. He was upset at first, but has become amazingly good-humoured about this situation. I have been surprised by my own reactions. Janet tells me that she has never enjoyed heterosexual relations; my own switch from enjoyment to distaste puzzles me.

I have read Nigel Nicolson's *Portrait of a Marriage* with great interest, because Vita Sackville-West's experiences seem so like my own. Her description of her relationship with Violet and Violet's emotions expressed in her letters seem very accurate to me, very familiar, and very true. The argument about Violet's marriage and the loss or retention of her virginity was the only thing in the whole account which did not strike a sympathetic chord with me.

It seems to me that my predominant sexual taste is for lesbianism, because in a general way I do not find men sexually attractive. I am attracted to women, usually on the basis of friendship, but I always feel that the right kind of friendship can develop into love and the physical expression of it. I now feel that my marriage may have been a deviation from the pattern, and that if I had been able to live with Janet I would probably not have been attracted to a man at all. It is difficult to tell about this, however, because I have loved only one woman and one man. I feel that these relationships have been with other *persons* and not representatives of one sex or the other. In general I feel that a loving relationship with another woman is perhaps more rewarding emotionally. I value the great tenderness and devotion that Janet and I feel for each other. We think that our sameness is an important part of our love – the sense of sharing we have as women. We feel a great balance in our sexual relationship, because we are each lover and loved at the same time; we have never felt quite this balance in a heterosexual relationship. I suppose that if I were suddenly left in need of an emotional involvement, I would look for it in another woman and not a man, but I also suspect that the person and his or her qualities might be more important to me than the person's sex.

I cannot consider my bisexuality to be the crucial element of my personality. It seems to me to be an important strand among many other important strands. This attitude may be due to some desire to reject my bi- or homosexuality, but I doubt it. Naturally, I like

Professor Adler's theory that the real neurosis or abnormality is exclusive hetero- or homosexuality, and that the normal behaviour in any individual encompasses many varieties. I suspect that unconventional sexuality indicates imagination and a basic eclecticism in one's approach to life.

I am a bit surprised at my complacency. I am not even very curious to know whether there are reasons for bi- or homosexuality or what those reasons are. I prefer literary works about lesbianism to factual studies of it. I have enjoyed Renée Vivien's poetry and Isabel Miller's *Patience and Sarah*, which strikes me as *the* perfect description of love between women. Much of what I have read on the subject was passed on to me by Janet, who has become interested in the history of lesbianism. I am interested in meeting other women who love women, but even if I were living with Janet I do not think I would like to make lesbian organisations the centre of my social life.

5 MILDRED

Born to upper-middle-class family (father, army officer; mother, the daughter of one and ex-wife of another who was also a peer) full of well-hidden skeletons in cupboards. My mother was strict, dominating, efficient and determined; my father softer (to me anyway), short and fat, kind and old-style Tory politically. He believes in greedy workers and is racist, but humanitarian, e.g. against the James White Abortion (Amendment) Bill. Don't remember any sexual feelings for father, though he used to tickle my back after the bath on Sunday nights up to about age eight, and this I loved and still do – still have one kind of very good orgasm when R. tickles my back for about ten minutes, then I squeeze thighs together and come.

Nannies looked after me till I was five, but my mother still had a lot to do with me. I was quite independent then but got shy, fat and dominated by my mother when we spent three years (six and a half to nine and a half) on the Sussex coast. My father came for week-ends from London. She didn't have any good friends and no job, only me to concentrate on. Looking back, I can't think what she did all day but read – she was no lover of housework and cooking, always had domestic help and sometimes real servants. Anyway, I got overwhelmed by her.

Then my parents went to Germany and I went to boarding school. Two terms at a strange place, then on to a school for army officers' daughters in the West Country, where I remained till I'd taken

A levels at nearly eighteen. I didn't like it at all. My mother went through the menopause with a lot of trouble and visits to gynaecologists when I was about eleven, and she and my father had many rows. I sided with my mother, and that continued really till she died when I was nineteen – though in fact she was oppressing me more than he did, directly.

I was quite a tomboy, though too fat to be good at games. I did ride and swim though. At school it was the done thing to be crushed on an older girl, so I made my choice and built a big thing out of it – romantic fantasies etc., birthday presents and blushes, till she left when I was nearly fourteen. We never touched, though some older girls did have kissing sessions with the younger ones. I never wanted that, though a group of us around twelve would spend Sunday afternoons pretending we were older and having kissing practice, and lying on top of one another.

I wanted to have breasts and periods. I saw them as symbols of growing up so I could cease to be an oppressed child and do what I wanted. My mother was over-protective, convinced a rapist lurked behind every bush, and the school very restrictive.

I had two half brothers (mother's first marriage); didn't see them much as they were away in the army, but they would arrive occasionally with presents and exciting tales. As I grew older, I identified more with the younger one who was kind, gentle, and loved by animals and children. The older, I found boring and unattractive, and still do though he was engaged three times, and has just left his wife much to her heartbreak, so he must have something. My father doesn't like him much. Anyway the younger was always pursued by women but never got engaged. Finally, when I was fourteen, it all came out – he was a homosexual. Somehow he was up in court (this was before the Act about consenting adults). The judge liked him and he had excellent references plus being upper class, so he was sent to a mental hospital to be 'cured'. Ha! After three weeks they gave him morphine, he turned out to be allergic, relapsed into a coma and died after three days. Killed by the State. I just told my friends he'd had a nervous breakdown – given the 'queer jokes' that proliferated I couldn't have done otherwise. For years I told no one and never mentioned it. I did tell a boyfriend when I was eighteen, feeling he ought to know. When G.L.F. started it all became O.K. of course, and if the subject comes up and it seems appropriate, I will tell people, or if people ask me about my family and 'what did your brother die of' etc.

Well, I was nearly sixteen when I first *really* fell in love with the vicar's son in the village my father had retired to and where he still lives. I became tongue-tied and idiotic (I thought) in his company, and he never showed much interest in me, or maybe he did and thought I didn't like him. Who knows? That passion lasted about a year. Meanwhile I slowly began kissing and groping with boys at parties, meeting them illicitly out of school. This pattern continued through the year of work between school and university (London and Cambridge) and the first year of university – by the end of which I would do anything *but* spend nights with men. Religious hang-over plus fetish of virginity. Finally 'lost' it in Gibraltar on the floor of a bar after closing time to the Gibraltarian bar owner of 27, good-looking guy, and never regretted it at all. That was summer 1967 . . .

So another year of university, men who were sexists, drugs, student revolt, demos about Vietnam, going to left male-dominated political meetings I didn't understand, getting drunk, music, festivals, the Round House – the whole late sixties scene. Meeting R. in my third year and him moving into the flat I shared with two women . . . getting II.i Hons. at the end of it all.

Oxford, working as a clerk, and then a quite interesting though capitalist job. Monogamy, isolation, friendlessness (relative). Bad sexual scenes with R. He wanted to fuck all the time and I never did. The old headache excuses; worries that I might be frigid but never getting it together to tell the middle-class mother-figures at the F.P.A.

Going to Women's Liberation in February 1970 – scared off. They all wore jeans and no make-up, seemed most unlike me, scared they'd think I was frivolous and silly. Going to a new group in September 1970 and never looking back. Now a convinced Marxist feminist, or feminist libertarian socialist, or some such label – *feminist* anyway.

June 1971, met H. at a party and BANG went two and a half years' dreary monogamy. R. got off with the woman who lived downstairs the same night, no jealousy. He's been jealous when he's had no relationship but not much. I've never been jealous of his relationships and other women, though a bit surprised and dismayed at some of them, when he's got very couple-ish. I really don't like couples especially as the woman usually loses her identity etc. Lesbian couples are slightly less destructive to the ego it *seems*, but are beset with silly jealousies.

Seems to me that jealousy is encouraged by the Bowlby style mother/child relationship, which produces neurotic dependence and fearful insecurity patterns in the baby and young child. This is reproduced in later sexual relationships in adulthood. This is one of the reasons I am involved in collective child care with four little kids now (plus taking burden of full-time motherhood away from the biological mother). I've always felt that my having nannies has helped me *not* to be so jealously possessive and insecure as other people I know. The nuclear family is, I'm sure, responsible for all the battered wives/children, jealous traumas shit. Plus all the other evils of capitalism of course.

So H. moved in (to the one room R. and I lived in) in October '71, and has been around ever since. I stopped sleeping with him a year ago (just sort of fizzled out), partly to wean myself from my intellectual dependency on him. I have always and still do, feel competitive with H., power struggles, never with R.

For a while H., R. and I slept in the same bed, but they weren't physically into each other; it's always been much better when there's been two women and one man, I've found. This started for me in 1972, and that was like the year of sexual freedom and exploration, all politically based. Lesbianism was becoming *the* thing if you were in Women's Liberation, and people went on about Reich a lot. I slept with several women but felt very unsure and anxious often (though nothing to compare with later traumas). I saw – and see – people as generally *sexual*. It's mainly conditioning that forces people into the heterosexual mould. Couldn't get over women being so *soft* at first, now I like it. A lesbian on bail fell in love with me and we had a five months' scene, though neither was monogamous or wanted to be at all. My main emotional ties were to men, specifically H. who was causing me much pain by his romantic, patronizing relationship to what I saw as a traditionally passive, weak woman. It made me very angry. We were involved in some heavy political scenes, busts and trials, and the lesbians I met round that time in London were really nasty to het. women, and ignored your presence. So that put me off political lesbians. It still is a very elitist scene unless you've paid your dues, and come with revolutionary credentials. I pass now because I'm a feminist activist and also have a lot more confidence than I did then. Provincial lesbians are much nicer than that London crowd anyway. What got me then was that they were all very nice to H. – a MAN – but seemed to treat me as his girl friend from the provinces.

Anyway the year ground to an end in a wave of prison sentences and post-trial depression. The first of our collective children was born and four of us moved north. 1973 we spent getting to know people. I had a not-very-successful scene with a woman (we are still very good friends and sleep together but don't *do* anything!), and slept with a few men. Then we moved down to a better house, another woman had a baby, and two more collective children and adults emerged. Now my life is poverty-stricken, and over-full of political activity which I endlessly try to cut down on. I seek reasonably O.K. part-time jobs, and teach women's health to adults. Have many friends. Three years ago I slept with lots and lots of men, now it's down to R. again, once or twice a week, and M. every six months or so. I had an abortion last June 1974, which decided me I never want any kids biologically – would get sterilized if I could.

Felt very freaked about sleeping with women the last two years, having been hurt by a woman in Oxford, but now it's much better, and I fantasize a lot. I did sleep with one, D., three times recently and it was fine, but I don't want the sort of intense relationship I feel she demands. I fell for one woman at a women's week recently, but shyness and passivity held me back. But I think we may get it on eventually though she lives 100 miles away.

I love our kids and wouldn't leave this town and my living situation because of them (communal with four other adults, three men including H. and R. and one woman, and four kids). Apart from H. and R. I'm not close to any men, but I'm much closer to lots of women.

At that time I was seeking a relationship with a woman and still sleeping with R. whom I've known for seven years. I was still on holiday from political work, too, working on the summer play scheme for under-fives, and shortly to go on the pre-school camp on the East Yorkshire coast. And trying to sort my head out and unwind from the tangles and tensions of the previous few hectic months.

During this time I was going to the women's discos which happened fortnightly at a pub. At one of these round the end of July, I exchanged a few words with C. I'd known her vaguely for ages, knew she was active in G.L.F. and another women's group, and a crèche like ours in another part of town. She has a kid who's three and a half being brought up semi-collectively there. I met her again on an excursion with kids to the park one hot Sunday, and then at another women's disco after the camp. We talked, went on to a party, and ended up going back to her place and sleeping together.

I was very pleased and it was really nice. Since then we see each other two or three times a week. At first it was hard to find time to see each other, both being so busy and involved with political work, kids and our own households. (She lives in a house with two other women.) Now some of my political work takes me over her side of town, so I've been spending say two days at a time based at her place, which I enjoy as it's a more realistic situation than just seeing someone socially. Neither of us would have any intention of dropping our lives and work to live in each other's pockets, so that's good.

At first I felt incredibly high about the whole thing, dancing along the park singing: 'I'm a Lesbian and I'm O.K.,' wearing G.L.F. and 'Glad to be Gay' badges, telling my friends, in fact 'coming out'. Although I first slept with a woman three and a half years ago, I've never felt the urge to do this till now. I do get embarrassed on my own about the badges and have to fight the urge to remove them, but I persevere. I've gone to a couple of G.L.F. meetings and activities and enjoy them – they are mixed. In many ways I'd rather they were all women, but the lesbian group I don't like. It's just a weekly social gathering at a pub, and everyone goes on to this horrible gay club afterwards, which I've always hated. Drinks are really expensive and there's a lot of role-playing. Nobody talks about anything in particular and it's boring. Yet when proper lesbian *meetings* have been tried most women just stop coming and it's down to the committed few. It's a shame only a few women come to G.L.F. I feel lesbians really need an identity as *women*, and a feminist consciousness, otherwise they don't change much, apart maybe from coming out of the closet, which is a big thing of course, but doesn't mean that solidarity with all women and all the oppressed necessarily follows.

I feel confused now. It's hard being bisexual. I still sleep with R. about once a week and don't intend stopping – he's been part of my life for so long. But this guy came to stay, and I found I could talk to him very easily, and felt attracted to him a lot, but felt very ambivalent about whether to act on it. I did, in the end, reckoning that if I felt it I might as well do it. But it was strange, I felt I'd betrayed sisterhood or something, certainly not C. I mean neither of us believe in being, or are, monogamous, and I really don't find jealousy a big problem. If a person I'm fond of, whether or not I'm sleeping with him/her, goes off with, or gets very friendly with, someone I distrust or dislike, then I'm pissed off and – yes – hurt. I wouldn't create a big scene about it. No, I just felt I shouldn't sleep with a man, then. As it was I didn't enjoy it much and thought why bother, when it's so much better with C.

But just recently I've felt different again, partly because C. and I don't really talk openly to each other. I have really felt a need to say some things about the way she is with the kid, the state of his room etc. but haven't as yet. *I will though.* I think I expect perfection (my ideal) in a woman, and feel disappointed when she doesn't fulfil all the criteria. I have to admire and respect the people I'm emotionally close to/sleep with – not admire in thinking 'they're great, I'm lousy', I don't mean putting myself down, but I couldn't go with someone for any length of time whom I didn't admire. Certainly sex has been very, very good with C. I feel nervous still about 'doing the right thing' and being able to satisfy her, but she seems to enjoy it and I know I enjoy it a lot. I do prefer women's bodies to men's I think (except men I've known a long time, like R., I don't experience as 'a man' but as 'R').

This is confused, reflecting accurately my state of mind. I have fantasies about other women, including the one I met in Scotland, and have begun to think 'she's attractive' about women in bars etc. in a way I didn't before. I don't know if that's good or bad. Also I've noticed a lot more lesbians around that I ever did before, and keep finding out about past lesbians – Janis Joplin, Virginia Woolf – people I never imagined would be.

6 AUDREY

I am fifty-one years old, and I have one brother three years younger than myself. I remember little of my early life and the arrival of my brother. I cannot remember him as a small baby, only when he was old enough to sit in a high chair. I have vague memories of staying with a strict aunt at this time. As a very small child I became interested in the penis, and drew pictures of 'matchstick' men urinating. (This carried on into my schooldays.)

My first attraction outside the family was a young man named Richard who lodged with us. I used to follow him around whenever he was at home.

At five I started in a small school run by nuns and was very happy there. My first friend was John. He was in my class and we used to walk home together. I also liked two older girls, Janet and Mary.

When I was eight a new school was built, the nuns left and we had lay teachers. I settled down without difficulty, and was very fond of my woman teacher. I was good at my lessons but never top of the class, usually third or fourth. I was a day-dreamer, rather lazy, not good at games and inclined to mild mischief. This school used the cane for punishment, so I had my share. Apart from my first teacher (I think I loved her), I had no 'crushes' on girls or teachers, but I did like two of the boys. I never told anyone of this as I thought I would be ragged. At home I was friendly with the boy who lived opposite me. We used to go shopping together and share our sweets.

I hated the teacher I had when I was about ten years old and she disliked me. I started to lie and steal. I think this went on for one or two terms, then I told my mother. I was deeply ashamed and begged her not to tell my father. She promised not to but she did tell him. He did not punish me, just talked to me. I didn't want to lose my standing with him and I never did.

I was eleven when my legs were burned in an accident during a science class. I was in hospital for a week and in bed at home for two months. I only missed a month or so of schooling as it happened just before the summer holidays started. My legs were badly scarred and I was very self-conscious about them. It was years before I went without stockings.

My main interest was the Brownies and, later, the Guides. I thoroughly enjoyed all the activities there. I had 'crushes' on two older girls, Peggy and Ruth, and one of the officers, but they were not strong or long-lasting. I liked one of the Scouts, Ian, but I only knew him slightly and was too shy to talk to him very much.

I never passed the 'scholarship' (11+), so I went to a local convent school when I was thirteen. I was miserable at first (although I'd longed to go there), as I was so aware of not being as well off as the other girls, and having only the bare minimum of uniform. (The latter was very important to me as I liked wearing uniform.) However, I settled down and did in fact become quite popular. I found my school work easier, and did particularly well at art so that I was known outside my own form. I enjoyed the praise and recognition. I had minor 'crushes' on two or three older girls, but became strongly attached to Alison, also a senior. This lasted for several years, even after I left school (I was only there for a year) although I only spoke to her once in all that time.

I had friends at school but seldom saw them outside. I mostly played with the children where I lived. They were not very reliable about arrangements, and I would often be left on my own with no one to play with. I would feel very lonely as I needed company and liked to be doing things. I felt frustrated indoors. I enjoyed drawing, painting and reading, but didn't find them sufficiently satisfying. I had dolls, pram, house, cot, etc., but I seldom played with them. I preferred roller-skating and climbing trees. I also liked acting, dressing-up and playing at churches and hospitals. I always read boys' books, but later started to read girls' stories and enjoyed them more. They were almost always school stories. I was still reading them after I left school. (I had two rag dolls when I was little, one blue and one pink, and I used to ill-treat the blue one and cuddle the pink one – a vivid memory!)

I wasn't happy about being a girl. I always thought boys had a better deal. Once I considered dressing myself as a boy so that I could become an altar server. I was embarrassed about my developing body, particularly when I was at the mixed school as I knew the boys discussed the girls' figures.

My periods started when I was thirteen. My mother had prepared me for it, but I still hated telling her. She often tried to talk to me about sex, but I would just walk away. I never told my friends my periods had started. I felt too embarrassed.

I didn't get on well with my mother. She was boss. There were constant rows about money and my father's inability to earn more (all in front of me and my brother). My father, who was quiet, usually ignored it but would sometimes fight back (verbally!). My mother always seemed to be nagging and discontented. She often talked of getting a job, and would probably have made a better business woman than housewife.

My father took more interest in me and my hobbies. He was more intelligent, more loving than my mother, but rather shy and self-effacing. He had a job well below his capabilities and must often have felt very frustrated, but he was rarely irritable or bad-tempered. I loved him.

I only liked my brother sometimes. Usually we argued and often fought (literally!), and my mother kept a cane for dealing with these situations. He was quite clever and nice looking, and I was aware that my mother preferred him. (When I was about fourteen she told me that she had wanted a boy when I was born.) I wasn't a pretty child. I was pale, bespectacled and rather awkward.

When I was about nine or ten years old a local tradesman used to take me for rides in his van. One day he offered me sixpence if I would let him touch me. With the lure of the money I agreed, and this happened on several occasions. He did no more than touch me and I didn't seem to care much about it. I also remember several cases of indecent exposure in parks and fields, but each time I was with friends. I was more afraid of this and we always ran away. I never told my mother about any of these incidents. Later in my twenties, I made the mistake of kissing a friend's father when I called (as she often kissed my father). It was only a casual kiss on the cheek, but he grabbed me and tried to kiss me on the mouth. I pushed him away and ran off, and I was always very scared of him after that.

I left school, completely untrained, when I was fourteen. I didn't want to leave. I wanted a higher education, but my mother didn't believe in education for girls (a fact that always made me angry). She didn't care what sort of job I had, and I felt she only regarded me as a source of income. I worked in several factories (getting the sack from one – too slow!) for a few weeks at a time, then in a wool shop for six months. I hated them all! In between I had periods of not working at all. I used to write stories and day-dream about my great 'crush', a film actor.

Just after the outbreak of war, when I was sixteen, I got an office job in the firm where my father worked. I liked it, and there were plenty of young people there so I made several friends. My special friend was Jim, the boy who worked with me. He was the first boy I got to know really well and felt at ease with. We used to go dancing with other friends (boys and girls) and usually all walked home together, but if he did see me home alone he always kissed me. He went into the Navy and used to write to me and sent me a present when he was abroad. I built him up as my 'big romance', but it was never the same when he came home. He eventually married another girl in the firm.

I had a long-lasting attraction for a woman, Patricia, whilst I was there, though I didn't know her well. (All the women I've liked have been adored at a distance.) I was quite shattered when she was transferred to the West Country.

I had made up my mind to join the W.A.A.F. when I was old enough, but my mother wouldn't hear of it. We had constant rows about it, but I never had the guts to go out and volunteer. When my mother died suddenly in 1943, I felt I couldn't go and leave my father (though he would never have stopped me). I was frustrated and resentful and ill-equipped for running a home – though my father did much of the work himself. I also had to transfer to the factory side of the firm, doing war work. I didn't like it much as the hours were long and I was slow at the work. My one bright spot was falling for my boss (also at a distance). I was enchanted by him, and then he too went to work at another branch.

After the war I returned to my office job, but I couldn't settle down. I became slower and slower and I was transferred from one department to another, eventually, after eight years, getting the sack. After this I worked as a teleprinter operator in several office jobs till, in my late twenties, I found the job I most enjoyed – in a drawing office. As it was a government department, they trained me for the work themselves. I was there for thirteen years, and then made things difficult for myself by resenting a new (female) colleague who was more experienced and better at the work than I was. On the advice of my boss (with whom I had a very good relationship) I accepted a transfer to another drawing office, but I never liked that so well. I then worked on the clerical side of the Civil Service for several years. I am now back in a drawing office and reasonably content, but I still don't see myself as a particularly efficient worker.

From 1951 till my father died in 1957, I ambled along fairly comfortably though always feeling frustrated. Most of my social activities were centred round the church where I had a good circle of friends. I was always looking for the 'right man', but never finding him! I went out with a few men but never more than once or twice. I felt (I still feel) that I was not particularly attractive to men. My brother married in 1950 and now has two grown-up children. Most of my own friends married about the same time. I thought I'd marry too, but was never very positive about it.

Since 1958 I have lived alone in a small flat in a block. My neighbours are friendly and I have a full social life – art classes, Scottish dancing, rambling clubs. For the past eighteen months I have been going out with a man I met at work. Robert is forty-six, a bachelor, kind, steady, reliable, but I cannot feel any emotion for him at all. I have attempted intercourse with him but it was unsuccessful. It was the first time for me and I don't feel I want to try again with him. I would be quite happy with companionship only.

My real attraction is for a woman who attends my art classes. We are not close friends but she gives me a lift to classes. I am attracted to her physically (I've never felt this for a woman before) and feel she may be a lesbian. It is my feelings for her and lack of feelings for Robert that have made me look at my emotional pattern and wonder if I *am* really bisexual. I have no real sexual experience, so I cannot be sure about it.

I should mention that during the war I had a Canadian boyfriend for eighteen months. He was rather like Robert in temperament, though more positive. I reacted to him better than I do to Robert.

7 CHARLES

My parents met each other in 1924 when my mother was thirteen and my father twenty. He was my uncle's best friend at college, and he had cycled from London to Wiltshire to stay with my mother's family. They met at Golden Gates, a romantic spot on a hill overlooking the Avon Vale. My mother says that they fell in love with each other from that first meeting. They wrote to each other at least once a day from that holiday until they married in 1930. On rare occasions she would visit him in London, and still reminisces, telling us of the bright lights, the theatres and museums. I have understood that sense of excitement and adventure that she expressed, on my first visits to London. She has always had dreams of a gayer life, but was unable to fulfil them because of my father's puritanical régime.

My mother is a very lively, energetic and loving person, who has given her life to her six children. I think she has always been confused in her mind by what are said to be serious subjects, party/power politics, economics and religion, and has always looked to my father, who knows about these things, for guidance. When it comes to making decisions from the heart she has no problem, because she knows how she really feels. She has a lot of common sense, which has enabled her to cope admirably with bringing up a large family on a shoe string. This practical ability means that in many areas of the household she wields considerable power, which she will not hesitate to use. She came from a family who were great chapel goers, and has since ceased practising that religion and now believes that she is a humanist. Spiritual beliefs and ideals make her suspicious and cynical. She needs to grasp something physical, where she can express herself practically. Churches always fascinate her from an aesthetic point of view rather than a spiritual one.

My father found in my mother his escape from London to the country. He does not like urban situations and will avoid towns and places with many people in them at all costs. He was a keen naturalist before moving to the country to live with my mother, but then having settled there, he was able to indulge in his hobby with enthusiasm and commitment. He would spend most of his free time out on nature trails with the local natural history society, or stuffing birds from the local museum. My father is a hard-working man, and put his all into his career and hobby. He became headmaster of our local primary school which we all attended. He had a good academic attitude towards children, believing in learning by exploration. He created a fine school, with an open-air theatre, swimming pool, garden plots and open space.

I was my parents' fifth child, and am eighteen months younger than my sister and eight years older than my younger brother who is the baby of the family. Consequently, I spent much of my early childhood playing with my sister. We were very good friends, and used to play shop, dressing up and making dens. Dolls and gollies were important in our games, and we spent hours knitting and sewing clothes for them. I learnt a lot about housewifery from the lessons my mother would give to my sister. When my sister went to school I was left at home with my mother and our daily. We spent many productive hours together, my mother teaching me how to thread and use a sewing machine, darn socks and do elementary cooking. During this year or so, I had little contact with men, my brother away doing his national service and my father mostly at work or out in the country. I do remember my brother coming home on leave, spit and polishing his boots, and then off back to base. The fourteen years between us meant that we hardly knew each other until we were much older.

It was an unfortunate position we found ourselves in at school. We had no choice over which school we would prefer to go to, and probably would have chosen my father's believing it to be the best and most progressive in town. My father was determined that we should have no preferential treatment, and often dealt out unfair punishment or made examples of us in front of our peers in order to prove his point. It was not a very happy time in my life. I was always teased either because of my relationship to the headmaster, or because of my physical weediness. I don't remember having many friends, and those that I did have were either chosen for me by my parents or their parents, thinking that we were socially suitable for each other. It was hard for me to relate to my contemporaries, particularly as we were not allowed to play with the council estate kids out on the street. I remember hanging on our front gate, wishing and wishing to join the kids who were roller-skating on the other side of the fence. It was not until I went to secondary school that I was able to make friends of my own choosing, and experience the pleasure of socializing.

We had a very large garden in which to play, part of which was left wild with an orchard and long grass. It was in many ways a child's paradise, allowing us a lot of freedom in which to use our imaginations. It was here that we had a mock wedding, and used to enact the Christmas story. In the garden shed, out of sight of the world, I made my first attempts at sexual intercourse with my sister's friends. We knew what to do in order to create a baby, but I lacked the ability and knowledge to get it together. It was a thing we did because it was daring, like running around the garden naked. Already at the age of nine, even before I could have an erection, I knew of the guilt that surrounded anything to do with the genital area.

Ritual seemed an important thing to me, even though we never went to church. When I was about ten, I wanted to explore and experience the different kinds of church ceremony, and in this I had encouragement from my parents. I think they were very confused in their ideas of how they wished us to think about the church, and so left me to find out for myself. They believed that education by experience is an ideal thing, so long as the areas of exploration fitted in with their moral values.

It was fortunate that my father had holidays at the same time as we did; thus we knew him better than most children know their fathers. Our activities with him were always planned and decided for us by him. Many hours were spent with him gardening or out bird watching and generally learning about natural history. I am grateful to him for giving me this knowledge. But I don't think I ever had a close relationship with him. It was usually one where he was the teacher and I the pupil; he always cut the hedge and I picked up the clippings. He found it hard to accept weaklings, and particularly so when his son was a physical weed like I was. I was a disappointment to him because I was useless at sports, and the more manly activities of the world. He would not be defeated by my inability to play football and took over coaching the school team, and he put me on the right wing.

My mother, to whom I related much more easily, openly and emotionally, had no expectations of me in this way. She had aspirations for me in other directions, and when I failed my 11+, they were both down on me like a ton of bricks. Combined with this failure, I seemed to be cracking up in other directions. I had a habit of crying if the least little thing went wrong – this, of course, made my father furious. It was a vicious circle; I was too afraid to ask for help because I thought he would shout at me 'grow up and be a man' and I would cry, or I would cry because I could not get help because I was too afraid. At this time I also developed a series of nervous twitches, which, looking back, must have been very upsetting for my parents. I would literally be unable to walk down the street without having to scratch my crotch, twitch my head, and blink my eyes almost continually. A series of visits were made to doctors, opticians etc. in the company of my father, who would always exonerate himself of any blame and then cast me into the lion's den. They always agreed with my father that it was my fault, and there was really nothing wrong with me.

I carried on twitching and taking phenobarbitone until I was about twelve or thirteen, and it was then that I was able to assume a little independence. Rather than send me to the local boy's secondary modern school, I went to a local art secondary school in a neighbouring town. This was probably one of the most fortunate things to happen to me. I was left to find my own way in the world without the social back-up from my parents' position. I travelled every day to and from school on the train unattended by adults, and to my surprise I could do it. I now had friends and a life of my own outside the family. I stayed at this school for five years which were very beneficial to me. I perhaps strayed further from the path my parents had chosen for me than they wished, but now I realize how much happier I was.

It was good for me to be able to make my own decisions and live a life out of the control of my parents. Being rebellious seemed to suit me, and gave me a lot of scope – from vandalizing trains to attempting a change in school policy. I was given even more freedom for development when, in my fourth year, my father had a heart attack. It did more for my relationship with my parents than any other single event. They were now dependent on me for my help and cooperation, and I felt I had more of an equal footing with them. I took over many of the jobs that my father used to do, and I was given greater responsibility and trust than before.

It was strange to me and also upsetting to be in such a confused state. Here I was helping my mother run the house as a man, and at the same time being treated like a schoolboy. I was small for my age and I felt physically inadequate. The other boys in my class were well developed, with broadening shoulders, light beards, and large cocks. I started dreaming of having hair on my chest and face, longing for a big cock and muscular body. No matter how hard I prayed my body still didn't change, and I put a lot of energy and time into praying to God, though I soon realized that he did not have supreme power. My mind became occupied with thoughts and visions of a strong manly body.

One summer term I caught chicken pox, and had to stay in bed for a long time. When I did finally get up and dress, my clothes were too short in the legs and sleeves: I had grown whilst in bed. I went back to school the following term as tall as my contemporaries, and I felt high, literally. Puberty, this enigma which had been discussed in biology classes and with my friends, was mine at last. Life seemed to become progressively better, I had girlfriends and I became one of the lads. The changes seemed rapid, no sooner had I experienced a first 'French kiss' than the next step, touching a breast, was followed by putting my hand up a skirt. I was now accepted as an equal with the rest of the boys in my class and started a good friendship with a boy called Stuart. We used to smoke grass together, and go out after school to mess about with girls. We would listen to the Beach Boys and the Animals, get incensed with energy and go out rampaging around the neighbourhood. Alas, I had to leave my friends and transfer to my local grammar school to take an 'A' level course.

Rules and regulations were much more in evidence at my new school, uniform was compulsory, and strict timetables were created to keep us in line. Here the children, despite my preconceptions, were immature and frightened because of five years of intense restriction. I found it hard to relate to many of them because they were so straight and obedient. Again I lucked out and spent much of my time in the art department with the livelier elements in the school. Here I had a very inspired and hard-working teacher who did much to help me. I worked very hard with and for her, and it was then that I decided to go to art school. At the time I thought she had a very outgoing and liberal consciousness, which did a lot to help me channel my energies into creative activities. I had a few good friends in the art department, some of whom were the friends of my sister who was also studying art. I think that because of my forwardness and promiscuity I was an embarrassment to her, and our relationship which had not been so good for a long time deteriorated even more.

I was very deeply influenced by the philosophy of free love and 'flower power', which was in its heyday. I spent much of my free time hitch-hiking to London to hang around Piccadilly and various discotheques that were popular at the time. I had many one night stands with women at this time, none of which grew into anything lasting. I learnt a lot, because of the social climate, about how to relate to people more openly and freely, in an apparently more loving way. It was a time of great change, gays were coming out and the parks were full of flower children and hippies; it was an exciting time to be in swinging London. I was determined to be 'where it was at', but never seemed to make it. I was still on the periphery.

I was ignorant of the joys of homosexuality until one day when out on a field trip with a friend, he suggested we go into the woods and mutually masturbate. This we enjoyed and repeated it many times in secluded secret places. Having finally related to a male sexually, I felt it much easier to get along with other men and start up new gay relationships. After masturbating in the woods and fields of Wiltshire, I started having a very exploitative relationship with a man who lived in West Kensington. This man, who was a dealer, based life and its worth on dope and money, would screw me and pay me off in dope or cash. I enjoyed being paid for the service I did him, because it added to the pleasure I got from the humiliation I felt from being screwed. It was also an exciting contrast to the clean, healthy life of the country and school. I gained confidence now that I felt I was getting something exciting and pleasurable out of life. Even though I felt good in gay relationships there was no way that I would admit to myself or the world that I was a 'browner', and I would counter each homosexual experience with a heterosexual one.

At school I just didn't seem to fit in. I was neither a 'rugger-bugger' nor an effeminate academic, and consequently most of my friends were girls with whom I had more in common. I was popular in some ways, particularly for my outgoing defiance of authority. In my upper-sixth I became appointed prefect, which was much against my principles. I went to see the headmaster, who told me that I was especially chosen to make me take responsibility and conform to the school system. I think he was surprised that I didn't want to control little boys and throw them out in the cold and wet at break times. I once swore as an eleven year old that I would never become a power maniac and do such cruel things, but I was forced to under threat of expulsion. I hated my duty, but found a way to enjoy it by starting lunchtime discos in the school hall. With the help of my good friend from field trip days, we got a good thing going. The next shock in my career as administrator and ruler was to be elected house captain. There was no way out of this situation because I was elected by my fellow house-mates. Fortunately I was able to minimize my duties, and had little to do except pick someone to read from the Bible at house prayers. I was supposed to choose a team and organize practices for sports day. I explained to my house that because of the destructive competitiveness of the event, I felt that sports day was a waste of time. If they wanted our house to enter, then it was up to them to form a committee to organize it. There didn't seem to be a competitive element in the house and so no team was entered. Sports day came, and I felt that I had let my house down. I could not stand the tension on the sports field, so went home feeling very depressed. I tried to think about how I would have felt if I had entered a team; there are always losers in any race, and I think, having been a loser too many times before, that I would have felt more depressed than I already did. It was an obvious assumption that we would be losers; I never seem to win when it comes to 'good honest sportsmanship'.

I had to use other methods to get ahead, and so I bluffed and hasseled my way into Art School, even going so far as to lie on my application form as to how many 'O' levels I had. When I was found out I was so well inched into college that I was able to tell the truth, which was that I believed my academic qualifications had little to do with my talents as an artist, and that misrepresentation of my exam results could do me nothing but good. I was right, and my story fell upon sympathetic ears and my principal did all he could to help me stay. I could never tell anyone else about this because I felt guilt for my dishonesty. Even now I don't think I could tell my father, because he would be shocked by my deceit. To him the truth is to be respected, lies and liars to be treated with contempt. Telling lies was worth it, and I spent four very happy and interesting years at college. Here I met many good friends, three of whom I live with now. It was an easy place to make contact with one's contemporaries and staff because it was an isolated community in a small English country town. The college was idyllic in its surroundings, a large stately home in glorious parklands and gardens.

In my pre-diploma year I had a tutor whom I became very fond of, who told us that he thought it was his job to help us unlearn all that we had previously been taught. I thought that this was strange, but as the weeks went by it clicked with me as to what he was trying to do. He was the seed of the process by which I started to find out about myself for myself, and to think about myself as what I was and not what society was making me. This is a continuing thing which has taken me in many directions, one of which was to take L.S.D. This hallucinogenic is an exciting, exhilarating and exhausting way of getting one's kicks. After each trip I would feel drained, for the most part, of the knowledge of my former self, and I would begin to re-create, in a way which seemed honest, my new self. This in itself is an hallucination, because I could only create for myself from the limits of my experience.

Taking drugs was an important and influential part of my life at college. It was more important to me than classes on three dimensional design or typography. I could rise at 2.30 a.m. for a trip at sunrise on a June morning, but I would find it hard to make it to the college for a 10 a.m. class. Some friends of mine moved into a flat which my art teacher had recently vacated. No. 8 became the centre of my life; here I had good friends who I could smoke with, and it was a refuge from my parents. It became a No. 8 custom to take cough mixture on a Saturday night. We would sit around and force ourselves to drink half a bottle of revolting mixture, because we knew it would give us something exciting to do all evening and something to talk about all next day. Everything became happy and often hysterical, and we would go for long walks in the park visiting spots which had become important landmarks to us. Bundled up in coats and wellington boots, we would trudge off into the November mists and fantasize in a world that was all our own. The people of No. 8 became very close and would usually meet together for coffee, lunch and tea in the cafeteria. We were a very large family who for the most part loved each other, and did most things together as a group. From the outside, we became known as drug-crazed hippies, who I think were often feared and revered.

Because of the new influences on my life, my relationship with a girl, Liz, with whom I had been going steady since I was at school, began to break up. The break-up was a slow and ridiculous thing which went on for about five months. We had only been seeing each other at week-ends and consequently grew apart, as we had less time together and less in common. There was also pressure from my parents, particularly my mother, to dissolve the affair. My first reaction to this pressure was to intensify the relationship, but then the pressure had the desired effect, and sad as it was, we parted company. We had had a sympathy for natural and man-made beauty which had brought us together. We had created a very romantic dream between us, one that we couldn't quite hold on to. There were times when we did succeed, like lying naked in a field of corn and making love – and how good I felt when I received a valentine embroidered with a message in hair plucked from her head, which told me how much she loved me. The illusion was too fragile and burst like a bubble, but we refused to believe that it had done so. We had spent week-ends in bed together and talked of having our own family, a cottage and a cosy life, but I knew that it would not work.

The summer of my first year I went away for a holiday with Vicky, a friend from No. 8. We were just good friends, and we expected everyone to believe us. Liz thought that I had ulterior motives, and at this point we finally split up. In retrospect, I think our parents took us seriously, and thought that it was good that we were going out to educate ourselves in art history and the culture of Italy. It was an amazing holiday and started out on a good note. I was introduced to Nick, a ballet dancer friend of Vicky's. I was fascinated by this man who was so overtly gay. It was extraordinary for me to meet someone who was not afraid to show himself for what he was. We spent an enjoyable evening together, and I again felt reassurance that I should be myself and not feel guilty, constantly hiding an important part of myself. It was also reassuring to see that Vicky's parents accepted him for what he was, and obviously liked him a lot.

It was my first holiday abroad and was full of all the adventure necessary to meet my wildest dreams of foreign travel. We spent the night stranded under a bridge in a very dramatic thunderstorm in

Bari, broke into a Youth Hostel in Brindisi, and were solicited in Naples to pose for pornographic pictures. All these events I enjoyed to their fullest. I certainly was getting my kicks. When feeling that we were in a particularly exhilarating or dangerous situation, we would sing a Shirley MacLaine number, 'If my friends could see me now'. It became our theme tune – our link with home. Having only each other to talk to meant that we got to know each other very well, and despite our isolation our relationship held together well.

The return to college was good. I felt I had achieved an important goal in my career. Travel had for me a status which I wished to have; and I found it important to impress upon people how glamorous I was. Vicky and I had remained 'just good friends', despite our friends' preconceptions that the relationship would blossom on the sexual front. I had no inclination, except when being offered money in Naples, to sleep with Vicky. Typically it was not until I read her diary when we returned that I realized how she felt. It was still a long time before we finally got it together; it was as if our friendship didn't need a sexual side to it. I don't think it did, and no great change took place after we had slept together.

My relationship to Julia was different, as it started out with a sexual communication. The first time I saw her was across a village hall sorting through jumble at a sale, and I thought what 'come to bed with me' eyes she had. I later met her briefly at No. 8, and then more regularly when I used to score for her. We never said much to each other except on one occasion when we happened to be on our own in the flat. It was hard to talk with her because I was constantly looking for the opportunity to turn the conversation around to getting her into bed with me. It was a while after this when Vicky, Julia and I were sitting around one evening coming down off a dose of cough mixture that we got to talking about the way we felt about women asking men to go to bed with them. We all agreed that it was fine, and that women should be able to get out there and get a piece of the action. It was easy to agree as we all felt secure enough not to be threatened by it. It was fine until Julia suggested that she and I should go to bed together. I could see no reason why not, and it was what I desired very much. The next morning was not so happy when I realized that I had hurt Vicky. I could not see why, when we had for a long time believed that sexual freedom was important.

I had bought a caravan and had parked it in a paddock belonging to a local doctor, who was liberal minded and gave me complete freedom. This is where we spent our first night together and soon we had a very domestic scene going. We realized after a while that we both needed more people around and started living at No. 8 again. We would return and live in the caravan again when pressures from the landlord forced us to leave, as he thought we were running a brothel. Sometimes we would leave No. 8 carrying bundles of pillows and blankets because we wanted to be on our own again.

There was a constant flow of people through No. 8, friends of people who lived there, friends of friends, new tenants, and the odd policeman. It was always a popular place to live and had a waiting-list of would-be tenants. It was a first floor and attic flat above a very old and smelly butcher's shop, a warren of rooms on different levels. I usually spent all my holidays there except during the summer. It was an attractive place to live, no warden, no supervisor, we ran the place ourselves. We had many jolly parties, spontaneous and planned. It was a hive of social activity where we would entertain and be entertained. I remember occasions when we would dress up and paint ourselves and go off to college dances. One time I dressed up as Diana Ross, Julia as a sadist/leather freak, Tim as a duchess and Hilary as a schoolboy. Dressing up seemed a creative way to spend an evening and we all had a lot of fun. There was plenty of make-up around and a junk room full of clothes and oddments. We were always good at borrowing and begging for things we needed to complete our images.

My time at college was very decadent – week-ends spent in country mansions with swimming pools and parties, time and more time to think about oneself. Corsham was a place where I felt what I had learnt, I'd learnt despite the college curriculum. The most important thing I learnt was the pleasure of friendship, and happy times spent in company other than my family.

Julia and I did most things together, going to festivals, parties and picnics. The countryside around Corsham lent itself to bathing in the river and picnics on the downs, or the occasional night trip to the beach. We grew to know and love each other very much, and the summer she went away to stay with her parents was very sad for us. It was the first time I had cried when parting with somebody. We were apart all summer and I felt very lonely and depressed. It was bad news to go and live with my parents again. I spent all summer working in a chicken packing factory, which was a real bring-down. I found that I was compelled to whistle at girls, and make rude comments at them each time they passed, and involve myself in horse play in the toilets and sneak off to the pub at lunch time. I had to assume a different personality in order to conform to the standards of bored chicken processors. Every job was extremely repetitive, and to break the monotony we would either sabotage the machinery and cause a breakdown, or pick on an old woman, or a young and frightened boy, and tease them unmercifully. Life in the factory was so dead and uneventful that huge arguments would take place among us over petty issues, like people taking a six instead of five minute break.

I was so pleased to have Julia back, and after reorientating ourselves, we found out how happy we were to be together again. Returning to college I met Carol who was a tutor of mine. She was an inspired woman who introduced me to new influences like Genet, and William Burroughs, both of whom changed my consciousness. She too, lived to some degree by their philosophies, which was the way I wanted to live. But there was and still is this continuous conflict between wanting to be adventurous, and, on the other side of the coin, wanting a happy, secure domestic scene like the rest of my family. We would discuss this problem and yet never came up with a solution. She no longer lived with her husband, and now went travelling around the world, with apparently no responsibility to anyone except herself. I was not and have not yet been in that position, because I need the 'security' of a domestic relationship, which I have grown more and more dependent on. Carol has drifted off to who knows where, and someone I had loved and grown to know well is like a dream to me now. Carol's visits once a week to college were a highlight, a glimmer of hope. She would arrive from Amsterdam with the latest issue of 'Suck' magazine, or from London with a file full of new drawings. She would bring news of the gay scene, and tell me about the most recent drag ball she had been to, or how David Hockney was. She was always looking for something, a harmony which she never knew, and could not find.

Julia quit college but continued to live in Corsham, and worked to support herself in various ways in the neighbourhood. At the end of the year she went to live in London, where I would go and visit her at week-ends. I then moved in with her for the summer, during which time I worked washing dishes in a canteen. I was so pleased that at long last I was living in a city. Though we had little money, it seemed like a fortune compared with a student grant, and we led a jolly and exciting life, eating out, shopping, going to movies, visiting and being picked up by men. It seemed that men found me attractive – never before had I felt so wanted, and it made me feel so good. I liked being picked up as a woman is, treated to drinks, and to be escorted to bed, never having to make a decision myself.

During this holiday I got a letter from college which told me that if

I didn't pull my socks up and start working I would be asked to leave. I didn't know quite what to do, stay in town and have a good time, or go back to college and complete my course. In true timidity I went back and worked. Julia came back as well, and Carol was there too, and all seemed to be centred around work. Julia was re-applying to art school, and I was applying to the Royal College. It was my final year and suddenly I seemed to be enjoying working, and received my first freelance work to illustrate a book about astrology. The author was a very strange man, steeped in occultism, which made him extremely fascinating. He and Julia seemed to get along very well together, and she started to live and work with him. I was left on my own, probably a good thing, but I didn't think so at the outset. I began to put my energies into my work and making new friendships. I realized then that I had to make my own decisions, and be generally more outgoing. It was difficult without Julia's support and help, and I missed her a lot. I realized that domestic 'bliss' is not as secure as I had thought, and came to the conclusion that one should never expect the total security of a relationship that I had. Not wanting to think about my new situation, I raced around completing work for my exhibition and plans to visit America. I was driven by the thought of finishing and leaving, leaving for good.

In America, I felt I had escaped and that I had my freedom. But that too I realized was not true, I was responsible to others, and I never could be an island. I met up with Julia in Florida where we had a glorious holiday and reunion. We travelled around together and finally parted in New York. When Julia flew back to London and her other man, my feelings were mixed. I was pleased to be in N.Y. but felt sad that I would not be sharing my life with Julia, and resented her going back to her lover. I knew I had no rights over her but I felt incredibly possessive and jealous. I stayed in N.Y. for a while and then returned to work in Florida.

In N.Y. I had met Juan, a Venezualan who had asked me to come and live with him in Caracas. Florida to me was a stepping-stone, a place to earn some money. I had been in Florida but two days when there was a phone call from Julia's mother, saying that Julia would be in Miami next afternoon. I was thrilled, I had felt so lonely in the previous two days that the prospect of Julia returning was too good to be true. She and I lived together for a year in our old apartment in the old downtown area of Stuart. Stuart is a redneck small-time town with big shot ideas. Of course the icing on the cake was thin, and great pressure was put on us to get married. We didn't want to get married as we believed it was a social imposition on our relationship which it did not need. Julia would receive delegations of aunts persuading her that marriage was the best thing for a woman, I was still intending to go to Caracas and live with Juan, which was something I had to do on my own, but I felt incredible pressure to get married in order to prove to the world that I was not gay. It was also advantageous to get married so that I could get the necessary status to stay and work in the States. After much deliberation, and because we were broke and couldn't really afford to leave Stuart, we got married.

We were now accepted into a society which treated us like newly-weds, and railroaded us more and more into playing traditional roles. Our wedding presents were for our home, and my career with Julia's uncle blossomed; another incentive for gaoling ourselves behind a white picket fence. From the day we got married it was Julia's sole intention to leave Stuart. Life in most ways was boring and the monotony was broken by visits from friends, drinking, smoking grass, and shopping trips to Palm Beach. I make it sound bad because for the most part that was how it was, living in a small town full of decrepit reactionary old people and shuffle board courts. To me it was fascinating to be living in a soap opera, but I was unable to see out and realize what was happening to us. I became possessed by the materialism, and struggled hard and climbed fast the ladder of 'success'. I was becoming successful, I was rich, I was hooked on the 'American Dream'.

We eventually left and returned to London. I felt the town was very claustrophobic, and could not believe how lethargic people were. Everything seemed small and complacent and I found it hard to tolerate. After a month of travelling around and visiting friends we decided to leave, and go and visit Julia's parents in Indo-China. I was pleased to leave England – it just seemed that nothing was happening. Anyway there was no status to be gained from living at home, and no privilege to be gained from being a native. There were many good things that I missed about America, the hospitality, and the outgoing personality of the people – not to mention their state of mind with regard to body consciousness. For example, wearing shorts in the streets in this country is unpleasant, because of the rude comments one gets shouted at one. Yet in America, whether you be tall, fat, thin or short, no one minds. Also while in Florida, I had grown to believe that it was important to make money in order to be happy, and I felt that the limited funds which most English people dispose of, limited one's scope for enjoyment and happiness.

How mistaken I was, and this I realized by living in Laos where people have very little and seem happier than they are in America.

Most people had smiles on their faces and were willing to be friendly and loving to each other. Probably because they did not have the worries of being a member of a 'dog eat dog' society, or the worries of having property and protecting it. Here I found out what exploitation and privilege was, because there was no middle class to smudge the boundaries between the ruling class and the serfs. I learnt the tyranny of colonization and imperialism and the merits of socialism. At the same time, I lived with Americans, probably the worst variety, Nixon diplomats. I went to diplomatic parties, and met many generals and attachés. I was a privileged person, but I found it nauseating to have so much when the majority had so little.

I was able to get a job teaching English to Lao people who wished to work for the Americans. This I enjoyed very much, mostly because it brought me in contact with Lao people who could speak English. I had three classes, one of middle-aged men with whom I found I could make little contact, and two other classes with students of about my own age, who I got on well with. It was hard and rewarding work, and I found it taxed my mind considerably. It was good to talk with these young people, and find out what they wished from life and how they viewed it. Life to them was slow and simple, as they were not hungry they could sit on the back of a water-buffalo, or smoke a pipe and watch the sunset and be happy. When I asked what they did with their time off they said that they slept. Sleep to them was a luxurious source of enjoyment. Their happiness in their simplicity of life made a great impression on me. I felt in the short time I was there that I had received an illuminating education which I would never forget.

We were sorry to leave, but living with one's in-laws becomes a strain. Our relationship seemed to deteriorate under these circumstances. We returned to London broke, but really grateful that we had had the experiences of Laos. London seemed extremely wealthy compared with Vientiane and Bangkok, and I seemed to find it much easier to fit in. It was wonderful to be no longer treated as a married couple but as ourselves again. I played around for the next eighteen months, not really knowing what I was doing or where I was going. I was in a state of confusion. Finally I got a job in a design agency which neither suited me nor my employers. This lasted a long five weeks. During this period I met David, who was a young and rich businessman who was a good friend while he still fancied me. I enjoyed myself with him, I liked the gay life he showed me. He treated me like most men treat their women. This I could take so much of, but being a man and having been conditioned to be assertive, I found the continuous humiliation hard to take. Our relationship ended when I was in Paris with him and would not sleep with him when and how he wanted. He could not understand that what he had paid for was not his to use and abuse at his whim.

I learnt a lot about the way women probably feel about their relationships with men, and about how I was treating Julia. I don't know how much I changed from my own initiative, but at this time Julia was getting involved in sexual politics, and I most definitely had to change in order to go on living with her. We were again living together as a couple in Hampstead, and when Julia became pregnant we had to move to a new home, and decided that we wanted to live with a group of people and not as a nuclear family. This we thought would allow us to be ourselves as individuals. We moved south of the river into a large flat with two friends from college.

It was our aim when we set up our household to break away from the traditional methods of housekeeping, and create a situation where both men and women cooked and cleaned, or fixed a shelf and did the decorating. A place where our child could see that she would not have to be good at cooking in order to get her man. A place where she could see the importance of women having freedom to do their own work, and not just look after the kids and house. A place where she could experience the strength of women and the tenderness of men. A place where reality could exist, where people could be themselves regardless of their sex. A place where people whose sexuality was of their own choosing could be together. A place where she could be cared for by people other than her biological parents.

In January, after six months of adjusting to being parents, Julia had a daughter. It was difficult to realize that this new situation was for keeps. I had great problems adjusting to the reality of the situation, and to take the great weight and seriousness of supporting my family on my shoulders. I had great hang-ups about not having a respectable career ahead of me as most men in my class and situation did. I would leave Julia each morning and go to work and come home in the evening to play with the baby. It was harder still for Julia who did not wish to be at home full time to fulfil her part of the bargain. These things conflicted greatly with our politics and Julia was not to be beaten. With her initiative, and help and support from her women's group, we have been able to resolve the situation to some degree by forming a neighbourhood crèche. A great amount of resentment built up in me because I thought I was doing more work than she was.

Now that a more equal responsibility for child care has developed in the household, I enjoy living with Bronnie. I find that having a child has brought me out in that I have to relate to more people purely because my daughter is so sociable. I am learning about how we are conditioned into having prejudices and guilts. Bronnie is constantly harassed by people, the media to be a sweet, pretty, innocent little maid who sucks up to men. It is sickening to see the power society wields over our children.

Through Julia's and Suzie's (the other woman who lives in our household) connection with the feminist movement, I joined a group of men who aim to break down the barriers of sexist stereotyping. Before I met these men the only man I had as a friend was Tim. I have been in this group for about eighteen months, and feel that these men are now good friends of mine. Because of my relationship with them I find it easier to relate to all men. I find that I can understand why men are as they are, and how I am more like them and they more like me. We have realized some of the things which make relationships between men difficult. I now recognize the conditioning that men experience to make them competitive and alienate them from their brothers. I see how we are dragged into the fight for the top where we are forced to be more productive to no gain, fight wars, and trample on our weaker brothers and keep them in their place. We are taught that it is unnatural for men to have emotional friendships, and is only encouraged when comradeship can be manipulated to make one group of men fight another.

John and I have been making out together for nearly a year now, making this the longest homosexual relationship I have had. When the relationship started it seemed that things went well, especially in bed. It was the first time that I felt I was having a sexual relationship that was equal. There was no dominant partner, no fucker and no fuckee, it was good and I felt that I had found what I had always been looking for. Having such good feelings about my new relationship made it possible for me to be more honest with Julia than I had been in the past. It seemed that all went well, Julia was extremely supportive and encouraged the relationship. Her only misgivings are that it is an exclusive relationship.

My relationship with John is not as strong as it used to be, sexually it is no longer equal, and socially we have little in common. I have tried to integrate John into the rest of my life, my work, the group etc., but the only times he has attempted to see me out of his little world have been when he came to visit me when the rest of the household were away. It is a shame that we don't live closer lives, because sex and gossip don't seem to have held the relationship together.

There seems to be a split between my gay life and my straight life. I am the only gay person in my household, and because I feel isolated in that area, I tend to divorce my gay life from my home life. I wish that there could be greater harmony between the two, but I have yet to accomplish it. There has never been any judgement made by my household or friends about my sexuality. It is the pressures of society which make it a problem to me. So until I can make my bisexuality a corporate sexuality in my mind I will not have resolved the problem.

8 GORDON

At the time of my birth my mother was forty and my father fifty-five. Father was a gentle and creative man, rather weak, who desired nothing but to bring up his family in peace and earn his living. He hated arguments. He was partly disabled (disorderly action of the heart and neurasthenia) from having been blown up and gassed in the 1914–18 war. He had no hobby but work. I do not think he had any friends. He did not get on well with my mother's relations who were all richer than us. Father loved us children deeply. Despite constant aggravation from my mother, I think he loved her too. He died in 1948 when I was twenty-five, and I missed him deeply. I still regret I did not know him better.

My mother is still alive, now in an old people's home, after living with me for the past ten years. I am the only one of the three children who would ever have had her live with them. In all my life I have never known my mother profess to be in good health. Ninety-nine per cent of her illness was pretence, and the other real. We have had frequent false death-bed scenes, etc. I think she is wicked, selfish, insincere, lazy, deceitful, vain and cunning. When she was younger she was attractive and very sociable. I was a latch-key child, returning daily from school to an empty cold dark house because Mother would be out playing cards every day – whist, poker etc. I now think that she probably had affairs too. Father earned a very good living (£9 per week pre-war) but we were always broke because my mother frittered the money away – mainly on herself. We were constantly in debt, yet we had a daily charwoman and even a maid at one time. Yet we owed money to shops and relations, and it was often a cause of shame to me. The home was neglected and comfortless. I wore my cousin's cast-off clothes. She tortured us by subtle alternate loving/neglecting. To this day she enjoys creating emotional situations and distress to all around her. My brother is still in a state about her – cannot face her alone, and my sister has regular nightmares about her childhood and the parental home of those days.

When I was pre-school I was sometimes mother's little special darling, and she sometimes spoiled me and created tension between me and my siblings. She indulged her own fancies; sometimes talked of running away from home and taking me with her. Other times she would ignore me. Once when I was nine I met her in the street with one of her woman friends; she ignored me, and when I spoke to her she said: 'Run away little boy. I don't know you!' – presumably because I was dirty and ragged and needed a haircut and she was ashamed of me.

Background of the family is Catholic on both sides. Father gave up Catholicism in despair in the trenches in 1917. Mother was an orthodox Catholic, full of superstition and ignorance about the whole subject.

I think my emotional development re sex was fairly normal up to the age of about ten, though I was a soft boy – often bullied at school. I had a somewhat girlish appearance and did not like rough sports. At about age ten or eleven, just before puberty, I had an unfortunate experience when I was slightly interfered with by a crank in a lavatory cubicle. He did me no harm, and did not expose himself. He could not have got much satisfaction from it as I was too frightened and too young to respond and did not get an erection. He tricked me into the lav with him on the pretence he would give me 'a special massage that would make me strong'. I was very scared, later very remorseful and eventually tearfully told my parents. I do not think the incident was important to my development.

I think I learned the facts of sex initially from school friends and got the details a bit mixed up. But soon I read a good book called *How You Began* which I got from the public library, and got that sorted out. I think I was about eleven when I came to puberty. I had thoroughly enjoyed playing with the genitals of other boys at school for some time before I had my first orgasm, and I think I had seen other boys ejaculate. I produced my first orgasm by masturbation in bed, and it may be significant that, needing some lubrication, I stole a pot of vaseline from beside my father's bed for the occasion. I had some mixed up feelings for a few days after my first orgasm, confused because I had not expected the intense feelings around my rectum when I came. I had visited the Zoo a few days previously and seen apes with hideous backsides, and I wondered if the same would happen to me! From then on there was much more sex play with other boys at school, which I found tremendously thrilling. I got caught once by the headmaster who took no action. There were daily mutual masturbation sessions at the school. This was the only sort of friendship I had to any extent. The other boys led me in the sex play, but, because I did not play games, I was not popular. There was one boy who I thought quite beautiful and we did have something of a friendship. It was with him that I first got the idea of wanting to put my penis into his rectum, but he would not let me. Eventually we went off each other. During school years from about twelve to fifteen I went out with girls sometimes, and there were a few timid kisses. There was one girl that excited me, and I got as far as investigating her breasts and vulva, but it did not occur to me to try and have intercourse.

I left school at fifteen. Up to that time I had never achieved anything else but mutual masturbation with other boys, and I generally self-masturbated at least once a day. When I was about thirteen I discovered rectal masturbation, a practice which I have never completely stopped. I used various phalli to excite my rectum while masturbating. I was nearly thirty before I discovered that I could have a good satisfying orgasm without having an erection. From fifteen to seventeen were lonely years. I started work but could not make contact with boys. There were one or two girl flirtations but I remained a virgin. When I was seventeen I went into the Army and soon found other young men who would indulge in sex play – not usually regularly, and most times when they were tipsy and I was pretending to be.

I did not seriously attempt intercourse until I was nearly nineteen, but I had a premature ejaculation and it was a failure. The frenchletter was inhibiting too. One girl whom I had known before I went into the Army was the object of some emotional feelings, and I was about nineteen when I thought I wanted to marry her. My mother put a stop to that, and I immediately got engaged on the rebound to the girl who was to be my first wife, Lucinda. She was a tall girl, taller than me, and a Roman Catholic. Very prim and prudish, stupid too, with all kinds of silly habits. It has always been a mystery to me why I went ahead with the marriage when I knew we did not have a thing in common. I think in retrospect, I would like to have married her younger sister, who would have nothing to do with me. This pattern was repeated later in my life, strangely enough. Before

I married Lucinda I had done no more than kiss her (lips only – not tongues). We were married when I was nineteen and she was, I think, twenty-eight. It was a disaster. She never had an orgasm during the five years of our marriage. I was very unhappy most of the time. I had many more orgasms from self-masturbation than from intercourse with her. She used to pretend to enjoy the sex and simulate orgasms, but I now realize they were false. We had two children who are now thirty-one and twenty-nine. Lucinda and I had constant arguments, and I thought she was stupid and unreasonable. I came out of the Army when I was twenty-three in 1945, and two years later I left her because I could stand her no longer, and feared I might kill her, she aggravated me so.

I moved to digs in Chelsea and for a little while I drank rather a lot. I met a few girls, but at first was not very successful in keeping them or satisfying them. I started to meet homosexual men, and I had several affairs and a few one-night-stands. I was disgusted with the queens. What I wanted was to meet a manly man and be the passive one, but I never met anyone I liked. I had an intense affair with a very nice girl and she wanted to marry me, and I went off her. Then, when very lonely and depressed one evening I went out with the intention of picking up a girl – any sort of a girl, and I met one called Carol. She was a bisexual girl, a virgin (or nearly) and we had an affair. Unfortunately, after a while I made her pregnant. Carol was a slut, and even if I had been free I would not have married her. But I offered her to live with me while she was pregnant, because her parents were ashamed to have her at home with a fat belly, on the strict understanding that she had the baby adopted when it came. Carol used to bring home girls, and I used to take an interest in them too. One girl she brought home was called Pamela. Eventually Pamela moved in with us, and we had a ménage-à-trois fairly successfully for a while. Then the baby came and we had a dreadful time while Carol made up her mind to part with it. After the baby went, she soon left, because my divorce from Lucinda had come through and Pamela wanted to marry me. I must explain that Pamela had a younger sister, Julia, and I was keen on her. But Pamela and I got married, and Julia wept at our wedding, and even on our wedding day I realized I had married the wrong one (AGAIN!). The marriage with Pamela was not a success. She did not have orgasms either, though her main reason in wanting us to be married was to overcome her difficulty in this respect. I was not unhappy, but not satisfied. I had a few light flirtations with men without success. Then I started to have an affair with Julia, Pamela's sister.

It was very good, and she appeared to have good orgasms. The relationship with Pamela deteriorated and she started to have affairs with other men. Eventually we broke up. There was a difficult period when Pamela and Julia went, and I tried going back to Lucinda for a while! I was so lonely and depressed, but of course that did not work, and I reverted to going with men. After a dreadful year, Julia at last agreed to come back to me, and we have been together for twenty-three years, having got married in Scotland.

Julia and I have four children and it is a very happy marriage. It works because she is tolerant and turns a blind eye to my escapades. When we first were married I was faithful to Julia, but after a few years I got very restless and unsatisfied. My sexual behaviour over the past eighteen or twenty-three years has been very mixed. I have lived with Julia and had sex with her. I have had intermittent relationships with men, and one or two longer friendships – the relationships invariably being broken off by me because I become bored or disgusted. I have done some things of which I am ashamed – like contact through cottaging on a few occasions. I did have a brief affair with a girl once during my marriage but it did not work – I did not have enough free time or money at that stage. Through all the years I have had some kind of sex experience almost every day – if only masturbation. The frequency of intercourse with Julia used to be three times weekly, but this has declined a little in recent years – my fault, I don't fancy her as strongly as I did because the intercourses are so brief (she is not a well woman and gets tired), and there are other factors which I don't want to write about.

About eight years ago I got entangled with an attractive woman, Carmen, sister of the cousin whose cast-off clothes I wore as a boy. When her marriage broke up she took a lover; when her affair broke up I flew to her side to comfort her, and was in bed with her inside ten minutes. We had a consuming, passionate affair that lasted about two years. Sex with Carmen was marvellous. Super orgasms and lots of them. But she was mentally kinky – had ex-boy friends all over the world who had run away from her because she was driving them mad. She is what I call a man-eater. She could have upward of twenty orgasms in one intercourse lasting an hour. And repeat it all two hours later. Eventually she wanted me to leave Julia and go to America with her. I nearly did, I was so besotted with her. My marriage was in danger and I was in a total psychological mess – obsessed with Carmen and my work going to pieces. I broke down and told Julia all about it. Disaster, it looked as if our marriage was on the rocks. But she fought to keep us together. One evening, when

I got very drunk, I told her about the attraction of Carmen, and how I could not cope with her, and yet she was sucking me dry of life. I confessed to Julia that I was a bisexual, and that the attraction of Carmen was that she is a really bossy butch woman – domineering yet attractive, tough-minded and very intelligent, professional yet sexually alluring. A real go-getter woman and she turns me on by canalising all the other half of my sex drive – the half I normally spent in the homosexual mode.

Julia was not surprised that I was gay. Apparently she had known all about me before we were married, and had not minded at all. She had learned about me from a doctor at the hospital where she had trained as a nurse. Apparently I had had a relationship with this young man. Even now she does not object to my having relationships with men as long as I keep it away from the family. The business with Carmen was terrible, and I was only able to break my obsession with her with professional psychiatric help which took months. The experience had a bad effect on my career too. Eventually I made a new start and Julia forgave me. I went back to something of a part-time gay life again, but I never found a satisfactory partner. One result of the psychiatry was to completely lose my faith in Catholicism. I am now an atheist and humanist.

The problem was that I was looking for a mirror-image of myself – a manly man to go to bed with which is a paradox. I sometimes am the passive and sometimes the dominant partner with a man – either with different men or the same man on different occasions. For about two years after the break-up with Carmen, I had odd affairs with men with varying degrees of success. Because I could not find a suitable partner for male sex I more or less gave up. I hoped to find someone perhaps a little younger than me, married and not a bit camp or effeminate. I sublimated this drive into social work, and helped in a youth club, and did befriending for others in trouble. Julia worked with me on some of the cases of married bisexuals, both of us using our personal experience.

Four years ago I met the second Carmen. I was not looking for a mistress, but the attraction was mutual and strong. I liked the smell of her. This affair has only just finished – I terminated it. She also was a bossy bitch. I do not know why it went on so long, for we had nothing much in common. We used to enjoy going to bed together, eating together and taking week-ends in my motor caravan. But there was constant sexual difficulty for she could only have orgasms if I stimulated her clitoris directly with my finger or tongue, but I enjoyed the bed bit very much with her. I put an end to the affair because I suddenly caught crabs and thrush – and I suspected she passed them on to me from other men. I had been away rather a lot on business, and she had lots of opportunities to pick up men. I have recently started an affair with a very nice man, Kurt, of whom I will write in a moment.

I should explain that Julia accepts that I go out by myself one or two evenings each week, and that I go away in the caravan several times each year. She believes that all these absences have been with men. She never knew about my new girlfriend.

Reverting to Kurt, he is around forty, very good-looking and married. He is less experienced than me and we are still experimenting. He seems to prefer the active role. I think there are terrible risks of V.D. in these relationships, and I worry lest he is going with other men. I do not see Kurt very often because I go away a lot on business and he works shifts. I must confess that already I am going off him; it is usually like this – a very strong attachment, mainly physical on my side – and then I want to finish the relationship. I do not fall in love with men, only desire them. But I do fall in love with women. I think now that I would like to have a new affair with a strong-minded rather bossy woman – perhaps a professional worker of some kind, who has a strong sex drive and would like to have sex with me once or twice a week, and come away with me in my motor caravan for week-ends now and again. Such a source of sexual satisfaction without much social involvement would satisfy my homosexual drive with greater dignity than I can do it with a man. I do not want a mannish woman – but she must be a bit bossy and commanding; this seems to work emotionally on me as if she were a man, and I find it satisfying.

I still sleep with my wife perhaps once a week, sometimes two or three nights. If I don't have sex with her or with a mistress or boy friend, I generally indulge in masturbation. I seem to have rectal masturbation once or twice a month if I don't get good satisfaction otherwise, and afterwards I am ashamed and remorseful. I am sure that if I find a suitable mistress I will absorb all my homosexual urges into the relationship as I have done before. I am very much driven by my sexual urge, and I rarely seem to get real satisfaction. I think I am fifty-fifty gay/heterosexual, but if I could find the right mistress I would be peaceful. Sex with Julia is not completely satisfying because she does not like sex-play; she wants to start quickly and finish in two minutes with little loving and playing about. I find it sexually satisfying but it leaves me strung up emotionally. I cannot explain this to her and have given up trying to make an adjustment.

9 WALTER

I have always been bisexual, although at various times my sexual activity goes from one to the other. I am equally attentive to both sexes, i.e. my over-attentiveness to other men is found strange, as is the lack of it with women. I do not think I want either a boy or a girl. It just does not enter into my thought. I pay little attention to what genitals someone has until I'm in bed.

I enjoy all sexual activity. I have given up trying to work out why I fancy someone. They are just people that, put all together, I want to make love to. I am usually dominant sexually with both sexes, but passive socially (perhaps just easy going).

Because of the totally different campaigns in acquiring boyfriends and girlfriends, I tend to spend six months at this and six months at that etc. This has nothing to do with a mobile sexuality. I tend to campaign and make love by a mental flow chart.

I prefer heterosexual boys. I tend to have discreet arrangements with boys who have regular girlfriends, etc. I do not like many homosexual boys. They always talk of them and us. With boys, (and I tend to have younger boyfriends) they are just people who I make friends with anyway, and when they know and like me well, I let my sexual orientation slip and be known. As anyone else who does this will tell you, many 'straight' guys then just can't wait to get to bed with you, as long as they know you're 'safe'. With girls, I go through the usual heterosexual routine of picking up girls at discos, etc.

I want to marry and settle down. But I won't give up my freedom. I am a happy person and can make others happy. My mother and grandmother were loving women. My father made me feel secure. I like the mixed company of a family, which is one of the reasons why I prefer homosexual relations with hetero- or bisexual men. I pick them up in gay pubs. Homosexual experience helps heterosexuality. I dislike a fixed gender role. It is false. We are all equal. It makes no difference that I am more erotic and adventurous with a woman. She is softer. Sex with a female is like homecoming. With men, sex has more sharpness. It is stiff and edgy. I have never hidden my homosexuality over the last five years.

I tend to think of bisexuality as normal. With some social stigma still lingering over homosexuality, I think normal behaviour is frustrated.

10 ALICE

This last autobiography differs from the others in that Alice's bisexuality remains in dreams and fantasies where love for her own sex is concerned. But she *thinks of herself as bisexual*.

Aged forty years, I am happily married to a fellow Catholic, aged forty-five. Two children aged twelve and nine. Father – a history professor, mother – a medical practitioner; stable marriage.

I have four brothers, all younger than myself. The youngest is fifteen years my junior. The two elder ones are happily married – it seems!

Apart from running a home and enjoying a happy family life, I teach at the University, and also at a College of Further Education. I have two degrees, the second being a Ph.D. and have wide intellectual and other interests – painting, making music, fell-walking, wild life, travel, etc. From 1960 to 1969 we lived in Ghana, and I've had the chance to visit countries like Russia, Finland, Israel and Ethiopia.

Altogether, I've had a full and rich life, and, surprising though it might seem, I now count my problems as part of the richness. Let me give some account of them.

For the first twenty or so years of my life I was conscious of being quite unreconciled to being female. I 'wished that I was a boy'. I was unable to throw myself into any form of activity which I and others saw as specifically feminine (e.g. dolls, 'feminine' clothes, female magazines, boyfriends, female gossip). I felt inadequate, insecure and awkward when in a 'female role' (e.g. at a party, in a party dress; with a boyfriend and so forth). As I was a very good-looking girl with, on the face of it, every advantage, there was no obvious reason why I felt so unequal to these things.

The activities I felt happy in were intellectual, artistic and sporting. *None* were specifically 'masculine' – like football, fighting, getting underneath cars. I preferred *poetry* to 'necking'. The clothes I felt happiest in were shorts and trousers – and jeans when they came into fashion.

All this must be true of many women. Hardly worth recording, one might think. At the time I just shrugged my shoulders, and didn't often think deeply about these things, miserable though they often made me. I put it all down to 'not being a boy when I wanted to be one', the 'position of women', the 'unfairness of men', and shyness which I would outgrow, etc.

However, I did sometimes give these things some thought. I wondered why I sometimes felt feminine and then lost that feeling suddenly, coming to feel masculine. Feeling 'feminine' was so difficult to sustain, even in a ball dress, and feeling 'masculine' usually embarrassed me because I 'knew' I was not masculine. I felt safest in neuter (or 'unisex' as we say now) clothes, and in situations which did not demand a lot of 'femininity', because I did not have to bother about jacking up my female image on those occasions, and I didn't have to watch it in case this image slipped a bit. In short, I could relax and forget about all that. Sometimes I did feel 'feminine'; other times I seriously wondered whether I ought not to change my sex. But if I had had the chance to do so (with the help of a wand, not a surgeon), I think I would always have refused.

When I married at twenty-five, the problem was less marked for some years. I felt more firmly 'feminine' during early marriage and child-bearing. I loved breast-feeding; I made clothes and so forth. The problem was fundamentally unchanged however. My interest in sex went in waves, and I noticed that it largely depended on whether I felt able to throw myself into womanhood or not. That ability was still shifting and elusive. Later, my husband and I adapted ourselves so that I could enjoy sex in more bi-sexual ways.

I've never had sex outside marriage. My husband attracts me very much, but other men do not. Many women have attracted me, but I 'can't think of' sex with them – it frightens me. In my dreams, I often make love to women who are unidentifiable usually – although one was quite clearly my mother, and another was a friend. About two years ago, I had a hilarious dream in which I was in a house full of lesbians. It was the greatest fun. The same friend was with me – although I'm not particularly 'attracted' to her in waking life. In actual life, she and I have a relationship of twenty years' standing, founded on a rich sharing of interests. (My husband and I have a similar relationship actually – sex apart. There's a great deal of sharing at all levels of experience.)

I think it's now time to tell you about other aspects of my psychological history.

At particular periods of my life I experienced a great increase of anxiety – particularly at ages seventeen, twenty-four to five, and thirty-four to eight. These periods were also characterized by sharp increases in physical symptoms which I have always had – back pain, migraine, inability to eat, etc. At age thirty-four, when I returned from Ghana to live in England, I was so ill physically that I sought help from Dr Wilfred Barlow and his 'Alexander Technique' in London. I expect you know about Dr Barlow and his colleagues.

After receiving medical treatment from him in the shape of restoring my muscles to a near-normal (rather than over-contracted) condition, and lessons in how to keep myself relaxed, etc., I began to realize how I had got into my screwed-up condition. I found that I was trembling with fear, and constantly trying to screw up again. I then sought the help of Dr R. M., a psychotherapist, in Manchester. I had a considerable analysis with him for three years and eight months, finishing in August, 1973. In the main, Dr R. M. was tackling my terror of the believed magical power of my thoughts, leading me to imagine that I was destroying others, and my intrapunitive aggression, my constant bashing of myself for being 'bad' and constantly falling short of perfection... However the picture was more complex than that, and my sexual condition was investigated. We found that *I am bisexual*, and I was helped to accept this, but I did not come to realize all that I realize now, until I heard *you* last Saturday. Now the picture seems to me to be decidedly clearer.

As you talked, I realized that you were talking about *me*. This surprised me, in spite of the fact that I thought you could hardly talk about something totally alien to me! My assumption was, as it has always been, that I'm really imagining it all; I'm just a 'normal' person, trying to fix a label to a muddle of my own making and anyone who has never 'done' anything sexual except get married can hardly be anything to write home about! But you weren't talking about anyone doing anything – you were talking about what certain people *feel* about themselves – and I recognized these feelings. All my life up to this day, I have had no lasting and firm sense of being a woman: I feel a kind of hermaphrodite. I don't always worry about it now. As I get older, and I've adapted myself to it – *and* I've had the permanent benefit of Dr R. M.'s help – I feel I can live with it. I don't know how much I feel 'masculine' and 'feminine' together. On the whole, I perhaps feel feminine for one split second and masculine the next... I don't know. It's hard to analyse, and all I can say is that my image of being 'feminine' is elusive and fluctuating. I've had to learn to live with myself as a kind of woman-man. I no longer want to 'be a man' at all – did I really ever want to be? (I could start analysing this, but I'll resist the temptation!)

Quite apart from all you told us about gender identity, other things you said most forcibly struck me. For instance, you told us that you once had always had a strong impression that love was something that took place between women only – and it was something with which men had nothing to do. *I*'ve always felt that. I firmly believed it until I met my husband and, in spite of his love, I still believe it in the case of all men but him! No reassuring can remove this feeling (naturally, since reasoning can never change a feeling, only *another* feeling can!).

I'm fully aware that I haven't gone into my relationships with my parents, what my grandparents were like, how I felt during puberty (increased anxiety of course), my relationships with my children, etc. There are some significant details where all these matters are concerned. My father is a deeply repressed and very unsatisfactory relative; his mother was undoubtedly a latent homosexual. Puberty was an agonising experience for me, a girl whose body was speaking a very different language from that of her psyche, and my children defy all these things by being thoroughly 'wholesome', secure about their gender identity and very interested in the opposite sex.

THREE DREAMS

From a collection of 160, almost all dreamt between January 1970 and the end of 1973, quoted verbatim from my notes.

1 I dreamt that I was going to be a minister of state, a very important man who made speeches, in some noble kingdom in the Middle East, it seems. In a way, I suppose it was heaven. I wore long flowing robes, and the ruler, who seemed inaccessible, was to be crowned that day. I had a front seat and felt very proud. I had a brother, a shadowy figure, also in a front seat, and we decided to go out for a stroll in the park while waiting. Suddenly, in the park, my brother disappeared and I was a crawling cripple struggling to return to the palace, but great lorries and horses were bearing down on me from everywhere. I had a terrible time avoiding them on hands and knees. At last I got back and was suddenly an upright, handsome, successful man again. The 'Queen Mother' greeted me at the door, and I felt she must know what I had suffered. So I staged a faint. She revived me and I took my place just as the ceremony was about to begin.

2 I dreamt that I became a trapeze artist with Nigel's encouragement, and I was walking about on the branches of trees among bushy clumps of twigs, holding the hand of a young, rather feminine, dancing boy. Quite a lot happened, which I can't remember, resulting in the boy being condemned to punishment. Then Napoleon shouted, 'He must be castrated!' I was horrified and tried to stop it – then woke up in terror.

3 I dreamt that a very beautiful medieval half-timbered house, one of a row in a historic village, had been tragically burned down. The National Trust were heartbroken! At the same time, I was

aware that there were whisperings around the village that there were 'awful goings-on' in the ruined house. I went along with an older woman, whom I can't identify, and we went all over the house. I was amazed that it was still possible to walk over its half-destroyed, charred floors. I can remember the details of the burnt timbers and flooring very clearly, and I can also remember my fear that I might fall through the floors as we gingerly walked along. To the sides of the main upper gallery were modern bedrooms, quite unscathed. There were two just ahead of me, and I was aware of one or two others behind me. This was where the 'goings-on' took place. It was Lesbianism, and I wondered how the Lesbians could keep it up while they were being prevented from doing so, as far as was possible, by their neighbours. As I thought of the Lesbians' determination I decided to join in. A very good thing. I surveyed my friends, wondering who could be my partner. I chose X [specifically identified], and was just going to start having a marvellous time when, alas, I was wakened. It was time to get up . . .

APPENDIX 1: BISEXUALITY AND ANDROGYNY

Bisexuality has been equated with androgyny, irrespective of the differences between the two. Psychiatrists and psychologists are particularly to blame for the mistake of identifying them. Androgyny has now become a favoured theme of their investigations. I have mentioned several papers which deal with psychological androgyny (chp. I). Both bisexuality and androgyny were, in fact, related to the Greek myth of Hermaphroditus. The legend goes that the nymph Salmacis fell in love with the beautiful son of Hermes and Aphrodite, and in answer to her prayer never to be separated from him, the Gods combined their sexes (chp. I). Hermaphroditus himself was a semi-god, and venerated as such. In this ancient myth, androgyny and bisexuality were one and the same. The divergence of meaning began when the world of magical ideas was superseded by rationality. But the concept of androgyny has never lost its mythical and spiritual quality, even in modern times. Its use in present-day psychology reveals the desire to give scientific status to an originally mythical notion.

The identification of bisexuality with androgyny is however justified in one respect, namely in the realm of gender identity with its repercussions on the self-image. I have pointed out that the natural gender identity of every human being is female/male or male/female, which is androgynous. In this sense, bisexuality is *inside the Self*, and identical with psychical androgyny. Here the two coincide, but they differ in most other respects.

1 Androgyny has retained the ancient flavour of myth and religion. The Greek legend of Hermaphroditus was probably taken

over from similar legends current in Asia and the Middle East, where in antiquity, androgynous goddesses were worshipped: the bearded Astarte in Phoenicia and Syria, and the androgynous Ishtar in Mesopotamia. Another less known female/male goddess was Nyame, who is worshipped up to this day as the genetrix of the universe among the Akan people of Ghana, according to the anthropologist, Eva L. R. Meyerowitz. (Personal communication.)

2 The concept of androgyny is also related to physical appearance, whereas bisexuality is not. One speaks of an androgynous girl or woman when she has broad shoulders and narrow hips, and looks altogether boyish. And the reverse is true of an androgynous man or boy.

3 The word androgyny only applies to human beings. Bisexuality on the other hand, is apparent in the whole of nature.

It was no accident that the first person to use the word bisexuality was a scientist, Charles Darwin. In 1868 he wrote in *The Variations of Animals and Plants under Domestication* that bisexuality alone could explain certain hereditary traits in both. He thus demonstrated that bisexuality has much wider implications than androgyny.

Ever since Darwin, bisexuality has puzzled psychiatrists and psychologists, and now androgyny has become its linguistic substitute. But apart from its much wider meaning, bisexuality is essentially different from androgyny in two other respects: first, it refers to the way of life of a considerable number of human beings, which androgyny does not; and second, bisexual people need not have androgynous physical features. In fact they do not differ in appearance from so-called normal people and come in all shapes and forms.

Even if it is not obvious in their day-to-day living and attitudes, all bisexual people are aware of their male/female gender identity, and therefore retain, consciously or unconsciously, a spark of the androgynous magic of love so beautifully illustrated in the legend of Hermaphroditus. And the cosmic spirit of the myth also lives on in them. Androgyny or *bisexuality inside the Self* is the basis of creative energy. It is impossible to isolate an individual's creative energy from cosmic energy which pervades all and everything. The whole of nature is under its spell. Human beings can perceive it in many ways: in love, in religion, in the arts, literature, scientific research, human relationships and many forms of ecstasy. Through such experiences they touch the sphere of what is generally called spirituality, which is the search for something lasting. Whatever word one may apply to this search, it expresses values which reject a materialistic view of the world.

Androgyny is the nature and tool of the artist and particularly the writer. How otherwise, could a novelist make characters of the opposite sex come alive? And painters also would be limited in the range of their art if they were unaware of their own 'double' nature. Androgyny is however most obvious in writers, whether it is combined with bisexuality in human relationships or not.

The following pages illustrate, through some outstanding examples from remote and present times, the combination of androgyny and bisexuality.

In the distant past, Sappho, the celebrated poet and archetype of female homosexuality, was in fact, androgynous *and* bisexual. Unfortunately there are only few fragments of information available about her, some of them probably not reliable. But remnants of her poems show that she loved women with an overwhelming aesthetic and sensuous love. Yet her poetry also celebrated marriage, and maternal love is tenderly expressed in a poem to her daughter Cleis.

It is a long jump from the third century B.C. to the twentieth century A.D., when the Bloomsbury Group provided examples of writers and artists who were both androgynous and bisexual. Although such women and men existed at any time, those of our own can be recalled most effectively and vividly.

Vita Sackville-West's androgynous and bisexual nature has been immortalized in fiction by Virginia Woolf who wrote *Orlando* about – and for – her. And Vita's own son Nigel recalled her androgynous being and her bisexuality in the famous biography of his parents *Portrait of a Marriage*. She fell in love with women, and at the same time loved her husband who adored her. He was himself bisexual, and although fixated on his wife, pursued homosexual adventures. Vita Sackville-West loved Virginia Woolf, a love which was requited in a rather sophisticated and somewhat reluctant way.

Virginia Woolf made snide remarks about Vita's sapphic friendships (Quentin Bell, *Virginia Woolf*, part 2), but I think this was her way of 'talking' and protecting herself.

I had several long conversations with Virginia Woolf in 1935. There was neither a particular emphasis nor any inhibition discernible when once she said to me: 'Leonard is my mother'. I have never forgotten these words. Her rejection of sexual stereotypes struck an enthusiastic note in me because she was, as far as I remember, the first person I had met who was aware of human sexuality in the round. Her androgyny of the mind was not matched by her bisexuality; her physical responses were weak. Her mental illness may have contributed to, or caused, her frigidity.

Virginia Woolf's friend, Lytton Strachey, writer and biographer, stands out as the perfect example of androgyny and bisexuality. His 'psychical hermaphroditism' was reflected in his physical posture and attire. In a still categorizing language, he would probably be called a homosexual, but he loved, emotionally and sensuously, men and women, though in different ways, and it is appropriate to include him in the wider range of bisexual individuals. He himself rejected sexual stereotyping and categorization, and would not tolerate any taboo against any kind of loving. The woman who meant most to him was the painter, Dora Carrington. She accepted everything from him for the price of being allowed to love him. He followed the dictate of his own needs and iconoclastic social ideas. His thoughts about love recall those of many participants of this study. He despised and rejected jealousy, as did many of the subjects in the younger age groups. Like him, they aspired to a non-capitalistic spirit in everything, particularly in human relationships. Like Strachey, they considered jealousy to be an expression of the possessive sense of a male-dominated society.

One could cite more examples of the co-existence of androgyny and bisexuality from the Bloomsbury Group. Suffice it to quote from Carolyn Heilbrun's book *Toward a Recognition of Androgyny*: 'It seems certain today that no one of them was without bisexual experience' (p. 123) – a remark which refers to both artists and writers of the Bloomsbury Group.

The lonely figure of Somerset Maugham, who was not allied to any group, is a special example of the combination of androgyny and bisexuality. He brilliantly created his female characters, from 'Liza of Lambeth' to 'Jane'. One of the most impressive is 'Jane', the heroine of a short story of that name. Jane is unique, and an outstanding example of a liberated woman (many decades before the Women's Liberation Movement started). Hers is the liberation from conventional taboos through nothing else but the freedom to be herself. A middle-aged widow, she marries a man twenty-seven years her junior. She leaves him for another man when their harmonious relationship runs out after three years, but during this time she transforms herself from a dowdy, provincial lady into a 'stunner' of exquisite taste and irresistible wit. Several actresses I know enthused about 'Jane', and wished for nothing better then to play her in a dramatised version of this story. Rachel Kempson achieved this ambition. In 1970, during a Somerset Maugham series on B.B.C. television, she gave a brilliant and unforgettable performance in 'Jane'.

Somerset Maugham is of particular interest to my subject because of the pointedness of his androgynous mind and his bisexuality. In Robin Maugham's *Conversations with Willie* (1978), a few years before his death, he said to his nephew in a tête-à-tête:

> One day it will be realised that there are people who are *born* homosexual or bisexual and there's nothing whatsoever they can do about it. I'm bisexual, but for the sake of my reputation I don't care to advertise the fact. But as you know, I've loved girls and I've loved boys – I've loved women and I've loved men. (p.107)

Dolores Klaich mentions in *Woman plus Woman* (p.198) that Somerset Maugham confessed to his nephew, Robin, that he had thought of himself as bisexual with much stronger hetero- than homosexual inclinations when in the prime of life. But the proportion became reversed with age. An unhappy marriage may have contributed to this change, together with other causes, probably of an endocrine and biographical nature.

As mentioned before, such changes occurred in both bisexual men and women of my study, through hormonal or psychological influences, or a mixture of both. Biographical events also favour the stronger development of the hetero- or homosexual side at one period or another. But the less developed and suppressed component makes itself felt with a particularly 'loud voice' at an appropriate time, the more so, the more it has been held in check.

Another fitting example of the *time factor* in hetero- or homosexual predominance of bisexual people is the French writer Colette. A sensuous and profound attachment to her mother, Sidonie, predisposed her from the start to loving women. But her sensuality comprised everything tasty, beautiful, graceful, be it men, women, animals or plants. This great lover and exquisite writer was, at one period of her life, a music-hall artist. At that time her lesbianism was evident when for five years she lived with the Marquise de Belboef.

But before that she had married her first husband, Willie, whom she passionately loved in spite of his cruel behaviour towards her. She married again late in life. But she always loved women sensuously and emotionally, and in her the frontiers between androgyny and bisexuality became blurred.

Finally, I want to mention two writers who were physically androgynous, but not bisexual in their way of life as far as I know.

Flaubert's remark 'I *am* Madame Bovary', (Heilbrun, book cited, p.156) puts the writer's psychological androgyny into relief.

Fyodor Dostoyevsky's androgyny of the mind is apparent in most of his novels, but particularly in *The Idiot*. Alyosha, the saintly fool, represents a perfect balance of male- and femaleness. Nastasya Filippovna, one of the most attractive women ever created by a novelist, reminds one of the hetairae who played such an important part in the Athenian civilization of ancient Greece and also on Sappho's Lesbos. Nastasya's femaleness is accentuated and heightened by characteristics of her maleness. She is both intuitive and intellectual. Her sense of adventure, her *presénce d'esprit*, her decisiveness in taking action and her idealism, are part and parcel of the unforgettable charm and uniqueness of her androgynous personality.

I have been mainly concerned to show the combination of bi-sexuality and androgyny in professional writers, and two of the autobiographies in chapter VIII are directly relevant to this. They are those of two creative women, Penelope and Alice. Both are university teachers and writers. Penelope is a poet of considerable talent, and Alice an original interpreter of folklore and a writer. Penelope (autobiography 4) identifies with Victoria Sackville-West. She has a successful marriage with an understanding husband, and a consuming lesbian love.

Although Alice (autobiography 10) has much in common with Penelope, she is of particular interest for other reasons. She is androgynous not only in mind but also in appearance. She is one of the few participants of my study who experienced the same-sexed aspect of their bisexuality only in dreams and fantasies. Although she has no physical lesbian relationships, she is fully aware of her bi-gender identity and the erotic attraction women have for her. The fact that she is happily married does not diminish her lesbian longings, nor do they make her feel guilty towards her husband and children.

These two women are examples of the close connection between love, in this case bisexual love, and creativity. They find that glimpse of the 'eternal' in both. Love lends its fire to the creative process and vice versa.

It is to be expected that gifted and creative people are able to articulate in words or art what others feel but can only dimly express. Yet the same desire for 'something lasting' which does not die under one's hands, is a common human desire. It is the innate mechanism which activates religious feelings and idealistic pursuits.

I had asked the participants of my study to write about their emotional and sexual experiences, as well as their own ideas about bisexuality. Their psychosexual experiences were the focal point of the empirical part of my investigation. They were therefore the dominant theme in the autobiographies of all the participants, but their humanity and idealism can be read between the lines. And practically all of them were united in the desire for a 'bisexual society'.

My subjects represented more or less a cross-section of society, a fact which is reflected in their autobiographies. Some are therefore not only more articulate but also of a wider scope than others, as for example those of two male artists, Adrian (autobiography 2) and Charles (autobiography 7). Adrian, a divorcé, nearly sixty years of age, is a disturbed personality, constantly fighting with himself. He suffers from depression and is tortured by guilt feelings. But this has not diminished his adolescent enthusiasm and his capacity for love and lust. His absorbing love for Ingrid did not lessen his homosexual needs. Both kinds of loving stimulate his creative energy, and are reflected in the androgynous style of his paintings. He is an eternal student, who tries to sublimate his bi-sexual love in art.

Charles, a much younger man, could have had a prosperous bourgeois career as a commercial artist, but he rejected prosperity and a secure income. His creative urge concentrated on a new way of life, which he vividly describes in his autobiography. His capacity for loving goes far beyond the personal, as he is actively concerned with the fight for an alternative society which would ensure a life without sexism. He did not hesitate to leave his lucrative profession as a designer to become a gardener, because he felt that he could get a sense of reality only through close contact with the earth.

The longest autobiography is that of Ingrid, who gave her profession as 'call girl'. There is something of the hetairae in this beautiful, intelligent, well-educated woman. She chose prostitution as a job because it gave her freedom from want and the luxury of a beautiful home into the bargain. Ingrid is able to carry out her profession with complete detachment because it does not touch her as a person, nor does it affect her capacity to love. Financial security and leisure enable her to follow intellectual pursuits and develop her literary gift. Although Ingrid loves men and women, she has recognized that she would find greater peace, and a deeper mutual understanding in lesbian, rather than heterosexual, love.

Bisexual and homosexual people have to break the set rules which are the 'blue print' of society's design for living. Since the Sexual Offences Act of 1967, the homosexual man has been able to do so more openly then before, because 'coming out' no longer spells unavoidable dangers. About the same time, the situation of the lesbian became uplifted through the Women's Liberation Movement, which gave her a new self-confidence to fight the mental persecution she still encounters from society. But bisexual people of both sexes are far more prone to lead a double life than homosexuals. They are inclined to retain conventional standards in their daily existence, and to live out their homosexual side more discreetly and more secretively than the homosexual does. But as I have shown in this book, no hard and fast rules can be made about either. Grouping and categorizing does not hold water anyway, as so-called heterosexuals are turned round in the same emotional and sexual carousel as bi- and homosexual people.

But bi- and homosexuals share the refusal to be regarded as second-class citizens, if not outcasts. Their protest creates in them a high level of nervous tension, irritability and restlessness. Aggressiveness and defiance are the natural consequences of such an emotional climate. People who feel rejected experience a sense of rootlessness which has a polarizing effect on the emotions. It makes for dissatisfaction with everything and everybody on one hand, and leads to expectation of something marvellous just round the corner on the other. Such a state of mind easily leads to an emotional brinkmanship where sexual 'greed' and emotional ambivalence are partners. They reinforce one another because of the notoriety of unorthodox sexuality in the eyes of 'normal' people. Nobody would classify anyone of a conventional life style as the heterosexual Mr or Mrs Somebody, but a homo- or bisexual person is first and foremost categorized as such. The focus on their 'orientation' is bound to make them acutely self-conscious and ill-at-ease.

Autobiography 8 (Gordon) illustrates emotional brinkmanship and sexual restlessness particularly well, as does autobiography 5 (Mildred). Both portray disturbed and rootless people who 'wander' from one person and one sex to the other in their search for 'happiness' and 'partnership'. Mildred, however, is different from Gordon in one respect: she has found satisfaction, if not 'salvation', through her love and care for children as a non-biological parent in the commune where she lives.

Another young woman, Ruth, (autobiography 3) a university student of high intelligence, finds her bisexual orientation emotionally enriching, but at the same time it causes her depressing conflicts.

She feels particularly insecure and at a disadvantage in her lesbian relationships. She approaches women with a preconceived sense of rejection. Yet she cannot resist opening up relationships with them. She became an ardent feminist, and made a name for herself in the Women's Liberation Movement, to which in fact, she gave her heart and soul. I do not believe that emotional problems can ever be solved by giving one's mind (and heart) to the many instead of the one. But in this case there was a direct connection between her personal and her super-personal love for women.

Autobiography 9, that of a very young man, was included for one particular reason: it shows the nonsense of sexual categorization. He speaks of his preference for heterosexual boys, which is a common feature in bisexual males. The same preference also applies to a certain number of bisexual women and lesbians, who attach themselves to heterosexual women.

I have already mentioned that androgyny is implicit in bisexuality, but that this is not the case the other way round. However, how closely the two are connected has been poignantly and beautifully expressed by Flaubert in one of his letters to his love, Louise Colet. Here is a quotation from the German edition, followed by my translation:

Du bist keine Frau, und wenn ich Dich mehr, und besonders wenn ich Dich *tiefer geliebt* habe . . . als jede andere, so deshalb, weil es mir vorkam, dass Du weniger Frau bist als eine andere . . . Denk darüber nach, und Du wirst sehen, ob ich mich täusche. Ich wollte, wir behielten unsere beiden Körper, und wären nur ein einziger Geist. An Dir als Frau will ich nur das Fleisch . . . Verstehst Du, dass dies keine Liebe ist, sondern etwas Höheres, so scheint mir, da diese Begierde der Seele für sie fast ein Lebensbedürfnis ist, ein Bedürfnis sich auszuweiten, grösser zu werden. Jede Empfindung ist eine Ausdehnung, deshalb ist die Freiheit die edelste der Leidenschaften. (Flaubert, *Briefe*, p.241)

You are not a 'woman', and I loved you more and *with a deeper love* than other women because I felt that you are less of a woman than all the others . . . Reflect about this, and you will find out whether I am wrong . . . I only wished that we remained physically as we are but were only one Soul. When I think of you as 'woman' I only want your body . . . You will understand that love is not lust, but is something higher. It seems to me that this desire of the Soul is the very essence of life, the need to stretch oneself and to become greater. All feelings stretch one's being, and because of this, freedom is the most noble passion.

These words by the apparently 'heterosexual' Flaubert imply that it is psychical androgyny which makes intimate relationships creative and lasting, independently of sex and sexual orientation.

APPENDIX 2:
STATISTICAL TABLES

How to read the tables

The thirty-one tables presented here list the *frequencies* with which individuals fall in particular categories. In Tables 1 to 6 the frequencies are listed under 'Number (Males)' for male participants and 'Number (Females)' for female participants. For example, in Table 1 there are 23 male participants in the sample of 75 who are aged under 30, 13 who are aged between 30 and 39, etc. As a further example taken from Table 1, there are 11 female respondents aged between 40 and 49.

In Table 7, and most subsequent tables, there are *two* variables as well as the sex of the respondent. For example, in Table 16 the two variables are (a) the participant's *age* (age levels are listed in the columns) and (b) the number of homosexual *lovers* that a participant reported having (the number of lovers are listed in the rows). In each table M = Male, F = Female. Thus, in Table 16 there are 3 male participants who are aged between 20 and 29 and who report having no homosexual lovers (an entry of 3 in the first column and the first row); similarly, there are, for example, 7 female participants who are aged between 30 and 39 and who also report having 6 or more homosexual lovers, etc. Totals appear at the right-hand margin (row totals) and, in most cases, at the bottom of the page (column totals). Thus, in Table 16 there are altogether 20 female participants who report having one homosexual lover, for example.

Statistical tests used

1 Kendall's *S-statistic* is used in order to assess whether there is

a significant correlation between two variables such as, for example, the age of a participant and the number of lovers. The test is used when both variables represent values which can be put in an order from one extreme to another: age is a variable which can be ordered from youngest to oldest, and number of lovers can be ordered from 0 to 1 to 2, etc. In each analysis the larger the value of S the greater the tendency for large values of one variable to be associated with large values of the other and vice-versa. In each case the value of z is that of the standard normal deviate; a correction for continuity was made in each test and when the correction changed the significance level conclusions were based on z (corrected) = z(c).

2 The *Chi-square* test is used when one or both of the variables cannot be ordered or when there are only two levels of both the variables. In each analysis, the larger the value of Chi-square the greater the relationship between the two variables. In each case the number of degrees of freedom (df) are given.

For both types of test a significant result is indicated by a value of *p* which is less than ·05; $p < ·05$ means the probability of getting the obtained relationship between two variables by chance is less than 5 chances in 100 and is, therefore, a significant relationship; $p > ·05$ indicates a non-significant result. Whether a 1-tailed or 2-tailed test is performed depends on whether or not a prediction is made in advance as to the direction of the difference or relationship between two variables. For all significant results, it is stated whether it is a 1-tailed (prediction in advance) or a 2-tailed (no prediction in advance) test. When the result is *not* significant, the probability stated is for a 2-tailed test.

The 'No Response' category appears in many tables but was always ignored in any statistical test or when citing percentages of individuals who respond in a particular way.

References
KENDALL, M. G. *Rank Correlation Methods* (4th Edition), London, 1969
SIEGEL, S. *Nonparametric Statistics*, New York, 1956

TABLE A – CLASSIFICATION OF SUBJECTS AND THEIR PARENTS ACCORDING TO OCCUPATION

Occupations	Subjects Men	Subjects Women	Fathers of m Subjects	Fathers of f Subjects	Mothers of m Subjects	Mothers of f Subjects
Education	15	21	3	7	6	15
Arts	13	14	3	2	2	4
Government Employee	9	4	12	14	3	1
Business						
Employed	5	8	8	10	7	11
Self-employed	4	5	11	12	1	1
Caring and Healing	6	15	6	6	1	7
Skilled Worker	13	2	18	16	8	3
Unskilled Worker	5	1	12	6	8	8
Unemployed/Retired	5	3	—	—	—	—
Housewifery	—	2	—	—	39	25

The grouping of people according to social class is out of tune with our time. I have therefore chosen to list the subjects of my study and their parents according to their occupation.

Points of special interest are a shift in the occupations of both male and female subjects compared with their parents, towards education and the arts, and in the case of women, also to the caring and healing professions; the fact that a considerable number (18) of the male subjects were manual workers; and that the number of unemployed or retired people was comparatively small.

TABLE 1 – AGE OF PARTICIPANTS

Age	Number (Males)	Number (Females)
Under 30	23	30
30–39	13	28
40–49	10	11
50–59	18	2
Over 59	11	4
Total	75	75

There is a *significant* difference between the ages of male and female participants (S = 1605; z = 3·13; p < ·002, 2-tailed test). Male participants are older (Mean Age = 42·0 years) than female participants (Mean Age = 34·1 years).

TABLE 2 – PARENTS' AGES AT PARTICIPANT'S BIRTH

Mother's Age	Number (Males)	Number (Females)
Under 20	3	2
20–24	16	12
25–30	24	21
31–35	19	25
36–40	8	10
Over 40	5	4
Don't Know	—	1

Father's Age	Number (Males)	Number (Females)
20–29	25	19
30–39	34	38
40–49	12	12
50–59	2	4
Over 59	1	—
Don't Know	1	2

There is *no* significant difference between the male and female participants, neither with respect to their mother's age at birth (S = 547; z = 1·07; p > ·05) nor with respect to their father's age at birth (S = 401; z = ·84; p > ·05).

TABLE 3 – PARTICIPANT'S AGE AT PARENTS' DEATH

Age (Mother's death)	Number (Males)	Number (Females)
0–3	2	1
4–7	1	1
8–12	1	—
13–18	—	1
Over 18 (or still alive)	71	72

Age (Father's death)	Number (Males)	Number (Females)
0–3	2	—
4–7	4	2
8–12	2	3
13–18	4	2
Over 18 (or still alive)	62	66
Don't Know	1	2

Only 5·3% of male participants and 4·0% of female participants lost their mother before the age of 19. Clearly the difference is not significant. 16·2% of male participants and 9·6% of females lost their father before the age of 19. These percentages are *not* significantly different (Chi-square = ·91; df = 1; p > ·05).

TABLE 4 – NUMBER OF SIBLINGS

Number of Brothers	Number (Males)	Number (Females)
0	32	32
1	27	30
2	12	9
3	3	3
Over 3	1	1

Number of Sisters	Number (Males)	Number (Females)
0	27	39
1	22	24
2	13	6
3	11	4
Over 3	2	2

There is *no* significant difference between the male and female participants in the number of same-sex siblings (S = 535, z = 1·03; p > ·05), nor in the number of opposite-sex siblings (S = 929; z = 1·79; p > ·05).

TABLE 5 – POSITION IN FAMILY

Position	Number (Males)	Number (Females)
Eldest	20	28
2nd	12	7
3rd	5	3
4th	1	1
5th or later	4	—
Youngest	20	21
Only Child	13	15

There is *no* significant difference between the family positions of male and female participants (Chi-square = 7·32; df = 6; p > ·05).

TABLE 6 – OLDER AND YOUNGER BROTHERS AND SISTERS

Older Brother(s)?	Number (Males)	Number (Females)
Yes	25	23
No	50	52

Younger Brother(s)?	Number (Males)	Number (Females)
Yes	25	23
No	50	52

Older Sister(s)?	Number (Males)	Number (Females)
Yes	31	17
No	44	58

Younger Sister(s)?	Number (Males)	Number (Females)
Yes	27	25
No	48	50

There is *no* significant difference between male and female participants in the number of same-sex older siblings (Chi-square = 1·62; df = 1; p > ·05), nor in the number of opposite-sex older siblings (Chi-square = 1·42; df = 1; p > ·05).

There is *no* significant difference between male and female participants in the number of same-sex younger siblings (Chi-square = ·03; df = 1; p > ·05), nor in the number of opposite-sex younger siblings (Chi-square = ·27; df = 1; p > ·05).

TABLE 7 – MARITAL STATUS AND CHILDREN

(a) *Of participants' parents*

	Males	Females
Happily married	39	40
Separated	5	6
Divorced	4	9
No response	27	20
Total	75	75

52·0% of males said their parents were happily married, compared with 53·3% of females – very similar.

(b) *Of subjects*

	Males	Females
Unmarried	32	37
Happily married	24	13
Not happily married	9	10
Separated	2	5
Divorced	3	8
Widowed	5	2
No response	—	—
Total	75	75

42·7% of males were unmarried compared with 49·3% of females. 72·7% of the married men were happily married compared with 56·5% of the married women. Not a significant result.

(c) *Do you have any children and what is your relationship to them?*

	Males	Females
Yes (have children)		
Loving	33	26
Indifferent	2	—
No response	1	1
No (no children)	28	39
No response	11	9
Total	75	75

There is no significant difference between the sexes in whether or not they have children. (Chi-square = 1·52; df = 1; p > ·05). 48·0% of males and 36·0% of females had children.

TABLE 8 – STEP-PARENTS

(a) *Having a stepmother before the age of 18*

	Males	Females
Yes	3	1
No	72	74
No response	—	—
Total	75	75

(b) *Having a stepfather before the age of 18*

	Males	Females
Yes	4	5
No	71	70
No response	—	—
Total	75	75

TABLE 9 – TRAUMATIC SEXUAL EXPERIENCE

(a) *In childhood*

	Males	Females
Yes	15	20
No	57	53
No response	3	2
Total	75	75

20·8% of males who responded reported a childhood traumatic sexual experience, compared with 27·4% of females. (*Not* a statistically significant difference.)

(b) *In adolescence*

	Males	Females
Yes	13	17
No	55	54
No response	7	4
Total	75	75

19·1% of males who responded reported an adolescent traumatic sexual experience, compared with 23·9% of females. (*Not* a statistically significant difference.)

TABLE 10 – INCEST

(a) *With same sex sibling*

	Males	Females
Yes	7	1
No	67	74
No response	1	—
Total	75	75

(b) *With opposite sex sibling*

	Males	Females
Yes	4	4
No	71	71
No response	—	—
Total	75	75

As predicted, there is a *significant* tendency for males to have more *homosexual* incest occasions with siblings (9·5%) than do females (1·3%). (Chi-square = 3·4; df = 1; p < ·05, 1-tailed test.)

(c) *With same sex parent*

	Males	Females
Yes	1	—
No	74	75
No response	—	—
Total	75	75

(d) *With opposite sex parent*

	Males	Females
Yes	1	2
No	74	73
No response	—	—
Total	75	75

TABLE 11 – EMOTIONAL ATTACHMENTS AND PREOCCUPATIONS

(a) *Emotional Attachment*

	Number (Males)	Number (Females)
Only Homosexual	6	4
Predominantly Homosexual	16	39
Both Sexes Equally	34	24
Predominantly Heterosexual	16	7
Only Heterosexual	3	—
No Response	—	1

(b) Predominant Emotional Preoccupation

	Number (Males)	Number (Females)
Homosexual	36	52
Heterosexual	25	12
No Response	14	11

There is a *significant* difference between the emotional attachments of male and female participants (S = 1666; z = 3·29; p < ·001, 2-tailed test). The emotional attachments of female participants are more homosexual than those of male participants; 29·3% of male participants reported homosexual emotional attachments compared with 58·1% of female participants.

There is a *significant* difference between the sexes in the orientation of their predominant emotional preoccupations (Chi-square = 6·38; df = 1; p < ·02, 2-tailed test). 59·0% of male participants reported predominantly homosexual emotional preoccupations, compared with 81·3% of female participants.

TABLE 12 – PAST DESIRES TO BE OF THE OPPOSITE SEX AND PARENTS' ATTITUDE

Mother desired respondent to be of opposite sex?	Sex	Yes	No	No Response	Total
Yes	M	5	5	—	10
	F	8	1	—	9
No	M	6	32	—	38
	F	14	20	—	34
Don't Know	M	15	12	—	27
	F	16	15	1	32
Total	M	26	49	—	75
	F	38	36	1	75

Father desired respondent to be of opposite sex?	Sex	Respondent desired to be of opposite sex?			
		Yes	No	No Response	Total
Yes	M	2	3	—	5
	F	10	4	—	14
No	M	10	33	—	43
	F	16	23	—	39
Don't Know	M	14	13	—	27
	F	12	9	1	22
Total	M	26	49	—	75
	F	38	36	1	75

There is a *significant* relationship between past desires to be of the opposite sex and the mother's desire that the participant was of the opposite sex, both for males (Chi-square = 3·49; df = 1; p < ·05, 1-tailed test) and for females (Chi-square = 4·71; df = 1; p < ·025, 1-tailed test). As predicted, participants of either sex were more likely to have wanted to be of the opposite sex if their mother had desired it. 50·0% of males and 88·9% of females wanted to be of the opposite sex if they thought their mother would have preferred them to be, compared with 15·8% of males and 41·2% of females if they thought their mother had no such preference.

There is *no* significant relationship between past desires to be of the opposite sex and the father's desire that the participant was of the opposite sex, neither for males (Chi-square = ·07; df = 1; p > ·05) nor for females (Chi-square = 2·69; df = 1; p > ·05).

There is a *significant* difference between the past desires of male and female participants to be of the opposite sex (Chi-square = 3·58; df = 1; p < ·05, 1-tailed test). As predicted, females more often wanted to be of the opposite sex than did males (34·7% for males, 51·4% for females).

There is *no* significant difference between the sexes in reporting that their mother desired them to be of the opposite sex (Chi-square = ·06; df = 1; p > ·05). 20·8% of males and 20·9% of females thought their mothers would have preferred them to be of the opposite sex. However, there *is* a significant difference between the sexes in reporting that their fathers wanted them to be of the opposite sex (Chi-square = 3·24; df = 1; p < ·05; 1-tailed test). As predicted, females more often thought their fathers would have preferred them to be of the opposite sex, females 26·4%, males 10·4%.

TABLE 13 – PRESENT DESIRES TO BE OF THE OPPOSITE SEX AND PARENTS' ATTITUDE

Mother desired respondent to be of opposite sex?	Sex	Respondent desires to be of opposite sex?			
		Yes	No	No Response	Total
Yes	M	3	7	—	10
	F	1	8	—	9
No	M	2	33	3	38
	F	—	34	—	34
Don't Know	M	9	16	2	27
	F	4	28	—	32
Total	M	14	56	5	75
	F	5	70	—	75

Father desired respondent to be of the opposite sex?	Sex	Respondent desires to be of opposite sex?			
		Yes	No	No Response	Total
Yes	M	1	4	—	5
	F	3	11	—	14
No	M	4	35	4	43
	F	—	39	—	39
Don't Know	M	9	17	1	27
	F	2	20	—	22
Total	M	14	56	5	75
	F	5	70	—	75

There is *no* significant relationship between present desires to be of the opposite sex and the mother's desire that the participant was of the opposite sex, neither for males (Chi-square = 2·51; df = 1; p > ·05) nor for females (Chi-square = ·52); df = 1; p > ·05). 30·0% of males who responded and 11·1% of females want to be of the opposite sex if they thought their mother would have preferred them to be, compared with 5·7% of males and 0·0% of females if they thought their mother had no such preference.

There is *no* significant relationship between present desires to be of the opposite sex and the father's desire that the participant was of the opposite sex for males (Chi-square = ·01; df = 1; p > ·05), but a *significant* relationship in the case of female participants (Chi-square = 5·30; df = 1; p < ·025, 1-tailed test). Females are more likely to want to be of the opposite sex if their fathers had wanted them to be; 21·4% compared with 0·0%.

There is a *significant* difference between the present desires of male and female participants to be of the opposite sex (Chi-square = 4·54; df = 1; p < ·025, 1-tailed test). As predicted, males more often want to be of the opposite sex than do females (20·0% for males, 6·7% for females).

TABLE 14 – ONSET OF BISEXUAL AWARENESS BEFORE 15 YEARS AND NUMBER OF LOVERS

Number of male *lovers*	*Bisexual awareness before the age of 15 years?*				
	Sex	Yes	No	No Response	Total
0	M	6	6	1	13
	F	1	—	—	1
1	M	—	3	—	3
	F	2	4	1	7
2	M	2	4	—	6
	F	2	10	—	12
3	M	—	8	—	8
	F	—	6	—	6
4	M	—	4	—	4
	F	1	11	—	12
5	M	1	2	2	5
	F	—	3	—	3
6+	M	8	26	2	36
	F	4	29	1	34
Total	M	17	53	5	75
	F	10	63	2	75

Number of female lovers	Sex	Yes	No	No Response	Total
0	M	1	2	—	3
	F	3	1	—	4
1	M	2	12	—	14
	F	2	17	1	20
2	M	3	7	1	11
	F	—	15	1	16
3	M	3	12	1	16
	F	1	8	—	9
4	M	3	6	1	10
	F	1	7	—	8
5	M	1	1	—	2
	F	—	2	—	2
6+	M	4	13	2	19
	F	3	13	—	16
Total	M	17	53	5	75
	F	10	63	2	75

Bisexual awareness before the age of 15 years?

There is *no* significant relationship between the onset of bisexual awareness before the age of 15 years and the number of *male* lovers, neither for male participants ($S = 129$; $z = .89$; $p > .05$) nor for female participants ($S = 147$; $z = 1.17$; $p > .05$).

There is *no* significant relationship between the onset of bisexual awareness before the age of 15 and the number of *female* lovers, neither for male participants ($S = 67$; $z = .40$; $p > .05$) nor for female participants ($S = 87$; $z = .63$; $p > .05$).

There is *no* significant difference between the sexes in the tendency to be aware of their bisexuality before the age of 15 (Chi-square = 1.97; df = 1; $p > .05$).

TABLE 15 – BISEXUALITY BETWEEN 15 AND 25 YEARS AND NUMBER OF LOVERS

Number of male *lovers*	Sex	*Bisexual between 15 and 25 years?* Yes	No	No Response	Total
0	M	7	5	1	13
	F	1	—	—	1
1	M	2	1	—	3
	F	6	1	—	7
2	M	5	1	—	6
	F	3	8	1	12
3	M	5	3	—	8
	F	5	1	—	6
4	M	4	—	—	4
	F	5	6	1	12
5	M	4	—	1	5
	F	1	2	—	3
6+	M	25	10	1	36
	F	20	12	2	34
Total	M	52	20	3	75
	F	41	30	4	75

Number of female *lovers*	Sex	Bisexual between 15 and 25 years?			
		Yes	No	No Response	Total
0	M	3	—	—	3
	F	3	1	—	4
1	M	9	5	—	14
	F	9	11	—	20
2	M	6	4	1	11
	F	9	5	2	16
3	M	10	6	—	16
	F	4	4	1	9
4	M	9	—	1	10
	F	6	2	—	8
5	M	2	—	—	2
	F	—	2	—	2
6+	M	13	5	1	19
	F	10	5	1	16
Total	M	52	20	3	75
	F	41	30	4	75

There is *no* significant relationship between the existence of bisexuality between the ages of 15 and 25 and the number of *male* lovers, neither for male participants ($S = 77$; $z = ·46$; $p > ·05$) nor for female participants ($S = 25$; $z = ·10$; $p > ·05$).

There is *no* significant relationship between the existence of bisexuality between the ages of 15 and 25 and the number of *female* lovers, neither for males ($S = 114$; $z = ·67$; $p > ·05$) nor for females ($S = 117$; $z = ·63$; $p > ·05$).

There is *no* significant difference between the sexes in the tendency towards bisexuality between the ages of 15 and 25 (Chi-square = $2·69$; df = 1; $p > ·05$).

TABLE 16 – NUMBER OF HOMOSEXUAL LOVERS FOR DIFFERENT AGE GROUPS

Number of Lovers	Sex	20–29	30–39	40–49	50–59	Over 59	Total
0	M	3	1	3	1	5	13
	F	2	—	1	1	—	4
1	M	2	—	—	—	1	3
	F	7	9	2	1	1	20
2	M	4	—	1	—	1	6
	F	8	6	2	—	—	16
3	M	3	1	—	3	1	8
	F	3	2	4	—	—	9
4	M	3	—	—	1	—	4
	F	3	3	1	—	1	8
5	M	1	1	1	1	1	5
	F	1	1	—	—	—	2
Over 5	M	7	10	5	12	2	36
	F	6	7	1	—	2	16
Total	M	23	13	10	18	11	75
	F	30	28	11	2	4	75

There is *no* significant relationship between the age of the participant and the number of homosexual lovers, neither for male participants ($S = 16$; $z = \cdot08$; $p > \cdot05$) nor for female participants ($S = 3$; $z = \cdot02$; $p > \cdot05$).

There is a *significant* difference between the sexes in the number of homosexual lovers reported ($S = 1425$; $z = 2\cdot73$; $p < \cdot01$, 2-tailed test). Males had significantly more homosexual lovers than did females.

TABLE 17 – NUMBER OF HETEROSEXUAL LOVERS FOR DIFFERENT AGE GROUPS

Number of of Lovers	Sex	20–29	30–39	40–49	50–59	Over 59	Total
0	M	2	—	—	—	1	3
	F	—	—	—	1	—	1
1	M	3	3	3	3	2	14
	F	3	2	2	—	—.	7
2	M	5	—	2	3	1	11
	F	4	6	2	—	—	12
3	M	3	5	1	5	2	16
	F	2	3	—	—	1	6
4	M	4	1	1	2	2	10
	F	4	4	2	—	2	12
5	M	2	—	—	—-	--	2
	F	—	2	1	---	—	3
Over 5	M	4	4	3	5	3	19
	F	17	11	4	1	1	34
Total	M	23	13	10	18	11	75
	F	30	28	11	2	4	75

There is *no* significant relationship between age of respondent and the number of heterosexual lovers, neither for males ($S = 64$; $z = \cdot 31$; $p > \cdot 05$) nor for females ($S = 237$; $z = 1\cdot 22$; $p > \cdot 05$).

There is a *significant* difference between the sexes in the number of heterosexual lovers reported ($S = 1429$; $z = 2\cdot 77$; $p < \cdot 01$, 2-tailed test). Females had significantly more heterosexual lovers than did males.

TABLE 18 – SIBLING ATTACHMENT AND PREDOMINANT EMOTIONAL PREOCCUPATION

(*a*) *Close relationship with* older same *sex sibling?*
Predominant emotional preoccupation?

	Sex	Hom.	Het.	No Resp.	Total
Yes	M	2	1	—	3
	F	4	—	2	6
No	M	34	24	14	72
	F	48	12	9	69

(*b*) *Close relationship with* younger same *sex sibling?*

	Sex	Hom.	Het.	No Resp.	Total
Yes	M	—	1	—	1
	F	4	1	2	7
No	M	36	24	14	74
	F	48	11	9	68

(*c*) *Close relationship with* older opposite *sex sibling?*

	Sex	Hom.	Het.	No Resp.	Total
Yes	M	10	4	1	15
	F	4	—	3	7
No	M	26	21	13	60
	F	48	12	8	68

(*d*) *Close relationship with* younger opposite *sex sibling?*

	Sex	Hom.	Het.	No Resp.	Total
Yes	M	3	4	—	7
	F	2	1	—	3
No	M	33	21	14	68
	F	50	11	11	72

There is *no* significant relationship between the orientation of predominant emotional preoccupation and having close relations with one's siblings: (a) older same sex sibling(s): Chi-square (Males) = $\cdot 11$; df = 1; p > $\cdot 05$: Chi-square (Females) = $\cdot 11$; df = 1; p > $\cdot 05$; (b) younger same sex sibling(s): Chi-square (Males) = $\cdot 03$; df = 1; p > $\cdot 05$: Chi-square (Females) = $\cdot 27$; df = 1; p > $\cdot 05$; (c) older opposite sex sibling(s): Chi-square (Males) = $\cdot 59$; df = 1; p > $\cdot 05$: Chi-square (Females) = $\cdot 11$; df = 1; p > $\cdot 05$; (d) younger opposite sex sibling(s): Chi-square (Males) = $\cdot 27$; df = 1; p > $\cdot 05$: Chi-square (Females) = $\cdot 01$; df = 1; p > $\cdot 05$.

There is *no* significant difference between the sexes in the existence of close relationships with (a) older same sex sibling(s) (Chi-square = $\cdot 47$; df = 1; p > $\cdot 05$); (b) older opposite sex sibling(s) (Chi-square = $2 \cdot 61$; df = 1; p > $\cdot 05$); and (c) younger opposite sex sibling(s) (Chi-square = $\cdot 96$; df = 1; p > $\cdot 05$). However, there is a significant difference between the sexes in the existence of a close relationship with a younger same sex sibling (Chi-square = $3 \cdot 30$; df = 1; p < $\cdot 05$, 1-tailed test). As predicted, females more often had a close relationship with a younger sister (9·3%) than did males with a younger brother (1·3%).

TABLE 19 – SIBLING ANTAGONISM AND PREDOMINANT EMOTIONAL PREOCCUPATION

(a) Antagonistic relationship with older same sex sibling?
Predominant emotional preoccupation

	Sex	Hom.	Het.	No Resp.	Total
Yes	M	6	4	1	11
	F	7	1	1	9
No	M	30	21	13	64
	F	45	11	10	66

(b) Antagonistic relationship with younger same sex sibling?

	Sex	Hom.	Het.	No Resp.	Total
Yes	M	4	—	3	7
	F	8	—	1	9
No	M	32	25	11	68
	F	44	12	10	66

(c) Antagonistic relationship with older opposite sex sibling?

	Sex	Hom.	Het.	No Resp.	Total
Yes	M	4	4	2	10
	F	5	1	2	8
No	M	32	21	12	65
	F	47	11	9	67

(d) Antagonistic relationship with younger opposite sex sibling?

	Sex	Hom.	Het.	No Resp.	Total
Yes	M	4	3	1	8
	F	5	2	—	7
No	M	32	22	13	67
	F	47	10	11	68

There is *no* significant relationship between the orientation of the participant's predominant emotional preoccupation and having antagonistic relationships with siblings: (a) older same sex sibling(s): Chi-square = ·08; df = 1; p > ·05 for males: Chi-square = ·00; df = 1; p > ·05 for females; (b) younger same sex sibling(s): Chi-square = 1·44; df = 1; p > ·05 for males: Chi-square = ·94; df = 1; p > ·05 for females; (c) older opposite sex sibling(s): Chi-square = ·03; df = 1; p > ·05 for males: Chi-square = ·17; df = 1; p > ·05 for females; (d) young opposite sex sibling(s): Chi-square = ·09; df = 1; p > ·05 for males: Chi-square = ·04; df = 1; p > ·05 for females.

There is *no* significant difference between the sexes in the existence of antagonistic relations with (a) older same sex sibling(s) (Chi-square = ·06; df = 1; p > ·05); (b) younger same sex sibling(s) (Chi-square = ·07; df = 1; p > ·05); (c) older opposite sex sibling(s) (Chi-square = ·06; df = 1; p > ·05); and (d) younger opposite sex siblings (Chi-square = ·00; df = 1; p > ·05).

TABLE 20 – GUILT FEELINGS ABOUT SEX

(a) *Guilt feelings about sex* inside *marriage (or marriage-like bond)*?

	Number (Males)	Number (Females)
Yes	10	5
No	57	66
No Response	8	4
Total	75	75

(b) *Guilt feelings about sex* outside *marriage (or marriage-like bond)*?

	Number (Males)	Number (Females)
Yes	16	15
No	54	59
No Response	5	1
Total	75	75

(c) *Guilt feelings about* homosexuality?

	Number (Males)	Number (Females)
Yes	21	11
No	47	62
No Response	7	2
Total	75	75

There is *no* significant difference between the sexes in their feelings of guilt about sex inside marriage (or marriage-like bond) (Chi-square = 1·47; df = 1; p > ·05). 14·9% of male participants and 7·0% of female participants reported such guilt feelings.

There is *no* significant difference between male and female participants in their feelings of guilt about sex outside marriage (or a marriage-like bond) (Chi-square = ·03; df = 1; p > ·05). 22·9% of males who responded felt guilty compared with 20·3% of females.

There *is* a significant difference between the sexes in their feelings of guilt about homosexuality (Chi-square = 4·16; df = 1; p < ·05, 2-tailed test). 30·9% of males who responded felt guilty about homosexuality, compared with 15·1% of females.

TABLE 21 – PSYCHOLOGICAL ILLNESS AND PARENTS' ATTITUDES

(a) Mother's attitude to respondent?

Have you had any psychological illness?

Attitude	Sex	Yes	No	No Response	Total
Loving	M	15	42	1	58
	F	17	32	1	50
Indifferent (or negligent)	M	6	9	—	15
	F	9	9	1	19
No Response	M	—	2	—	2
	F	4	1	1	6
Total	M	21	53	1	75
	F	30	42	3	75

Father's attitude to respondent?

Have you had any psychological illness?

Attitude	Sex	Yes	No	No Response	Total
Loving	M	9	30	1	40
	F	17	29	1	47
Indifferent (or negligent)	M	10	19	—	29
	F	11	10	—	21
No Response	M	2	4	—	6
	F	2	3	2	7
Total	M	21	53	1	75
	F	30	42	3	75

(b) Mother's attitude to respondent?

Have you ever been a patient in a mental hospital?

Attitude	Sex	Yes	No	No Response	Total
Loving	M	4	54	—	58
	F	7	43	—	50
Indifferent (or negligent)	M	4	11	—	15
	F	3	15	1	19
No Response	M	—	2	—	2
	F	—	5	1	6
Total	M	8	67	—	75
	F	10	63	2	75

Father's attitude to respondent?	Sex	Yes	No	No Response	Total
Loving	M	4	36	—	40
	F	6	40	1	47
Indifferent	M	4	25	—	29
(or negligent)	F	4	16	1	21
No Response	M	—	6	—	6
	F	—	7	—	7
Total	M	8	67	—	75
	F	10	63	2	75

Have you ever been a patient in a mental hospital?

There is *no* significant relationship between the *mother's* attitude to the participant and the incidence of psychological illness, neither for male participants (Chi-square = ·52; df = 1; p > ·05) nor for female participants (Chi-square = ·73; df = 1; p > ·05). *Neither* is there any relationship between the *father's* attitude to the participant and the incidence of psychological illness for males (Chi-square = ·58; df = 1; p > ·05) or females (Chi-square = ·85; df = 1; p > ·05).

There *is* a significant relationship between the *mother's* attitude towards the participant and the incidence of hospitalization in a mental hospital for male participants (Chi-square = 2·96; df = 1; p < ·05, 1-tailed test) but there is no relationship in the case of females (Chi-square = ·01; df = 1; p < ·05). As predicted males, with a loving mother were less likely to enter a mental hospital (6·9%) than males with an indifferent or negligent mother (26·7%). On the other hand, there is *no* significant relationship between the *father's* attitude and the chances of having entered a mental hospital (Males: Chi-square = ·01; df = 1; p > ·05; Females: Chi-square = ·12; df = 1; p > ·05).

There is *no* significant difference between the sexes either in their mother's attitude (Chi-square = ·61; df = 1; p > ·05) or in their father's attitude (Chi-square = 1·39; df = 1; p > ·05).

There is *no* significant difference between the sexes in their reporting psychological illness (Chi-square = 2·28; df = 1; p > ·05) or entering a mental hospital (Chi-square = ·10; df = 1; p > ·05).

TABLE 22 – PARENTS' FAVOURITE CHILD

(a) Who was your mother's favourite child?

Favourite	Males	Females
Self	23	12
Same sex sibling	12	7
Opposite sex sibling	6	17
No favourite	19	22
No response	2	2
Only child	13	15
Total	75	75

There *is* a significant difference between the sexes in the tendency of the mother to make a favourite of the participant (Chi-square = 3·14; df = 1; p < ·05, 1-tailed test). 56·1% of males who reported that their mother had a favourite claimed that they were the favourite, compared with 33·3% of females who reported that their mother had a favourite.

There *is* a significant tendency for the mother to make a favourite of boys rather than girls (Chi-square = 8·22; df = 1; p < ·005, 1-tailed test). 85·4% of males who reported that their mother had a favourite, claimed the favourite was a *male* child and 47·2% of females reported that the favourite was a *male* child.

(b) Who was your father's favourite child?

Favourite	Males	Females
Self	9	18
Same sex sibling	5	5
Opposite sex sibling	20	3
No favourite	25	32
No response	3	2
Only child	13	15
Total	75	75

There *is* a significant difference between the sexes in the tendency of the father to make a favourite of the participants (Chi-square = 9·23; df = 1; p < ·005, 1-tailed test). 26·5% of males who reported that their father had a favourite, claimed that they were the favourite, compared with 69·2% of females who reported that their father had a favourite and claimed that they were the favourite.

There *is* a significant tendency for the father to make a favourite of girls rather than boys (Chi-square = 12·01; df = 1; p < ·001, 1-tailed test). 58·8% of males reported that their father's favourite was a *female* child, and 88·5% of females claimed the same.

TABLE 23 – EMOTIONAL ADVANTAGE OF BISEXUALITY

Number of Male Lovers	Sex	Is bisexuality an advantage emotionally?			
		Yes	No	No Response	Total
0	M	9	3	1	13
	F	1	—	—	1
1	M	1	1	1	3
	F	4	1	2	7
2	M	5	1	—	6
	F	5	7	—	12
3	M	5	2	1	8
	F	1	5	—	6
4	M	1	2	1	4
	F	8	4	—	12
5	M	3	2	—	5
	F	1	2	—	3
6+	M	19	16	1	36
	F	21	12	1	34
Total	M	43	27	5	75
	F	41	31	3	75

Number of Female Lovers	Sex	Yes	No	No Response	Total
0	M	1	—	2	3
	F	2	2	—	4
1	M	7	7	—	14
	F	13	6	1	20
2	M	8	3	—	11
	F	6	8	2	16
3	M	7	8	1	16
	F	4	5	—	9
4	M	7	2	1	10
	F	5	3	—	8
5	M	—	1	1	2
	F	1	1	—	2
6+	M	13	6	—	19
	F	10	6	—	16
Total	M	43	27	5	75
	F	41	31	3	75

There is *no* significant relationship between the number of male lovers and the perception of bisexuality as an advantage emotionally, neither for male participants (S = 224; z = 1·45; p > ·05) nor for female participants (S = 125; z = ·75; p > ·05).

There is *no* significant relationship between the number of female lovers and the perception of bisexuality as an emotional advantage neither for males (S = 110; z = ·68; p > ·05) nor for females (S = 11; z = ·06; p > ·05).

There is *no* significant difference between the sexes in their perception of bisexuality as an advantage emotionally (Chi-square = ·14; df = 1; p > ·05). 61·4% of males who responded considered it an advantage emotionally compared with 56·9% of females.

TABLE 24 – MENTAL ADVANTAGE OF BISEXUALITY

Number of Male Lovers	Sex	Yes	No	No Response	Total
0	M	8	4	1	13
	F	1	—	—	1
1	M	—	2	1	3
	F	4	1	2	7
2	M	3	2	1	6
	F	9	3	—	12
3	M	7	—	1	8
	F	3	3	—	6
4	M	2	1	1	4
	F	9	3	—	12
5	M	4	1	—	5
	F	3	—	—	3
6+	M	18	15	3	36
	F	24	9	1	34
Total	M	42	25	8	75
	F	53	19	3	75

Number of Female Lovers	Sex	Yes	No	No Response	Total
0	M	1	—	2	3
	F	3	1	—	4
1	M	5	8	1	14
	F	11	8	1	20
2	M	7	4	—	11
	F	10	4	2	16
3	M	8	7	1	16
	F	6	3	—	9
4	M	9	—	1	10
	F	7	1	—	8
5	M	—	1	1	2
	F	2	—	—	2
6+	M	12	5	2	19
	F	14	2	—	16
Total	M	42	25	8	75
	F	53	19	3	75

There is *no* significant relationship between the number of male lovers and the perception of bisexuality as an advantage, mentally, neither for male participants ($S = 124$; $z = ·86$; $p > ·05$) nor for female participants ($S = 16$; $z = ·11$; $p > ·05$).

However, there *is* a significant relationship between the number of female lovers and the perception of bisexuality as an advantage, mentally both for male participants ($S = 260$; $z(c) = 1·66$; $p < ·05$, 1-tailed test) and for females ($S = 303$; $z(c) = 1·91$; $p < ·05$, 1-tailed test). As predicted, for both sexes the more female lovers a participant had the more likely he/she was to find bisexuality an advantage mentally; 52·5% of males and 65·2% of females with 3 or less female lovers found bisexuality an advantage mentally, compared with 77·8% of males and 88·5% of females with more than 3 female lovers.

There is *no* significant difference between the sexes in their perception of bisexuality as a mental advantage (Chi-square $= 1·44$; df $= 1$; $p > ·05$). 62·7% of males who responded found bisexuality an advantage mentally, compared with 73·6% of females.

TABLE 25 – CREATIVE ADVANTAGE OF BISEXUALITY

Number of Male Lovers — *Is bisexuality an advantage creatively?*

Number of Male Lovers	Sex	Yes	No	No Response	Total
0	M	8	4	1	13
	F	1	—	—	1
1	M	—	2	1	3
	F	6	—	1	7
2	M	6	—	—	6
	F	7	3	2	12
3	M	5	—	3	8
	F	5	1	—	6
4	M	2	—	2	4
	F	10	1	1	12
5	M	3	2	—	5
	F	2	1	—	3
6+	M	20	14	2	36
	F	26	6	2	34
Total	M	44	22	9	75
	F	57	12	6	75

Number of Female Lovers	Sex	Yes	No	No Response	Total
0	M	—	—	3	3
	F	3	1	—	4
1	M	8	6	—	14
	F	12	6	2	20
2	M	8	3	—	11
	F	13	1	2	16
3	M	6	7	3	16
	F	6	2	1	9
4	M	8	—	2	10
	F	6	1	1	8
5	M	—	1	1	2
	F	2	—	—	2
6+	M	14	5	—	19
	F	15	1	—	16
Total	M	44	22	9	75
	F	57	12	6	75

There is *no* significant relationship between the number of male lovers and the perception of bisexuality as an advantage creatively, neither for male participants (S = 138; z = 1·02; p > ·05) nor for females (S = 48; z = ·40; p > ·05).

There is *no* significant relationship between the number of female lovers and the perception of bisexuality as an advantage creatively for the male participants (S = 152; z = 1·06; p > ·05) but there *is* a significant relationship in the case of the female participants (S = 233; z(c) = 1·80; p < ·05, 1-tailed test). Females were more likely to find bisexuality a creative advantage if they had more female lovers, as predicted. 77·3% of females with 3 or less female lovers reported bisexuality a creative advantage, compared with 92·0% of females with 4 or more female lovers. The corresponding figures for males were 57·9% and 78·6% respectively.

There *is* a significant difference between the sexes in their perception of bisexuality as a creative advantage (Chi-square = 3·74; df = 1; p < ·05, 1-tailed test). As predicted, females more often found bisexuality a creative advantage (82·6%) than did males (66·7%).

TABLE 26 – SOCIAL ADVANTAGE OF BISEXUALITY

Number of Male Lovers	Sex	Yes	No	No Response	Total
0	M	5	7	1	13
	F	—	1	—	1
1	M	—	3	—	3
	F	1	4	2	7
2	M	3	3	—	6
	F	3	8	1	12
3	M	2	4	2	8
	F	2	4	—	6
4	M	1	2	1	4
	F	6	6	—	12
5	M	3	2	—	5
	F	1	2	—	3
6+	M	13	21	2	36
	F	9	21	4	34
Total	M	27	42	6	75
	F	22	46	7	75

Is bisexuality an advantage socially?

Number of Female Lovers	Sex	Yes	No	No Response	Total
0	M	—	2	1	3
	F	—	4	—	4
1	M	1	13	—	14
	F	5	14	1	20
2	M	6	5	—	11
	F	4	8	4	16
3	M	5	9	2	16
	F	2	7	—	9
4	M	4	5	1	10
	F	5	3	—	8
5	M	1	—	1	2
	F	—	1	1	2
6+	M	10	8	1	19
	F	6	9	1	16
Total	M	27	42	6	75
	F	22	46	7	75

There is *no* significant relationship between the number of male lovers and the perception of bisexuality as an advantage socially, neither for males ($S = 5; z = \cdot 03; p > \cdot 05$) nor for females ($S = 35; z = \cdot 24; p > \cdot 05$).

There *is* a significant relationship between the number of female lovers and the perception of bisexuality as a social advantage in the case of male participants ($S = 418; z(c) = 2 \cdot 56; p < \cdot 01$, 1-tailed test) but *not* for female participants ($S = 235; z = 1 \cdot 57; p > \cdot 05$). As predicted, males were more likely to find bisexuality a social advantage if they had more female lovers. Only 29·3% of those males with 3 or less female lovers found bisexuality a social advantage compared with 53·6% of those with 4 or more female lovers. The corresponding figures for female participants are 25·0% and 45·8%, respectively.

There is *no* significant difference between the sexes in their perception of bisexuality as a social advantage (Chi-square = ·42; df = 1; p > ·05). 39·1% of males who responded found bisexuality a social advantage, compared with 32·4% of females.

Number of Female Lovers	Sex	Yes	No	No Response	Total
0	M	—	2	1	3
	F	—	4	—	4
1	M	1	13	—	14
	F	5	14	1	20
2	M	6	5	—	11
	F	4	8	4	16
3	M	5	9	2	16
	F	2	7	—	9
4	M	4	5	1	10
	F	5	3	—	8
5	M	1	—	1	2
	F	—	1	1	2
6+	M	10	8	1	19
	F	6	9	1	16
Total	M	27	42	6	75
	F	22	46	7	75

There is *no* significant relationship between the number of male lovers and the perception of bisexuality as an advantage socially, neither for males ($S = 5; z = ·03; p > ·05$) nor for females ($S = 35; z = ·24; p > ·05$).

There *is* a significant relationship between the number of female lovers and the perception of bisexuality as a social advantage in the case of male participants ($S = 418; z(c) = 2·56; p < ·01$, 1-tailed test) but *not* for female participants ($S = 235; z = 1·57; p > ·05$). As predicted, males were more likely to find bisexuality a social advantage if they had more female lovers. Only 29·3% of those males with 3 or less female lovers found bisexuality a social advantage compared with 53·6% of those with 4 or more female lovers. The corresponding figures for female participants are 25·0% and 45·8%, respectively.

There is *no* significant difference between the sexes in their perception of bisexuality as a social advantage (Chi-square = ·42; df = 1; p > ·05). 39·1% of males who responded found bisexuality a social advantage, compared with 32·4% of females.

TABLE 28 – NUMBER OF HOMOSEXUAL CASUAL SEX ENCOUNTERS FOR DIFFERENT AGE GROUPS

Number of Encounters	Sex	20–29	30–39	40–49	50–59	Over 59	Total
0	M	4	2	2	1	4	13
	F	14	12	8	2	1	37
1–10	M	10	1	3	3	3	20
	F	14	15	3	—	3	35
11–20	M	2	1	—	4	2	9
	F	2	1	—	—	—	3
21–80	M	4	4	2	5	1	16
	F	—	—	—	—	—	—
81–150	M	2	2	2	—	1	7
	F	—	—	—	—	—	—
151–300	M	1	2	—	4	—	7
	F	—	—	—	—	—	—
Over 300	M	—	1	1	1	—	3
	F	—	—	—	—	—	—
Total	M	23	13	10	18	11	75
	F	30	28	11	2	4	75

There is *no* significant relationship between age of participant and the number of homosexual casual sex encounters, either for males ($S = 55$; $z = \cdot 26$; $p > \cdot 05$) or for females ($S = 177$; $z = \cdot 98$; $p > \cdot 05$).

There is a *significant* difference between the sexes in the number of homosexual casual sex encounters reported ($S = 3288$; $z(c) = 6 \cdot 47$; $p < \cdot 001$, 2-tailed test). Males had significantly more homosexual encounters than did females; in fact no woman had more than 20 encounters.

TABLE 29 – NATURE OF SEXUAL DREAMS AND FANTASIES

(*a*) *Do you fantasize crude heterosexual intercourse?*

Orientation of sex dreams?	Sex	Yes	No	No Response	Total
Mainly own sex	M	6	12	—	18
	F	7	7	2	16
Mainly both sexes	M	20	7	1	28
	F	25	12	2	39
Mainly opposite sex	M	9	4	2	15
	F	6	3	1	10
No Response	M	6	7	1	14
	F	2	8	—	10
Total	M	41	30	4	75
	F	40	30	5	75

(*b*) *Do you fantasize anal intercourse?*

Orientation of sex dreams?	Sex	Yes	No	No Response	Total
Mainly own sex	M	13	5	—	18
	F	2	12	2	16
Mainly both sexes	M	24	3	1	28
	F	6	28	5	39
Mainly opposite sex	M	6	6	3	15
	F	1	9	—	10
No Response	M	6	6	2	14
	F	—	10	—	10
Total	M	49	20	6	75
	F	9	59	7	75

(*c*) *Do you fantasize fellatio?*

Orientation of sex dreams?	Sex	Yes	No	No Response	Total
Mainly own sex	M	15	3	—	18
	F	4	10	2	16
Mainly both sexes	M	26	1	1	28
	F	18	17	4	39
Mainly opposite sex	M	11	2	2	15
	F	6	4	—	10
No Response	M	10	2	2	14
	F	3	7	—	10
Total	M	62	8	5	75
	F	31	38	6	75

(*d*) *Do you fantasize cunnilingus?*
Orientation of

sex dreams?	Sex	Yes	No	No Response	Total
Mainly own sex	M	6	11	1	18
	F	9	4	3	16
Mainly both sexes	M	23	4	1	28
	F	29	7	3	39
Mainly opposite sex	M	8	5	2	15
	F	7	3	—	10
No Response	M	9	3	2	14
	F	4	6	—	10
Total	M	46	23	6	75
	F	49	20	6	75

(*e*) *Do you fantasize mutual masturbation?*
Orientation of

sex dreams?	Sex	Yes	No	No Response	Total
Mainly own sex	M	15	2	1	18
	F	8	4	4	16
Mainly both sexes	M	18	9	1	28
	F	27	8	4	39
Mainly opposite sex	M	11	3	1	15
	F	4	5	1	10
No Response	M	5	7	2	14
	F	3	7	—	10
Total	M	49	21	5	75
	F	42	24	9	75

There *is* a significant relationship between the orientation of sex dreams and the existence of *crude heterosexual intercourse* fantasies in the case of male respondents ($S = 265$; $z(c) = 2·09$; $p < ·025$, 1-tailed test), but *not* in the case of female respondents ($S = 109$; $z = ·97$; $p > ·05$). 33·3% of males who dreamt mainly about their own sex fantasized crude heterosexual intercourse compared with 69·2% of those who dreamt mainly about the opposite sex. The corresponding figures for female respondents are 50·0% and 66·7%, respectively.

There is *no* significant relationship between the orientation of sex dreams and the existence of fantasies about *anal intercourse*, neither for male respondents ($S = 93$; $z = ·93$; $p > ·05$) nor for female respondents ($S = 16$; $z = ·20$; $p > ·05$).

There is *no* significant relationship between the orientation of sex dreams and the existence of *fellatio* fantasies, neither for male respondents (S = 25; z = ·35; p > ·05) nor for female respondents (S = 186; z = 1·61; p > ·05).

There *is* a significant relationship between the orientation of sex dreams and the existence of fantasies about *cunnilingus* in the case of male participants (S = 204; z(c) = 1·65; p < ·05, 1-tailed test), but *not* in the case of female participants (S = 16; z = ·16; p > ·05). As predicted, males were more likely to fantasize cunnilingus if they dreamt mainly about the opposite sex (61·5%) than if they dreamt mainly about their own sex (35·3%); the corresponding figures for females are 70·0% and 69·2%, respectively.

There is *no* significant relationship between the orientation of sex dreams and the existence of fantasies about *mutual masturbation*, either for males (S = 77; z = ·75; p > ·05) or for females (S = 83; z = ·86; p > ·05).

There are *no* differences between the sexes in their reporting of fantasies of crude heterosexual intercourse (Chi-square = ·01; df = 1; p > ·05), cunnilingus (Chi-square = ·14; df = 1; p > ·05) or mutual masturbation (Chi-square = ·37; df = 1; p > ·05). However, there *are* significant differences between the sexes in their reporting of fantasies of anal intercourse (Chi-square = 44·5; df = 1; p < ·001, 1-tailed test; males 71·0%, females 13·2%) and of fellatio (Chi-square = 28·0; df = 1; p < ·001, 1-tailed test; males 88·6%, females 44·9%).

There is *no* significant difference between the sexes in their sex dream orientations (S = 111; z = ·30; p > ·05).

TABLE 30 – SEX DREAMS AND THE ORIENTATION OF SEXUAL FANTASIES

(a) *Fantasies about person(s) infatuated with?*

Orientation of sex dreams?	Sex	Yes	No	No Response	Total
Mainly own sex	M	16	2	—	18
	F	15	—	1	16
Mainly both sexes	M	22	4	2	28
	F	38	1	—	39
Mainly opposite sex	M	11	3	1	15
	F	8	1	1	10
No Response	M	11	2	1	14
	F	9	1	—	10
Total	M	60	11	4	75
	F	70	3	2	75

(b) Fantasies about casual acquaintances?

Orientation of sex dreams?	Sex	Yes	No	No Response	Total
Mainly own sex	M	11	5	2	18
	F	9	6	1	16
Mainly both sexes	M	16	8	4	28
	F	25	12	2	39
Mainly opposite sex	M	7	6	2	15
	F	5	3	2	10
No Response	M	8	4	2	14
	F	4	6	—	10
Total	M	42	23	10	75
	F	43	27	5	75

(c) Fantasies about dream people?

Orientation of sex dreams?	Sex	Yes	No	No Response	Total
Mainly own sex	M	5	11	2	18
	F	6	9	1	16
Mainly both sexes	M	14	10	4	28
	F	21	16	2	39
Mainly opposite sex	M	9	5	1	15
	F	4	4	2	10
No Response	M	5	7	2	14
	F	6	4	—	10
Total	M	33	33	9	75
	F	37	33	5	75

There is *no* significant relationship between the orientation of sex dreams and the tendency to fantasize about people with whom the participant is infatuated, either for males ($S = 68$; $z = ·79$; $p > ·05$) or for females ($S = 60$; $z = 1·36$; $p > ·05$).

There is *no* significant relationship between the orientation of sex dreams and the tendency to fantasize about casual acquaintances, either for males ($S = 79$; $z = ·79$; $p > ·05$) or for females ($S = 30$; $z = ·27$; $p > ·05$).

There is *no* significant relationship between the orientation of sex dreams and the tendency to fantasize about dream people, either for males ($S = 198$; $z = 1·84$; $p > ·05$) or for females ($S = 85$; $z = ·73$; $p > ·05$).

There are *no* significant differences in the orientations of sexual fantasies of males and females in the cases of casual acquaintances

(Chi-square = ·04; df = 1; p > ·05) and dream people (Chi-square = ·03; df = 1; p > ·05). However, there *is* a significant difference between the sexes in their tendency to fantasize about people with whom they are infatuated (Chi-square = 4·10; df = 1; p < ·025, 1-tailed test). As predicted, females more often fantasized about people with whom they were infatuated (95·9%) than did men (84·5%).

GLOSSARY

adrenals (ad-renals): two endocrine glands situated above the kidneys. The adrenals play an important part in the regulation of blood-pressure and other vital functions, as well as emotional and sexual reactions. They consist of a cortex and a medulla, each of which secretes different hormones into the bloodstream, i.e. the corticoids (cortex), adrenalin, noradrenalin, etc. (medulla).

adreno-genital syndrome: a form of pseudo-hermaphroditism in men and women, produced by an overdose of androgens in foetal life. Symptoms lead to far more severe disturbances in females than in males. The abnormal function of the adrenals produces, unless treated, severe masculinization in women. There are two forms of the condition, as explained in Chapter II.

Albany Trust: founded in 1958, was the first organization to care for people with unorthodox sexual and emotional difficulties. Its first director, Antony Grey, was one of the founders of the Law Reform Society which changed the law against homosexuality. The Albany Trust gave counsel and other help to many clients, but in any case where deeper-seated emotional difficulties were suspected, the people concerned were referred to psychiatrists. At this time the Albany Trust called itself a referral agency. In recent years, it has concentrated more on sex-education through pamphlets, the media and special courses for teachers and social workers, without neglecting counselling.

ambisexuality (ambisexual): identified by some authors on sexology with bisexuality. This is incorrect. Ambisexuality means vacillation of object choice, easily turning from homo- to heterosexual love objects. The situation is different in bisexuality.

amorphous: without shape or form.

androgen-insensitivity syndrome: is also called testicular feminizing syndrome. It is a condition where the male hormones produced in the foetal testes are without effect on the body cells. In these cases, body tissues react to female sex hormones which are also produced in the testes. This is a condition of pseudo-hermaphroditism with 'female' external genitalia. Breasts are generally well developed.

androgens: male hormones produced either by the adrenals or the testes, and also by the ovaries.

androgyny (androgynous): having attributes of both sexes in equal measure.

animus, anima: terms coined by C. G. Jung, representing unconscious psychic forces responsible for the choice of love objects in women and men. These forces have a decisive influence on the emotional and mental life.

anxiety neurosis: a state of mind in which irrational fears govern reactions and behaviour.

archetype, archetypal: terms used by C. G. Jung's analytical psychology, relating to the original concepts of woman and man, with idealizing overtones.

Aristophanes: ancient Greek playwright, mainly of comedies. Also famous for his speech in Plato's *Symposium*.

autonomic nervous system: is intrinsically connected with the endocrine system and hypothalamus. It innervates the internal organs and blood vessels. It sustains and controls biological and emotional functions.

bi-emotionality (bi-emotional): predominantly emotional attachment to either sex, which may or may not include sexual acts.

bio-energetics: form of psychotherapy which aims at making people aware of their kinaesthetic sense and positive forms of aggression. Bio-energetics tries to free people from wrong inhibitions by releasing their aggressive impulses through 'physical' contact with the psychotherapist. This therapy is modelled on Alfred Adler's ideas and practice.

bio-psychological: combination of psychological and physiological reactions affecting body, mind and emotion.

bisexuality (bisexual): the innate disposition of men and women to possess psychical (and sometimes also secondary physical) attributes of the opposite sex. Bisexuality may or may not lead a person to choose men and women as love objects (see Chapter III). The concept has nothing to do with physical hermaphroditism.

C.H.E. (Campaign for Homosexual Equality): the largest homosexual organization in this country. Originally founded by men, it now has both male and female members (see Chapter VI).

chromosomes: infinitesimal, rod-shaped particles contained in the nuclei of the cells. They are the bearers of the genes which transmit hereditary traits. The discovery of the chromosomes (1952) considerably enlarged biological knowledge, particularly that of sexual variations and other bio-psychological conditions of genetic origin.

C.O.C. of Amsterdam: the three letters stand for *Cultuur en Ontspannunscentrum* (Cultural and Relaxation Centres). Founded in 1948, the C.O.C. has since then given service to the homo- and bisexual population of Holland free of charge. It was assisted from the beginning by the churches, medical organizations, social services, psychiatrists, and last but not least, by the Government of the Netherlands itself. The C.O.C. was built on the principles of human rights. Its services and social clubs are open to women and men.

consciousness-raising: comparatively new form of psychotherapy. It teaches people a greater awareness of their own perceptive and tactile

proclivities, thereby enlarging consciousness of themselves and others.
contrary sex: opposite sex.
cunnilingus: taking the labia and clitoris into the mouth, touching them with the tongue, producing sexual excitement often leading to orgasm in the passive partner. Cunnilingus is practised by both sexes.
Cushing's syndrome: the product of a prenatal endocrine disorder of the adrenals, affecting both sexes. Comprehensive description of symptoms is given in Chapter II.

endocrine glands: glands which secrete their products, called hormones, directly into the bloodstream. They are of vital importance in sustaining biological and bio-psychological functions.
eroticism (erotism): refers to sensuous and aesthetic attraction between people, which affects the emotions, the imagination and libidinous wishes, but does not necessarily include sexual activity. The term is derived from Eros, the god of love.
erotogenous zones: term introduced by S. Freud to describe selective regions of the body which are highly sensitive to touch, releasing sensuous and/or sexual reactions. The region of the mouth (oral zone) and the external genitalia (genital zone) are erotogenous zones par excellence.
estrogen (oestrogen): female hormone secreted by the ovaries (female sex glands), but also present in the testes (male sex glands).

fellatio: kissing and sucking the penis, which often induces orgasm in both partners. Practised by men and women.
Fröhlich's syndrome: endocrine disorder which goes with sexual infantilism, affecting men and women. Comprehensive description is given in Chapter II.

Gay Liberation Front: homosexual community with left-wing political attitudes.
Gay switchboards: during the last few years, several homosexual organizations, for example, 'Friend' and 'Ice-breakers', have provided a befriending and counselling service for homo- and bisexuals, through telephonic communication. It is a kind of service resembling that of the Samaritans.
gender identity: to be differentiated from sexual identity. It is the subjective erotic and emotional image a person has of him/herself.
genetics: study of heredity.
GH (growth hormone): one of the numerous hormones of the pituitary gland. The most striking functions of GH are its influence on skeletal growth and therefore body build, and its considerable effect on metabolism. GH excretion occurs mostly during the night, and affects sleep rhythms.

hirsutism: excessive hairiness in both men and women. In women, it generally means hair on the face and breast.
homoemotionality, homoemotional: predominantly emotional love for one's own sex, generally expressed sensually and erotically, and often, but not necessarily, sexually.
homosexuality: love for one's own sex. Homos means same. The term

has often been misunderstood, and taken to mean sexual love between men.

hypothalamus: part of the diencephalon or mid-brain. It regulates many vital functions, including sexual and emotional reactions. It is intrinsically connected with the pituitary gland. One section of the latter is, in fact, part of the hypothalamus itself.

inversion (sexual): like deviance, a term used to describe homosexuality. It implies that homosexuality is abnormal and perverted.

kinaesthetic: function of the muscular sense, relating to the feeling of one's own movements and postures.
Klinefelter's syndrome: a condition of chromosomal anomaly which goes with under-developed sexual organs and sterility, emotional infantilism and mental retardation (see Chapter II).

lateral thinking: a method of thought devised by de Bono, relating to intuitive side-lines of associations diverging from the straight line of logical thinking. Lateral thinking is supposed to encourage a more creative and fuller understanding of mental function.
libido, libidinous: sexual desire.

masochism: term coined by R. von Krafft-Ebing, means emotional and sexual pleasure derived from pain and injuries inflicted by other people on oneself.

narcissism, narcissistic: in psychoanalytical language means self-love which precludes love for other people. This contrasts with Melanie Klein's interpretation of the Greek legend of Narcissus (see Chapter I).
nervous breakdown: relates to a state of mind where the person is unable to cope with him/herself and others. It goes with lack of self-confidence, incapacity to make decisions, and withdrawal from the world. Yet because of their failure to cope with life, people who experience a nervous breakdown are utterly dependent on others. Frequent symptoms are depression and thoughts of – or even attempts at – suicide.
neuroendocrine: denotes the interaction between endocrine glands and the autonomic and central nervous systems.
neurosis (psychoneurosis): patterns of maladaptive behaviour of which the patient is aware. Neuroses have their roots in traumatic incidents which can date from childhood or any other period of life. Symptoms vary from floating anxiety to definite anxieties and phobias. Neurosis often goes with depression because of the patient's incapacity to deal properly with ordinary living. Well known examples are *agoraphobia*, which is fear of open spaces, preventing the patient from leaving his/her house, or *claustrophobia*, which is the fear of being enclosed in circumscribed spaces. This condition is generally accompanied by fear of meeting people.

paederasty: love and sexual attraction of grown-ups, mainly men, for children of either sex.

paranoia, paranoid: a mental illness characterized by ideas of reference and persecution. Patients often have lucid intervals between attacks of illusory sufferings.

Parmenides: enlightened Greek philosopher.

pituitary gland or hypophysis: an endocrine gland situated in the sella turcica, deep in the brain. This gland is of the utmost importance for biological functions in general, and psycho-sexual function in particular. It is called the conductor of all the endocrine glands.

pre-structured knowledge: a theory propagated by Chomsky in regard to language, which means that knowledge has an innate, rudimentary structure on which learning through imitation and teaching is built.

pseudo-hermaphroditism: a condition of hermaphroditic appearance in physical and psycho-biological attributes. The gonads are not, however, hermaphroditically mixed, but are either male or female.

psychosis, psychotic: denotes a mental illness such as schizophrenia or manic-depressive psychosis. Must be clearly differentiated from neurotic illness.

sadism, sadistic: term coined by R. von Krafft-Ebing meaning emotional and sexual pleasure derived from inflicting pain on others.

sado-masochism: term also coined by R. von Krafft-Ebing meaning love of inflicting pain on others, and at the same time love of suffering pain inflicted by others. The sado-masochistic syndrome plays a considerable part in psychological and psycho-analytical diagnosis.

schizoid: denotes a state of mind of divided, even contradictory, feelings and thoughts, which leads to constant conflict, and difficulties in adaptability and relationships.

sense of maleness and femaleness: in both sexes, mainly based on endocrine function and affects all human beings. Androgens and oestrogens are present in the sex glands of men and women. The production of androgen is part of adrenal function in both sexes. The effect of oestrogens and androgens on the brain is similar in both sexes, and influences emotional and mental reactions.

The bisexual nature of all human beings is evident, but it is particularly well illustrated in woman's menstrual cycle. At the pre- and post-menstrual period and the time of ovulation, oestrogen output is at its highest, and supersedes the secretion of progesterone, which is a powerful steroid similar to androgen. A woman's sense of *maleness* is closely connected with the latter, her *femaleness* with the former. Although the menstrual cycle allows for a more obvious explanation of maleness and femaleness (bisexuality) in women, the situation in men is similar because of the presence of male and female hormones in the blood stream.

sex centres: represent and mirror specific psychosexual dispositions in the brain. They are seated in the hypothalamus region.

sexism: a comparatively new term which means the over-estimation of sex in general, and of male sexual arrogance in particular.

sexology: a branch of knowledge combining psychology, endocrinology and genetics.

Stein-Leventhal syndrome: a condition in women which goes with enlarged and polycystic ovaries, hirsutism and sterility (see Chapter II).

syndrome: a group of symptoms characteristic of unusual conditions, or illnesses, either physical, psychological or mental.

syzygy: Greek work meaning being yoked together, a pair of correlatives, opposites, or otherwise related things (Webster's Dictionary).

testosterone: male hormone produced by the testes, but also in minor quantities by the ovaries.

transsexualism (transsexual): a person's conviction that he/she is born into the wrong sex.

transvestism (transvestite): men and women who have the compulsive desire to wear the clothes of the opposite sex. Transvestite males are particularly compelled by the wish to buy and wear women's underclothes.

Turner's syndrome: a condition of chromosome abnormality in females which leads to infantilism (physical, sexual and emotional), and sterility (see Chapter II).

variable: a quantity which can assume many different sets of values.

visuo-spatial ability: well developed visual sense, and the ability to focus accurately on objects in space, judging distances and having a clear stereoscopic picture. This capacity encourages confidence and accuracy of movement, and is most valuable in the pursuit of sports and games.

BIBLIOGRAPHY

ADLER, A. *Understanding Human Nature* (1st edition, 1928), London, 1969
ALTMAN, D. *Homosexual Oppression and Liberation*, U.S.A., 1971, U.K., 1974
BARNES, D. *Nightwood*, London, 1974
BARR, M. L. *The Human Nervous System*, New York, 1974
DE BEAUVOIR, S. *Nature of the Second Sex*, London, 1968
The Second Sex, London, 1969
BELL, Q. *Bloomsbury*, London, 1968
Virginia Woolf, London, 1972
BEM, S. L. 'The Measurement of Psychological Androgyny' in *Journal of Consultative and Clinical Psychology* (Vol. 42, pp. 155–62), 1974
'Sex Role Adaptability: One Consequence of Psychological Androgyny' in *Journal of Personal and Social Psychology* (Vol. 31, pp. 634–43), 1975
BENJAMIN, H. *The Transsexual Phenomenon*, New York, 1966
'Transvestism and Transsexualism in the Male and Female' in *Journal of Sex Research* (Vol. 3, No. 2), 1967
'Newer Aspects of the Transsexual Phenomenon' in *Journal of Sex Research* (Vol. 5, No. 2), 1967
BINET, A. *Revue Philosophique*, Paris, 1887
BLOCH, J. *Das Sexualleben unserer Zeit*, Berlin, 1908
BONAPARTE, M. *Female Sexuality*, London, 1953
BRECHER, R. and E. (eds.) *An Analysis of Human Sexual Response*, London, 1967
BRILL, A. A. *Lectures on Psychoanalytic Psychiatry*, London, 1948
BROWN, J. A. C. *Freud and the Post-Freudians*, London, 1976
BRUN, R. *General Theory of Neuroses*, New York, 1951
BUBER, M. *Between Man and Man* (3rd impression), London, 1949
BURNS, R. K. 'Role of Hormones in Differentiation of Sex' in W. Young (ed.) *Sex and Internal Secretion* (Vol. 1), London, 1961
CHESLER, P. *Women and Madness*, New York, 1972
CHEVALIER, J. *L'Inversion Sexuelle*, Paris, 1893
CLEMENT, C. and CICOUS, H. *La Jeune Née*, Paris, 1975

COSENTINO, F. and HEILBRUN, A. B. 'Anxiety Correlates of Sex-Role Identity' in *Psychology Reports* (Vol. 14, pp. 729–36), 1964

DARWIN, C. *The Variations of Animals and Plants Under Domestication*, London, 1868

DEUTSCH, H. *The Psychology of Women* (Vols. I and II), New York, 1946

DÖRNER, G. 'Zur Frage Einer Neuroendokrinen Prophylaxe und Therapie Angeborener Sexualdeviationen' *Deutsche Med. Wochenschrift* (Vol. 94), 1969

'Sex Hormone-Dependent Differentiation of the Hypothalamus and Sexuality' in *Hormones and Brain Function*, Budapest, 1971

'Environment-Dependent Brain Differentiation and Fundamental Processes of Life' in *Acta Biologica* (Vol. 33, pp. 129–48), 1974

'Hormone Dependent Brain Differentiation and Neuroendocrine Function' in *Biological Rhythms in Neuroendocrine Activity*, Tokyo, 1974

Endocrinology of Sex, Leipzig, 1975

Hormones and Brain Differentiation, Amsterdam, 1976

DOSTOYEVSKY, F. *The Idiot*, Penguin, London, 1955

DOUGLASS, J. *Bisexuality*, London, 1976

ELLIS, HAVELOCK, *Studies in the Psychology of Sex* (Vols. I and II), New York, 1942

My Life, London, 1967

FAIRBAIRN, R. *Psychoanalytic Studies of the Personality*, London, 1952

FELDMAN, M. and BROADHURST, A. (eds.) *Theoretical and Experimental Bases of the Behaviour Therapies*, London, 1976

FELDMAN, M. and MACCULLOCH, M. *Homosexual Behaviour Therapy and Assessment*, Oxford, 1971

FENICHEL, O. *The Psychoanalytic Theory of Neurosis*, New York, 1945

FLAUBERT, G. *Briefe*, Stuttgart, 1964, 2nd ed. Zurich, 1977

FLIESS, W. *Vom Leben und Vom Tod*, Jena, 1914

Das Jahr im Lebendigen, Jena, 1918

FORD, B. *Nonscience*, London, 1971

FREUD, S. *Collected Papers, Vol. II*, London, 1949

(a) 'Hysterical Phantasies and their Relation to Bisexuality', 1908
(b) 'Civilized Sexual Morality and Modern Nervousness', 1908
(c) 'On the Transformation of Instincts with Special Reference to Anal Eroticism', 1916
(d) 'A Child Is Being Beaten', 1919
(e) 'The Psychogenesis of a Case of Homosexuality in a Woman', 1926

Ibid. *Vol. III*, London, 1949

(a) 'Fragment of an Analysis of a Case of Hysteria', 1905
(b) 'Analysis of a Phobia in a Five Year Old Boy', 1909
(c) 'A Case of Paranoia (Dementia Paranoides), The Schreber Case', 1911
(d) 'From the History of an Infantile Neurosis', 1918

Ibid. *Vol. IV*, London, 1949

(a) 'On Narcissism', 1914
(b) 'Repression', 1915
(c) 'Instincts and their Vicissitudes', 1915

Ibid. *Vol. V*, London, 1949

(a) 'Some Psychological Consequences of the Anatomical Distinction between the Sexes', 1925

(b) 'Female Sexuality', 1931
(c) 'Termination of Analysis', 1937
The Ego and the Id (5th impression), London, 1949
The Origins of Psychoanalysis, Letters to W. Fliess, London, 1954
Three Essays on the Theory of Sexuality, London, 1967
GAGNON, J. H. and SIMON, W. *Sexual Conduct – the Social Sources of Human Sexuality*, London, 1974
GARDINER, M. *The Wolf-Man and Sigmund Freud*, London, 1972
GREEN, A. 'Aggression, Femininity, Paranoia and Reality' in *International Journal of Psycho-Analysis* (Vol. 53, p. 205), 1972
GREEN, R. *Sexual Identity Conflict*, London, 1974
GRIFFITHS, P. D., MERRY, J. etc. 'Homosexual Women: an Endocrine and Psychological Study' in *Journal of Endocrinology*, (Vol. 63, pp. 549–56)
GRODDEK, G. *The Book of the Id*, London, 1950
HAMPSON, H. J. L. and HAMPSON, J. 'The Ontogenesis of Sexual Behaviour in Man' in W. Young (ed.) *Sex and Internal Secretion* (Vol. II, pp. 1401–33)
HEILBRUN, A. B. and FROMME, D. K. 'Parental Identification of Late Adolescents and Level of Adjustment: the Importance of Parental Model Attributes, Ordinal Position and Sex of the Child' in *Journal of Genetic Psychology* (Vol. 107, pp. 49–50), 1965
HEILBRUN, C. G. *Toward a Recognition of Androgyny*, New York, 1973
HEINE, M. *Confessions et Observations Psycho-Sexuelles*, Paris, 1936
HIRSCHFELD, M. *Die Homosexualität des Mannes und des Weibes*, Berlin, 1914

Sexual Pathology, New York, 1947

Sexual Anomalies and Perversions, compiled by his pupils (12th impression), London, 1962
HOLROYD, M. *Lytton Strachey*, London, 1967
HORNEY, K. *The New Ways in Psychoanalysis*, London, 1947
Feminine Psychology, London, 1967
HUMPHREYS, L. *The Tearoom Trade*, London, 1970
HUTT, C. *Males and Females*, London, 1972
JONES, E. *Sigmund Freud, Life and Work, Vol. I*, London, 1953
JUNG, C. G. *Das Unbewusste im normalen und Kranken Seelenleben*, Zurich, 1929
Collected Works, Vol. IX (Part II, ch. III), London, 1963
Memories, Dreams, Reflections, London, 1963
KINSEY, A. C. *Sexual Behaviour in the Human Male*, New York, 1948
Sexual Behaviour in the Human Female, New York, 1953
KLAICH, D. *Woman plus Woman*, New York, 1974
KLEIN, M. *Envy and Gratitude*, London, 1953
Contributions to Psychoanalysis, London, 1968
KLEIN, M. and RIVIERE, J. *Love, Hate and Reparation*, London, 1967
KLEIN, M., HEIMANN, P., ISAACS, S. and RIVIERE, J. *Developments in Psychoanalysis*, London, 1952
KLIMMER, R. *Die Homosexualität* (3rd edition), Hamburg, 1965
KOLODNY, MASTERS, HENDRIK and TORO 'Plasma Testosterone and Semen Analysis in Male Homosexuals' in *The New England Journal of Medicine* (Vol. 285, pp. 1170–74), 1971

KRAFFT-EBING, R. V. *Psychopathia Sexualis* (English ed.), London, 1965
KRETSCHMER, E. *Korperban und Charakter* (9th and 10th edition), Berlin, 1931
LEACH, E. *Lévi-Strauss*, London, 1973
LÉVI-STRAUSS, C. *Totemism*, London, 1962
LORENZ, K. *King Solomon's Ring*, London, 1952
MAUGHAM, R. *Conversations with Willie*, London, 1978
MAUGHAM, S. *The Summing Up*, London, 1938
Complete Short Stories, Vol. 2, London, 1951
MASTERS, W. H. and JOHNSON, V.E. *Human Sexual Response*, London, 1966
MEAD, M. *Male and Female*, London, 1975
Coming of Age in Samoa, London, 1975
MILLETT, K. *Sexual Politics*, London, 1972
Flying, London, 1975
MITCHELL, J. *Psychoanalysis and Feminism*, London, 1975
MITCHELL, Y. *Colette*, London, 1975
MONEY, J. 'Sex Hormones and Variables in Human Eroticism' in *Sex and Internal Secretion* (Vol. II, pp. 1383–1401), London 1961
'Progestin-induced Hermaphroditism: and Psychosexual Identity in a Study of Ten Girls' in *Journal of Sex Research* (Vol. 3, p. 83), 1968
MONEY, J. and ERHARDT, A. *Man and Woman, Boy and Girl*, Baltimore, 1972
MONEY, J. and TUCKER, P. *On Being a Man or a Woman*, London, 1976
NAGERA, H. *Basic Psychoanalytic Concepts on the Libido Theory*, London, 1969
NEWMAN, L. E. and STOLLER, R. 'Gender Identity Disturbances in Intersexed Patients' in *American Journal of Psychiatry* (Vol. 124, No. 9), 1968
NICOLSON, N. *Portrait of a Marriage*, London, 1973
OAKLEY, A. *Sex, Gender and Society*, London, 1972
ORGLER, H. *Alfred Adler, the Man and his Work* (4th edition), London, 1974
PLATO, *The Symposium* (Penguin Classics), London, 1974
RANDELL, J. 'Indications for Sex-Reassignment Surgery' in *Archives of Sexual Behaviour* (Vol. I)
REDHARDT, R. *Zur gleichgeschlechtlichen männlichen Prostitution, Beitr. z. Sexualf.*, Vol. V, 1954
SACKVILLE-WEST, V. *The Edwardians*, London, 1930
SANTS, J. and BUTCHER, H. J. (eds.) *Developmental Psychology, Selected Readings*, London, 1975
SARTRE, J.-P. *The Psychology of the Imagination*, London, 1950
SCHLEGEL, W. *Sexualinstinkte des Menschen*, Bern, 1966
Sexuelle Partnerschaft, Gütersloh, 1969
SINGER-KAPLAN, H. *The New Sex Therapy*, London, 1975
SOCARIDES, C. 'The Desire for Sexual Transformation – a Psychiatric Evaluation of Transsexualism' in *American Journal of Psychiatry* (Vol. 125), 1969
STOLLER, R. *Sex and Gender*, London, 1968
Splitting, London, 1974
'Hostility, Mystery, Perversion' in *International Journal of Psychoanalysis* (Vol. 55, p. 425), 1974
The Transsexual Experiment, London, 1975

THOMPSON, SCHWARTZ, MCCANDLES and EDWARDS. 'Parent-Child Relationships and Sexual Identity in Male and Female Homosexuals and Heterosexuals' in *Journal of Consultative and Clinical Psychology* (Vol. 41, pp. 120–27), 1973

WALLON, H. *L'Evolution Psychique de l'Enfant* (Vol. I), Paris, 1941

WARD, J. 'Prenatal Stress Feminizes and Demasculinizes the Behaviour of Males' in *Science* (Vol. 175, pp. 82–4), 1972

WEININGER, O. *Geschlecht und Charakter*, Wien, Leipzig, (26th edition), 1926

WILLIAMS, R. (ed.) *Textbook of Endocrinology* (5th edition), Philadelphia, 1974

WILSON, G. and NAIS, D. *Love's Mysteries – the Psychology of Sexual Attraction*, London, 1976

WOLFF, CH. *The Human Hand* (3rd edition), London, 1949
On the Way to Myself, London, 1969
Love Between Women, London, 1971

WOLFF, W. *The Experimental Study of Forms of Expression in Character and Personality*, Vol. II, London, 1932–33
The Expression of Personality, New York, 1943

WOOLF, L. *Sowing*, London, 1960
Growing, London, 1961

WOOLF, V. *Orlando*, London, 1974
A Room of One's Own, London, 1929

INDEX OF NAMES

Authors, artists and female politicians

Adler, A., 31, 159
Aristophanes, 1, 3
Aristotle, 7–8

Bem, Sandra, 38–9
Benjamin, H., 34–5, 53
Benkert, K., 9
Bhavnani, 48
Binet, A., 9–10, 30
Blawatsky, Helene, 45
Bloch, I., 31
Bonheur, Rosa, 45
Burroughs, W., 180

Casper, I., 8
Caudrey, D., 69, 70
Chesler, Phyllis, 57
Chevalier, J., 12
Chomsky, N., 89
Cosentino, F., 38

Darwin, C., 9
de Bono, E., 49
Deutsch, Helene, 5, 24–5, 82
Dorner, G., 42–3, 63, 80, 82

Ecclesiastes, 17
Eliot, George, 45, 49
Ellis, Havelock, 8, 9, 15, 16, 27–30
Erhardt, Anka, 35, 43–4, 48, 49, 52, 53, 63, 82

Fairbairn, R., 27
Fenichel, O., 64, 100
Fliess, W., 2, 17–18, 22–3, 24, 29

Ford, B., 16
Forel, A., 30
Freud, S., 2–5, 7, 10–12, 16, 17–22, 24, 26, 28, 29–30, 34, 35, 56, 62, 103
Fromme, D., 37–8

Gagnon, J. H., 57, 63
Genet, J., 108
Ghandi, Indira, 45
Gley, E., 10
Goethe, W. v., 23
Gonsharowa, 49
Green, A., 52–3, 72
Griffiths, P. D., 46
Groddek, G., 26–7

Heilbrun, A., 37–8
Heimann, Paula, 4
Hiller, Josche, 26
Hirschfeld, M., 16, 23, 29, 30–1, 32, 46
Horney, Karen, 5, 25–6, 82
Humphreys, L., 63, 100–1
Hutt, Corinne, 46–50

Ischlondsky, 30

Jonckheere, R. A., 69
Jones, E., 11
Joplin, Janis, 165
Jung, C. G., 2–5, 7, 56, 89, 103

Kaltenbach, 11
Kinsey, A., 30, 31–2, 47, 100
Klein, Melanie, 3–4, 5–7, 17, 18, 89
Klimmer, R., 7–8, 9, 100

Kolodny, R. C., 63
Koster, 29
Krafft-Ebing, R. v., 9, 10–16, 17, 18, 30, 34
Kris, E., 17

Laycock, 29
Leonardo da Vinci, 23
Lévi-Strauss, C., 17
Liepmann, E., 26
Lonsdale, Dame Kathleen, 45
Lorraine, J., 46

Mascia, D. N., 42–3
Matisse, H., 144
Mead, Margaret, 32–4, 56
Michelangelo, 23
Miller, Isabel, 159
Millet, Kate, 50
Modersohn-Becker, Paula, 49
Moll, A., 28, 29, 32
Money, J., 35, 42–3, 43–4, 47, 48, 49, 52–3, 63, 82

Nash, J., 37
Nefertiti, Queen, 51
Nicolson, N., 158

Parmenides, 7–8
Piaget, J., 36
Picasso, P., 144
Plato, 1, 3

Randall, J., 36
Redhardt, R., 101
Reich, W., 162
Rosenthal, Miriam, 104–5

Sackville-West, Vita, 158
Sand, George, 25
Sappho, 75
Schumann, R., 23
Simon, W., 57, 63
Singer-Kaplan, H., 63
Smythe, Ethel, 49
Soutine, 49
Steinach, E., 30
Stoller, R., 15, 35–6, 53, 55, 56, 57, 62, 72
Swoboda, 22

Thatcher, Margaret, 45

Ulrichs, K. H., 8–9, 30

Vivien, Renée, 159

Wallor, H., 36
Ward, Ingeborg, 43, 57
Weininger, O., 22, 23–4, 45
Westphal, C., 9
Williams, R., 42, 62–3
Williams, Shirley, 45
Wolff, W., 23
Woolf, Virginia, 49, 165

Organizations and publications

Albany Trust, 67, 107, 108

Beaumont Society, 36, 60, 62, 67, 70

C.H.E. (Campaign for Homosexual Equality), 58, 107, 112, 121
C.O.C. of Amsterdam, 118

Friend, 107
Friends Homosexual Fellowship, 107

Gay Liberation Front, 9, 107, 121, 160, 163, 164
Gay Switchboards, 107

Institut fur Sexualwissenschaften (Institute of Sexological Science), 30, 31,
Integroup, 107
International Foundation of Full Personality Expression, 36

Kenric, 67, 107, 108

Men Against Sexism, 84, 94, 121

Scottish Minority Group, 107

Women's Liberation Movement, 38, 39, 51, 91, 93, 94, 153, 161
World League for Sexual Reform, 30

Gay News, 67, 108
Guardian, The, 36

Listener, The, 105

Sappho (also lesbian organization), 45, 67, 107, 108, 117
Spare Rib, 67
Suck (magazine), 180

Time Out, 67

INDEX OF SUBJECTS

Adopted children, 74, 75
Adrenals, 42, 45, 49; enlargement of, 42; dysfunction of, 45; hormonal secretions of, 42; *see also* pituitary and sex glands
Aggression, aggressive, 25, 33, 49–50, 54, 64, 147, 149; *see also* endocrine system
Alternative society, *see* bisexual society
Ambisexuality, ambisexual, 4, 63, 80
Anal intercourse between males, 78–84, 99, 100, 101, 120, 191; day dreams of, 104; rape, 80, 121
Androgen, androgenic, 42–5, 48, 49, 57; and aggression, 49; androgenized girls, 43; deficiency of in males, 43; hormones, 42; and intelligence, 44, 45, 48; levels of, 48, 49; overdose of in females, 43
Androgyny, androgynous, 1, 38–9, 66, 84–5, 90; psychological, 36, 38
Anima/animus, concept of, 2, 5, 89
Anthropology, anthropological, 31, 32–4
Anxiety states, 103
Aphrodisiac, 50
Archaic, 2, 17
Archetypal, 2
Artefacts in relation to human beings, 53, 65
Authenticity, authentic, 27, 65, 109
Auto-eroticism, auto-erotic, 15
Autonomic nervous system, 42; *see also* endocrine system, hypothalamus
Behaviourism, 7, 10

Bi-gender identity, 1, 58, 59, 62, 80, 91; *see also* gender identity and gender assignment
Bio-energetics, 94
Biological, 28, 30, 36, 40, 46, 54, 56; make-up, 80
Bio-psychical, bio-psychological, 1, 23, 30, 50, 55
Bisexual, disposition, 72; inclination, 62; orientation, 1; predisposition, 11; society, 106, 109, 122; *see also* sexual orientation

Casual sexual contacts (encounters), 98, 101, 102, 238–9; female, 99, 103; male, 98, 99, 103
Central nervous system, 42; *see also* autonomic nervous system and endocrine system
Cerebral lateralization in relation to different capacities in males and females, 47
Chauvinism, female, 51; male, 51
Child psychoanalysis, 18
Christianity, 8, 10; morals of, 9, 10, 18
Chromosomes, 40, 41
Classification of subjects, 69–70
Claustrophobia, 77, 182; *see also* anxiety states and neurosis
Climacterium, male, 55
Clitoris, clitoral, 21, 25, 26, 28, 40, 43, 45, 79, 153, 197; *see also* sex centres, pseudo-hermaphroditism and syndromes

Communes, living in, 163
Communication, high level of in women, 48
Congenital disposition to physical bisexuality, 41
Consciousness raising, 94
Contrary sex, cross-sexed, (= opposite sex), 9, 15, 17, 35, 60; desire to be of, 217, 218, 219
Core gender identity, 36, 55
Creativity, creative, 47, 48–9, 56, 106, 235–6; in women, 48, 49
Cunnilingus, 104

Delinquency, in men with sex chromosomes XYY, 41
Depression, 103; effect on output of androgens in pregnant women, 43, 57, 63; effect on output of testosterone in homosexual men, 63; possible effect on hormonal balance in all human beings, 63
Developmental psychology, 36, 37, 50
Dreams, 6–7, 29, 59, 69, 103–5, 240–1; Freudian interpretation of, 17, 103–4; of masochism, 120

Echo, 2, 5
Electra, 2
Embryology, 46
Embryonic, 41, 45
Emotional attachments, 90–3, 98, 202–3; *see also* marriage of subjects
Emotional preoccupation, 92, 217, 226; especially between women, 96, 244
Endocrine, changes, 55; constitution, 46; disturbances, 43; dysfunction, 45, 84; factor, 84; functions, 42; make-up, 43, 46, 72; psycho-endocrine, 46
Endocrine system, 41–2, 46, 55, 72; anomalies of, 42–5, 89–90; *see also* syndromes
Endocrinology, 40; experiments in, 30
Erections, 55, 60, 63, 146, 187, 188
Eros, 2
Eroticism (erotism), 27, 29, 57; infantile, 88
Erotogenous zones, 88, 89, 101
Estrogen (oestrogen), 42, 50; overdose of, 43; *see also* sex centres and hypothalamus
Exhibitionists, exhibitionism, 50, 79

Fantasies, sexual, 19, 59, 69, 80, 104, 129, 132, 150, 239–44; infantile, 4; sadomasochistic, 19–20; of anal intercourse, 240, 241, 242; of crude heterosexual intercourse, 240, 241, 242; of cunnilingus, 240, 241, 242; of fellatio, 240, 241, 242; of mutual masturbation, 240, 241, 242
Fellatio, (fellate), 61, 99–100, 101, 104, 143, 145, 146
Femaleness, 29, 31, 36, 55, 56, 59, 60, 65
'Femininity', 'feminine', 2, 8, 11, 14, 21, 23–5, 32, 34–8, 53, 54, 55, 60, 65, 66, 153
Feminization, 42, 43
Fiction, 56
Foetal, 42, 43, 44; hormones, 42, 43; *see also* hypothalamus and sex centres

Gender assignment, 12
Gender identity, 12–13, 24–5, 33, 35, 43, Chapt. III; 72, 82, 83, 94, 97; reversal of, 53; male/female, 58, 65
Genes, 40
Genetics, genetic, 40, 41, 45, 72, 80, 154; abnormalities, 41, 62, 63; dysfunction, 63; make-up, 72
Genital abnormalities, 41, 46
Genius, 49
Greek legends, 2–3, 89
Growth hormones (GH), 88; *see also* pituitary
Guilt feelings, re homosexuality, 7, 55, 94, 95, 98, 228; re sex in general, 228
Gynecomastia, 12

Hermaphrodite, 1, 2, 11, 41, 53; sexual, 3
Hermaphroditic, creature, 3; image, 1, 2, 7; legend, 2; monsters, 3
Hermaphroditism, 1, 3–4, 7, 11, 41, 53; mental, 8, 9; psychical or psychological, 2, 8, 9, 10, 13, 16, 17, 28, 38; psychosexual, 1, 3, 35
Hermaphroditus, 1, 2
Hirsutism, 45, 50
Homoemotionality, homoemotional, 91–2, 117
Hormones, hormonal, 30, 35, 40, 42, 46, 63, 80; abnormalities, 62, 63; balances, 42, 43, 63; disturbances, 43, 45; dysfunction, 63; female hormones, 42, 43, 44, 49; functioning – alterations in, 59; influences, 42, 43, 57; male hormones, 43, 44, 153; secretions, 42; sex hormones, 63; *see also* endocrine system
Hypothalamus, 42, 43, 45; male and

female sex centres situated in different parts of, 42; mixed male/female sex centre in, 43; *see also* sex centres

Identity, personal, 52, 83, 97
Illegitimacy, illegitimate, 74, 75–9
Incest, 19, 202; emotional, 57; homosexual, 91; in children, 18, 80–1, 84
Intelligence (IQ), 44–5, 47–8; unusually high, 86
Inversion, inverts, sexual deviance, 9, 10, 11, 12, 28, 29, 31, 63; theory of, 16

Judaism, 8, 10, 100

Kinaesthetic sense, 45

Lateral thinking, 49
Libido, libidinous, 19, 22, 27, 55, 88
Logos, 2, 17

Maleness, 20, 31–2, 36, 55, 56, 59–61, 65
Marriage of subjects, 93–8, 115, 117, 200
'Masculinity', 'masculine', 2, 11, 13, 14, 19, 21, 23, 24, 25, 26, 29, 32, 34–8, 53–5, 60, 65, 66, 82, 113, 153
Masculinization, 28, 37, 38, 43, 44, 49
Masochism, masochistic, 16, 25; dreams of, 120; fantasies of, 19, 20
Masturbation, 78, 79, 88, 89, 90, 145, 153, 174, 187–8, 190, 192; between schoolmates, 79; in dreams, 104; mutual between men, 99–100, 101, 104, 188; anal self-masturbation, 188
Matriarchy, matriarchate, 51
Morphogenic, 50
Mother complex, 75
Mullerian ducts, 40
Mythology (myth), 1, 2, 7, 17, 34; legend of Hermaphroditus, 1; Narcissus myth, 4–5; Klein's interpretation of, 4–5

Narcissus, 2
Narcissism, 4–5, 89
Nervous breakdown, 103, 126, 160
Neurosis, 18, 26, 28, 77, 103, 111, 159, 161, 229
Numerology, 22

Obscenity, 30
Oedipus, 2
Oedipus complex, 20, 27, 88
Orgiastic rituals, 100

Ovaries, 40, 43, 45

Paederasty, 8, 9
Paedophily, hetrosexual, 79; homosexual, 79
Parental expectations, 47
Parental favouritism, 82–7, 119, 231–2; in mother/child relationship, 35, 37–8, 47, 104–5, 111, 116, 119, 147, 161
Parental influences, 6, 46, 53, 72–4, 81–2, 103, 116, 167, 172–3, 186–7, 229–30; on illegitimate children, 74–9 passim
Parental preferences, 47
Penis envy, 5, 20, 25, 26, 165
Periodicity, 22–3, 23–4, 29
Pituitary (hypophysis), 42, 45, 84, 88 (GH); *see also* adrenals, endocrine systems, hormones, hypothalamus
Pre-oedipal attachments, 4, 21
Pre-structured knowledge, 89
Progestine (female hormone), 44, 49
Promiscuity, 76, 91, 174
Prostate gland, 40
Prostitution, female, 88, 98; homosexual, 98; male, 98, 100
Pseudo-hermaphroditism, pseudo-hermaphroditic, 43, 44; *see also* adrenals, androgen, estrogen, and syndromes
Psychoanalysis, psychoanalysts, psychoanalytic, 2, 3, 4, 6, 11, 17, 18, 20, 24, 25, 26, 27, 29, 30, 31, 34–6, 40, 58, 62, 64, 89, 103, 105
Psycho-motor function, 36
Psychosexual, 27, 58, 108; behaviour, 46, 63, 90; characteristics, 42; constitution, 42; functions, 42; identity, 66; life, 5
Psychosexuality, 21, 56
Psychosis, psychotic, 18, 103
Psycotherapy, 75, 103, 229
Public lavatories, as venue for homosexual activities, 100, 101, 102

Radical lesbians, 95, 96

Sadism, 5–6, 16; fantasies of, 19–20, 120
Sauna baths, as venue for homosexual activities, 102
Schizoid, 95, 109
Self-image, sexual (erotic), 52, 57
Self, alienation from, 52; – image, 53; other-sexed, 2, 58; real, 46
Sex centres (eroticising centres), 42, 43, 45; female, 42, 43; male, 42, 43;

260

same for both, 43; reversed, 42, 43; *see also* hypothalamus
Sex chromosome combinations, 40, 41; abnormal, 41, 63; *see also* syndromes
Sex glands, 40, 41, 42; female, 40, 41, 42; male, 40, 41
Smell, sense of, 50
Sound, sensitivity to (auditory stimuli), 47
Sexual, abnormalities, 30; camps, 79; early experiences, 77; hyperaesthesia, 9, 30; pathology, 8, 16, 28, 31; perversion, 31
Sexual, differentiation, 42; identity, 5, 14, 33, 35, 52, 53, 57, 72, 94; orientation, 13–14, 29, 30, 33, 35, 36, Chapt. III, and 55, 94, 109; orientation in dreams, 69, 104; variations, 16, 31, 32, 34, 46, 59, 63, 106, 107, 108, 123, 157
Sexual, group activities, 94
Sexual minorities, 46, 58, 67, 107
Sperm count, in primary homosexuals, 63
Sterility, in exclusively homosexual men, 63
Syndromes, 63; adreno-genital, 44; androgen insensitivity, 43; Cushing, 45; Fröhlich, 45; Kallman, 45; Klinefelter, 41, 63; sado-masochistic, 16; Stein-Leventhal, 45; Turner, 41

Territory, psychosexual, 108
Testes, 40; foetal, 41, 43; *see also* sex glands and sex centres
Testosterone (male hormone), 43, 63; *see also* sterility
Tomboys, 44, 82, 154, 160
Touch, sense of, 50
Transcendental meditation, 113
Transsexualism, 10–15, 34–5, 52–3, 59–62, 219–20; in children, 72
Transsexuals, 36, 53, 62, 67, 82; boys, 56, 57, 83, 94; men, 60; position of, 61; women, 35, 60, 61
Transvestism, 35, 60, 62
Transvestites, male, 36, 54, 60, 62, 67, 82, 94; female, 60
Trauma, early sexual, 79, 97, 154
Traumatic experience, 54; of a parent's death, 73

Uranism, 9
Urinals as venue for homosexual activities, 99, 100

Vagina, role of in orgasm, 21
Vaginal, reactions and masturbation in early childhood, 4, 26
Variables, 49, 70, 71, 208, 209
Visuo-spatial abilities, 47

Wechsler tests, 48
Wolffian ducts, 40

INDEX TO APPENDIX I
Names and Places

Asia, 200

Belboef, Marquise de, 203
Bell, Q., 201

Carrington, D., 202
Cleis, 201
Colette, 203; Sidonie (Colette's mother) 203; Willie (Colette's husband), 203

Darwin, C., 200
Dostoyevsky, F., 204

Flaubert, G., 203, 207

Ghana, 200
Greece, 204

Heilbrun, C., 202, 203
Kempson, R., 202

Klaich, D., 203

Lesbos, 204

Maugham, S., 202, 203
Maugham, R., 203
Mesopotamia, 200
Meyerowitz, E. L. R., 200
Middle East, 200

Nicolson, N., 201

Phoenicia, 200

Sackville-West, V., 201, 204
Sappho, 201, 204
Strachey, L., 202
Syria, 200

Woolf, L., 201
Woolf, V., 202

Index of Subjects

Aggressiveness, 206
Akhan people, 200
Alternative society, 205; (*see also* bisexual society)
Ambivalence, emotional, 206
Androgynous, 199, 200, 201, 203–205; goddess, 200
Anthropologist, 200
Antiquity, goddesses of, 200
Archetype, archetypal, 201
Astarte, 200
Athenian civilization, 204

B.B.C. Television, 203
Bisexual, 200–207; society, 205
Bloomsbury Group, 201, 202

Commune, 206
Cosmic, energy, 200; spirit, 200
Creative, energy, 200, 205; people, 204; process, 204; urge, 205
Creativity, 204

Depression, 205
Dreams, 204

Endocrine, 203

Fantasies, 204
Femaleness, 204
Feminist, 207
Frigidity, 202

Gender identity, 199, 200; male/female, 199, 200; female/male, 200; bi-gender identity, 204
Guilt feelings, 205

Hermaphroditism, psychical, 202; (androgyny of the mind), 204, 207
Hermaphroditus, legend of, 199, 200
Hereditary traits, 200
Hetairae, 204, 205
Hormonal, 203

Iconoclastic, 202
Ishtar, 200

Magic, magical, 199, 200
Maleness, 204
Myth, (Greek), 199, 200
Mythical, 199; notion, 199; quality, 199

Non-biological, 206
Nyame, 200
Nymph, Salmacis, 199

Persecution, mental, 206
Prostitution, 205
Psychosexual experiences, 205

Religion, religious, 200, 204

Self, image of, 199
Semi-God, 199
Sexism, 205
Sexual, categorisation, 202, 207; orientation, 206
Sexuality, unorthodox, 206
Sexual Offences Act of 1967, 205
Spirit, 207
Spiritual, spirituality, 199, 200

Women's Liberation Movement, 202, 206, 207